5 Longman Academic Writing Series

ESSAYS TO RESEARCH PAPERS

Alan Meyers

With love, to the newest members of my family: Dylan, Michael, and Anne, and to my companion and wife for fifty years, Ann.

Longman Academic Writing Series 5: Essays to Research Papers

Copyright © 2020, 2014 by Pearson Education, Inc.
All rights reserved.

Pearson, 221 River Street, Hoboken, NJ 07030

Staff Credits: The people who made up the *Longman Academic Writing Series 5* team, representing content creation, design, marketing, manufacturing, multimedia, project management, publishing, and rights management, are Pietro Alongi, Margaret Antonini, Eleanor Barnes, Gregory Bartz, Rosa Chapinal, Aerin Csigay, Gina DiLillo, Gina Eide, Warren Fischbach, Ann France, Shelley Gazes, Sarah Hand, Gosia Jaros-White, Stefan Machura, Amy McCormick, Bridget McLaughlin, Lise Minovitz, Linda Moser, Dana Pinter, Liza Pleva, Katarzyna Starzynska-Kosciuszko, Joseph Vella, Peter West, and Autumn Westphal.

Cover Images: BrAt82/Shutterstock (quill pen), Evgeny Karandaev/Shutterstock (laptop)
Text Composition: TSI Graphics
Cover Design: Page Designs International

Library of Congress Cataloging-in-Publication Data

Meyers, Alan.
  Longman Academic Writing Series, Level 5 : essays to research papers / Alan Meyers.
  ISBN-13: 978-0-13-291274-7
  ISBN-10: 0-13-291274-0

  1. English language—Rhetoric. 2. Report writing. 3. Research—Methodology.
  4. Academic writing. I. Title.

  PE1478.M45 2013
  808'.042—dc23

                                                                2013013188

ISBN 13: 978-0-13-683855-5 (Student Book with App, Online Practice, and Digital Resources)
ISBN 10: 0-13-683855-3 (Student Book with App, Online Practice, and Digital Resources)

ISBN 13: 978-0-13-683866-1 (E-book with App, Online Practice, and Digital Resources)
ISBN 10: 0-13-683866-9 (E-book with App, Online Practice, and Digital Resources)

Printed in the United States of America
6 2022

CONTENTS

CHAPTER 4 Cause / Effect Essays 64

CHAPTER 7 Summary / Response Essays 128

APPENDICES

TO THE TEACHER

Welcome to Level 5 in the *Longman Academic Writing Series*, a five-level series that prepares English language learners for academic coursework. This book is intended for advanced students in university, college, or secondary school programs who need to write longer essays and research papers. *Longman Academic Writing Series: Essays to Research Papers* offers a carefully structured approach that focuses on writing as a process. It teaches rhetoric and sentence structure in a straightforward manner, using a step-by-step approach, high-interest models, and varied practice types. It also addresses the writing, research, and documentation of papers in different academic areas. Each chapter explores a different rhetorical genre—classification, process, cause / effect, definition, summary / response, argumentation, and the research paper—as it applies to academic writing across the curriculum.

This book integrates instruction in organization and sentence structure with the writing process. It carefully guides students through the steps of the writing process to produce the well-organized, clearly developed essays and term papers that are essential to academic writing in English. You will find a wealth of realistic models to guide writers and clear explanations supported by examples that will help your students through typical rough spots. These explanations are followed by the extensive practice that learners need to assimilate writing skills and write with accuracy and confidence. Interactive tasks, including pair work, group work, and full-class discussions, engage students in the learning process and complement the solitary work that writers must do. The tasks progress from recognition exercises to controlled production and culminate in the chapter Writing Assignments. The extensive appendices and a thorough index make the text a valuable and easy-to-use reference tool.

Features

- **Theme-based chapters** that focus on a particular academic area and rhetorical genre;
- **Chapter objectives** provide clear goals for instruction;
- **Realistic writing models** with academic content present the type of writing students will learn to produce in the end-of-chapter Writing Assignments;
- **Two vocabulary sections**, Noticing Vocabulary and Applying Vocabulary, highlight useful words and phrases from the writing models and allow students to practice the new vocabulary and use it in their writing assignments;
- **Organization** sections explore the structure of papers in a variety of organizational patterns;
- Sections on **Grammar** and **Sentence Structure** provide practice with the structures that pose the most difficulties for advanced students;

- A **Preparation for Writing** section reinforces learning and develops the research skills needed for the writing assignment;
- Step-by-step **Writing Assignments** make the writing process clear and easy to follow;
- **Timed Writing** practice develops students' writing fluency;
- **Writing Guides** for each rhetorical genre give students the tools they need to improve the flow of ideas in their papers;
- **Citation guidelines on MLA** and **APA formats** provide students with the documentation skills needed to write papers for a variety of academic fields.

The Online Teacher's Manual

The Teacher's Manual is available on the Pearson English Portal. It includes general teaching notes, chapter teaching notes, answer keys, reproducible writing assignment scoring rubrics, and reproducible chapter quizzes.

Acknowledgments

I am grateful to the members of the Pearson ELT team for the expertise and dedication they brought to this project, particularly Amy McCormick, Lise Minovitz, Eleanor Barnes, and Joan Poole. I would also like to thank Barbara Weisberg for her careful editing of the first four chapters of this book. I would also like to acknowledge the members of the writing team for this new edition of *LAWS*: Jennifer Bixby, Linda Butler, Jane Curtis, Lara Ravitch.

I am grateful for the help and suggestions provided by my colleagues at Truman College, Chicago, in particular Anne Close, Kim Steffen, Kate Gillespie, and the aforementioned Lara Ravitch, who now teaches at the University of Oregon. I especially wish to express gratitude to my friends and colleagues Gerald Graff and Cathy Birkenstein, whose trailblazing work has inspired the writing guides. And I am indebted to my loving and pro bono editor, my wife Ann.

I extend one last thank you as well as congratulations to the students at Truman College, Chicago, who shared samples of their writing with me, which have been adapted for this book: Aksana De Bretto and Ksenia Laney; and which appear in the *Teacher's Manual:* Helosia Costa Ramos and Lidia Ziegler.

My thanks go out as well to the following reviewers, who contributed to our planning for this new addition to the *Longman Academic Writing Series* with their suggestions: **Cynthia M. Durham-Gonzalez**, Seminole State College, Florida; **Mary Goodman**, Everest College, Florida; **Emily Knox**, Bridge Language School; **Ruth Moore**, University of Colorado at Boulder, Colorado; **Barbara Smith-Palinkas**, Hillsborough Community College, Florida; **Amy Weinberg**, Bridge English, Colorado.

I would also like to thank the following people for their feedback on our online survey: **Eric Ball**, Langara College, British Columbia, Canada; **Mongi Baratli**, Al Hosn University, Abu Dhabi, United Arab Emirates; **Jenny Blake**, Culture Works ESL, London, Canada; **Karen Blinder, Ph.D.**, English Language Institute, University of Maryland, Maryland; **Bob Campbell**, Academic Bridge Program, Doha, Qatar;

Nancy Epperson, Truman College, Illinois; **Kemal Erkol**, Onsekiz Mart University, Çanakkale, Turkey; **Russell Frank**, Pasadena City College, California; **Jeanne Gross**, Cañada College, California; **Lisa Kovacs-Morgan**, English Language Institute, University of California at San Diego, California; **Mary Ann T. Manatlao**, Qatar Foundation, Academic Bridge Program, Doha, Qatar; **Brett Reynolds**, Humber Institute of Technology and Advanced Learning, Ontario, Canada; **Lorraine C. Smith**, CUNY Queens College, New York.

Alan Meyers

Longman Academic Writing Series, Level 5, Essays to Research Papers, offers a carefully structured approach to advanced academic writing. It features instruction on the writing process, the organization of essays and term papers, research and documentation, sentence structure, word forms, and grammar.

Four-color design makes the lessons engaging.

Realistic writing models present the type of writing students will learn to produce in the end-of-chapter Writing Assignments.

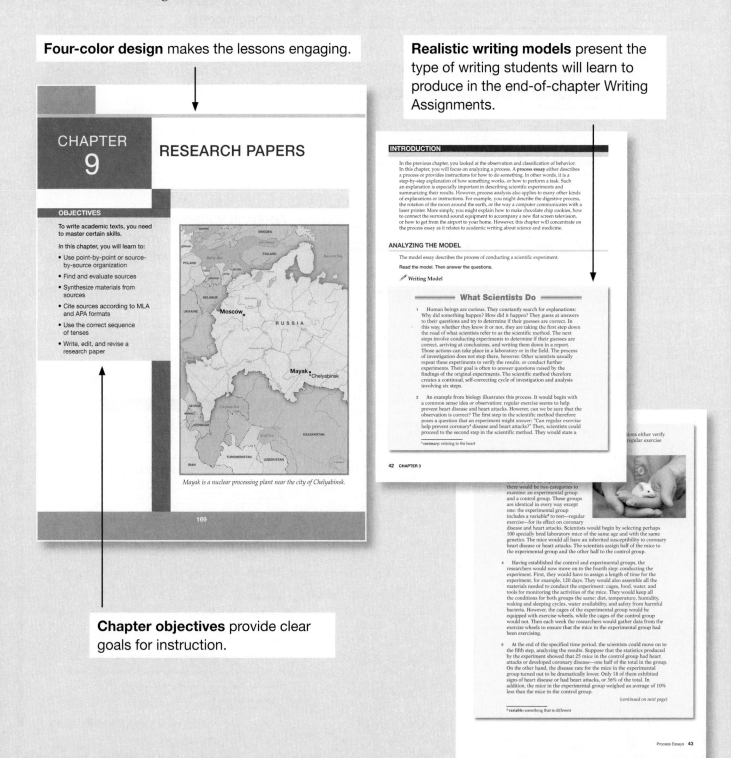

Chapter objectives provide clear goals for instruction.

Noticing Vocabulary: Irregular Plurals from Latin and Greek

Chapter 2 explained that the plural of the word *criterion* is *criteria*. This is because the word comes from Greek, which has retained its original plural forms for some words. Likewise some words that come from Latin have irregular plural endings; they do not add *-s* endings to the singular form. These words can be placed into four categories, which include many words used in scientific writing.

PRACTICE 1   Singular and Plural Forms of Irregular Nouns

A Look at the writing model again. Find irregular nouns for each category in the chart. The beginnings of each word have been included to help you.

CATEGORY 1: NOUNS FROM LATIN	
Singular (-*um*) Ending	Plural (-*a*) Ending
medium	media
1. _____	bac_____
2. _____	dat_____

CATEGORY 2: NOUNS FROM GREEK	
Singular (-*is*) Ending	Plural (-*es*) Ending
thesis	theses
1. ana_____	
2. hyp_____	_____
3. bas_____	_____

CATEGORY 3: NOUNS FROM GREEK	
Singular (-*on*) Ending	Plural (-*a*) Ending
criterion	criteria
1. _____	phe_____

CATEGORY 4: SINGULAR NOUNS FROM GREEK WITH NO PLURAL FORM	
Singular (-*ics*) ending	
mathematics	
1. gen_____	
2. sta_____	

B Complete the chart with the singular or plural form of each noun, where possible.

Process Essays   **45**

Noticing Vocabulary points out useful words and phrases from the writing models.

Applying Vocabulary allows students to practice the new vocabulary and then use it in their writing assignments.

Applying Vocabulary: Using Words Related to Cultural Change

Before you begin your writing assignment, review what you learned about the words in Practice 1 on page 131.

PRACTICE 7   Forming Different Parts of Speech

A Work in pairs or small groups. Fill in the appropriate word form for each. Use a dictionary as needed. As you work, look for recurring patterns.

VERB	NOUN	ADJECTIVE
1. acquire	*acquisition*	acquisitive
2. conflict	conflict	_____
3. reconcile	reconciliation	_____
4. assimilate	_____	assimilated
5. devote	_____	devoted
6. perceive	_____	perceived

B Change these nouns into verbs. Most, but not all, of the verbs will follow a consistent pattern. Consult your dictionary as needed.

NOUN	VERB
1. demonstration	_____
2. integration	_____
3. education	_____
4. definition	_____
5. invitation	_____
6. conversation	_____
7. evolution	_____
8. resolution	_____

C Choose the word form from Parts A and B that best completes each sentence.

1. When people get married, they pledge their complete ____*devotion*____.

2. Young children learn to _____ in a second language more quickly than most adults.

3. The _____ of a new language can be very challenging.

142   CHAPTER 7

Organization sections explore essay structure in a variety of organizational patterns.

POINT-BY-POINT ORGANIZATION

You are already familiar with this organizational pattern from Chapter 8. As mentioned in that chapter, a point-by-point pattern is particularly well suited to complex issues and longer papers, which makes it a useful way to organize a research paper. A partial diagram of how a point-by-point organization might be used in a research paper looks like this:

Body Paragraphs

The first major point is discussed and then supported by synthesized information/views on this point taken from several sources.

↓

The second major point is discussed in several sources, supported by synthesized information/views on this point from all of them.

↓

The first major point is discussed and then supported by synthesized information/views on this point taken from several sources.

↓

Further major points are developed in later paragraphs using similar support.

SOURCE-BY-SOURCE ORGANIZATION

A source-by-source organization is somewhat similar to a block organizational pattern in that it groups the information in blocks according to the source.

Body Paragraphs

The first few paragraphs contain a summary of key points covered and supported by specific information/views from one source.

↓

The next set of paragraphs contains a summary of key points covered, supported by specific information/views from a second source.

↓

The next set of paragraphs contains a summary of key points covered, supported by specific information/views from a second source.

↓

Further major points are developed in later paragraphs using similar support.

Make sure to connect your sources by discussing related key points and by using transitional phrases to show similarities and differences among the sources. For an example of a source-by-source organizational style, return to the writing model from Chapter 5 on pages 87–89.

174   CHAPTER 9

Grammar and **Sentence Structure** sections provide practice with the most challenging structures for advanced students.

PHRASAL MODALS

Another tool for making recommendations, suggestions, and demands is using a **phrasal modal** (or semi-auxiliary). A phrasal modal consists of two or more separate words and functions somewhat like a modal verb. It expresses ability, offers advice, makes recommendations, or discusses possibilities or probabilities. However, unlike a modal verb, which has one form, phrasal modals change according to person and aspect.

RULES	EXAMPLES
1. Use *be able to* + [the base form of the verb] for expressing achievement.	They have been able to make significant changes in research methods.
2. Use *be likely to* + [the base form of the verb] for expressing probability.	This change is likely to have profound effects.
3. Use *be going to* + [the base form of the verb] for expressing certainty with.	This change is going to benefit millions of people.
4. Use *have to* + [the base form of the verb] for expressing necessity. **Note:** The negative of *have to* means something is not necessary. It differs from *must not*, which means it is prohibited.	We have to conduct more research. We don't have to use animals in all experiments.
5. Use *had better* for expressing warning.	You had better be careful when working with dangerous chemicals.
6. Use *would rather* (without *to*) for expressing preference.	Most students would rather apply for a scholarship than take out a loan.

PRACTICE 3   Using Phrasal Modals

Choose five of the sentences you wrote in Practice 2 and rewrite them using phrasal modals.

1. _____

2. _____

3. _____

4. _____

5. _____

Practice Activities reinforce learning and lay the groundwork for the end-of-chapter Writing Assignment.

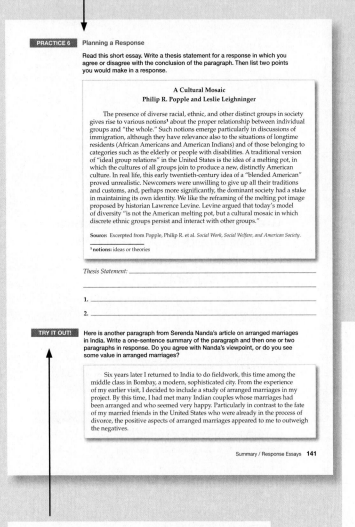

PRACTICE 6   Planning a Response

Read this short essay. Write a thesis statement for a response in which you agree or disagree with the conclusion of the paragraph. Then list two points you would make in a response.

A Cultural Mosaic
Philip R. Popple and Leslie Leighninger

The presence of diverse racial, ethnic, and other distinct groups in society gives rise to various notions[1] about the proper relationship between individual groups and "the whole." Such notions emerge particularly in discussions of immigration, although they have relevance also to the situations of longtime residents (African Americans and American Indians) and of those belonging to categories such as the elderly or people with disabilities. A traditional version of "ideal group relations" in the United States is the idea of a melting pot, in which the cultures of all groups join to produce a new, distinctly American culture. In real life, this early twentieth-century idea of a "blended American" proved unrealistic. Newcomers were unwilling to give up all their traditions and customs, and, perhaps more significantly, the dominant society had a stake in maintaining its own identity. We like the reframing of the melting pot image proposed by historian Lawrence Levine. Levine argued that today's model of diversity "is not the American melting pot, but a cultural mosaic in which discrete ethnic groups persist and interact with other groups."

Source: Excerpted from Popple, Philip R. et al. *Social Work, Social Welfare, and American Society.*

---
[1] **notions:** ideas or theories

Thesis Statement: _____

1. _____
2. _____

TRY IT OUT!   Here is another paragraph from Serenda Nanda's article on arranged marriages in India. Write a one-sentence summary of the paragraph and then one or two paragraphs in response. Do you agree with Nanda's viewpoint, or do you see some value in arranged marriages?

Six years later I returned to India to do fieldwork, this time among the middle class in Bombay, a modern, sophisticated city. From the experience of my earlier visit, I decided to include a study of arranged marriages in my project. By this time, I had met many Indian couples whose marriages had been arranged and who seemed very happy. Particularly in contrast to the fate of my married friends in the United States who were already in the process of divorce, the positive aspects of arranged marriages appeared to me to outweigh the negatives.

Summary / Response Essays   **141**

Try It Out! activities challenge students to apply what they have learned.

Quoting, **paraphrasing**, and **summarizing** instructions provide useful tools for research-based writing.

Writing a Good Paraphrase

A good paraphrase:

- identifies the source of the original
- shows that you have fully understood the material
- differs enough from the original that it is clearly your own writing
- does not merely substitute synonyms for the words in the original sentence

Here is an example of a paraphrase from Wade and Tavris, whose work was discussed in the model:

ORIGINAL MATERIAL

Learning explanations of language acquisition assume that children are rewarded for saying the right words and punished for making errors. But parents do not stop to correct every error in their children's speech, so long as they understand what the child is trying to say (Brown, Cazden & Bellugi, 1969). Indeed, parents often reward children for incorrect statements! A 2-year-old who says, "Want milk!" is likely to get it; most parents would not wait for a more grammatical (or polite) request.

PARAPHRASED MATERIAL

Carole Wade and Carol Tavris say that children do not acquire language from parents praising their correct speech and punishing their errors. For example, if parents can understand a child's request for milk, even if it is ungrammatical, they will give the child the milk. In effect, say Wade and Tavris, the parents "reward the child for incorrect statements" (2011).

Note that the paraphrase identifies the source and restates its ideas without copying them. It also integrates a short quotation from the original when it borrows the exact language.

Writing Tip

To write a good paraphrase you will need to follow a process:

1. Read the original passage carefully more than once, underlining the main points in the passage.
2. Cover the material so you cannot refer to it.
3. To help you restate the material in your own words, imagine that you are explaining the material to a good friend.
4. Finally, compare the original to your restatement to see if it expresses the same meaning—without using the same phrases.

Writing Tips provide useful strategies to help students produce better writing.

102   CHAPTER 5

Preparation for Writing develops the research and documentation skills needed for the writing assignment.

PREPARATION FOR WRITING

You have already learned basic research practices in Chapter 4, page 79. Now you can build on them. Begin your research on the topic by asking yourself a question. Here are some examples.

- Have experts discovered new findings on the topic?
- Is there a debate on this topic that you should explain to readers?
- Do new studies on the topic challenge or change previously held beliefs?
- Has research revealed an important problem that is worth exploring and discussing causes or solutions that people may not have considered before?

Think about the writing model and the research questions Ksenia Laney may have asked herself when she started her research. For example, how and why did the disaster happen? What were its effects on the people, the crops, and the animals surrounding the facility?

NARROWING YOUR FOCUS

The next step is to ensure that your research question is not too broad; otherwise, you may end up writing a book instead of a five- to twelve-page paper! Note how these broad research questions have been narrowed:

TOO BROAD What are the causes of obesity?

NARROWER Do carbohydrates contribute more to obesity than other food groups?

TOO BROAD What is autism?

NARROWER Why is autism so difficult to treat?

TOO BROAD Are artificial sweeteners dangerous?

NARROWER What has research revealed about the long-term effects of aspartame?

PRACTICE 5   Forming and Narrowing Research Questions

Work in small groups. Choose a topic and generate possible research questions to pursue. Remember to ask questions that begin with *how? when? where? why? who?* and *should?* or *could?* Decide if your research question is sufficiently narrow.

TOPICS

- College admissions standards and the makeup of U.S. colleges and universities
- The wave of immigration to the United States that occurred from 1989 to the present
- Down syndrome
- Medical technology
- Music therapy for mentally or physically impaired people

Research Papers **179**

Sections on **finding** and **evaluating information from sources** provide students with essential research skills.

Finding Information from Sources

Once you have narrowed your research question, use only sources that relate to the question, and read selectively. In books, consult the table of contents or the index to help you find the most relevant parts. Scan long articles, looking especially at the subheadings. Follow this procedure.

1. Be curious as you read, and ask yourself: Is the information important and usable in this paper? Does it raise more questions to explore? What additional research might answer these questions?
2. Annotate as you read. Underline important passages, highlight key points, and make notes in the margin about how and where the information might be used in your paper. Take notes and record your sources, along with the page numbers, on note cards. (See Chapter 6, pages 120–123.)
3. If you print out material, make notes directly on these pages. Highlight passages you may want to quote or paraphrase. Use note cards to jot down a brief summary of each important passage, abbreviate a source (using either the title or the author), and record the page numbers so you can return to them later in the original.
4. Again use note cards to write your own commentary on source material. Make sure, however, that you clearly distinguish that commentary from your source information.
5. Then organize your note cards by subtopics, especially by grouping the evidence that supports the claim of each subtopic.

Evaluating Sources

Not every source is reliable or objective. Many writers reveal a particular point of view or bias. Even the data they include or the people they quote may be influenced by their political, philosophical, or theoretical viewpoints. Moreover, with the growth of Internet use, virtually anyone can create a website, author a blog, or post an entry on a blog. Therefore, it is extremely important that you evaluate your sources for their reliability, objectivity, and stance on the issue you are researching. Keep the following guidelines in mind.

Timeliness

Your subject matter will determine whether a work is outdated. For scientific, psychological, sociological, and technical issues, the most recent publications generally provide the most useful information. However, if you are researching the life of a famous politician, author, or historical figure, older publications may be perfectly good sources of information.

Objectivity and Bias

Authors often have strong feelings about their subject matter, or even a financial or personal interest in the issue. Strongly worded opinions, though, do not necessarily mean that the author is unfair. The main test is whether the person's argument is balanced, giving equal, or nearly equal, treatment to more than one side of an issue.

180 CHAPTER 9

Step-by-step Writing Assignments make the writing process clear and easy to follow.

4. A person who fits into a new culture is said to be _____.

5. When someone gets new eyeglasses, the person's visual _____ may improve.

6. When a person feels divided between one feeling and another, he is said to be

_____.

WRITING ASSIGNMENT

Your assignment for this chapter is to write a summary and response essay on a topic related to culture. Write an essay of at least five paragraphs on one of the topics below or one that your teacher suggests. Follow the steps in the writing process.

POSSIBLE TOPICS

- Cultural identity
- Cultural diversity
- Cultural differences
- Adapting to a new culture
- Cultural assimilation
- Cultural practices in education

Explore   **STEP 1: Explore your topic, audience, and purpose.**
- Choose your topic from the list above.
- Research an Internet article on your topic.
- Read the article carefully, highlighting or taking notes of main points for your summary.
- Consider who might be interested in this article and a response; they are your audience.
- Consider what you wish to accomplish in your response; this is the thesis of your response.

Prewrite   **STEP 2: Prewrite to get ideas.**
- Freewrite, brainstorm, or cluster to uncover your ideas.
- Draft a preliminary thesis statement for your response.
- Brainstorm examples from your personal experience or the experiences of others that support or refute the article's thesis or supporting points.

Organize   **STEP 3: Organize your ideas.**
- Select the ideas to include in the summary.
- Outline the response, listing each claim.
- Select passages that you will paraphrase or quote as support for your claims.

Summary / Response Essays **143**

Peer Review and **Writer's Self-Check Worksheets** at the back of the book help students collaborate and sharpen their revision skills.

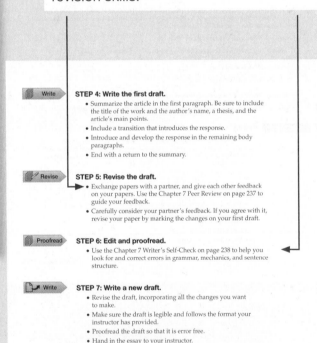

Write   **STEP 4: Write the first draft.**
- Summarize the article in the first paragraph. Be sure to include the title of the work and the author's name, a thesis, and the article's main points.
- Include a transition that introduces the response.
- Introduce and develop the response in the remaining body paragraphs.
- End with a return to the summary.

Revise   **STEP 5: Revise the draft.**
- Exchange papers with a partner, and give each other feedback on your papers. Use the Chapter 7 Peer Review on page 237 to guide your feedback.
- Carefully consider your partner's feedback. If you agree with it, revise your paper by marking the changes on your first draft.

Proofread   **STEP 6: Edit and proofread.**
- Use the Chapter 7 Writer's Self-Check on page 238 to help you look for and correct errors in grammar, mechanics, and sentence structure.

Write   **STEP 7: Write a new draft.**
- Revise the draft, incorporating all the changes you want to make.
- Make sure the draft is legible and follows the format your instructor has provided.
- Proofread the draft so that it is error free.
- Hand in the essay to your instructor.

Self-Assessment encourages students to evaluate their progress.

SELF-ASSESSMENT

In this chapter, you learned to:
- ○ Analyze a summary / response essay
- ○ Distinguish between objective and subjective points of view
- ○ Summarize an essay in an introductory paragraph
- ○ Plan and write a response to the essay
- ○ Use active and passive voice in appropriate contexts
- ○ Write, edit, and revise an essay about culture

Which ones can you do well? Mark them ☑

Which ones do you need to practice more? Mark them ♪

144   CHAPTER 7

EXPANSION

 TIMED WRITING ◄───────────────

Timed Writing activities develop students' writing fluency under pressure.

Return to "A Cultural Mosaic" in Practice 6 on page 141. Now summarize and write a full response to the passage. You will have 45 minutes. To complete the expansion, you will need to budget your time accordingly. Follow this procedure.

1. Reread the passage, underlining or highlighting the statement of the main argument and key supporting points. (10 minutes)

2. Write a one-paragraph summary of the passage. State the main argument and key supporting ideas you have located. Omit any long examples and explanations. (10 minutes)

3. Then write a response, beginning with a smooth transition and a thesis statement. Make your position clear. Do you agree or disagree with the argument, or is your response mixed? Refer back to the article to support your claims. What in your own experience, or the experience of others you know, can you cite as backing for your claims? Cite examples. (15 minutes)

4. Revise and edit your work. Be sure your summary and thesis are clear. If you write by hand, you may make changes above the lines in the margins. (5 minutes)

5. Check your summary and response for errors. Correct any mistakes. (5 minutes)

6. Hand in your paper to your instructor.

 RESEARCH AND RESPOND ◄───────────────

Additional writing tasks encourage students to further develop the writing skills in each chapter.

Do an Internet search using the key words "bilingual education" or "bilingual immersion." Find a short article that argues either for or against one of these topics. Summarize the article and respond, using the same procedures you have followed in the chapter.

Writing Guides provide students with tools to improve the flow of ideas in different types of essays.

APPENDICES

APPENDIX A WRITING GUIDES

The following are *writing guides*, or fill-in-the-blank sentences that can help you establish logical relationships as you write. These guides will provide you with models of wording that will make the introduction of ideas or the transition between ideas smoother. At times, you may wish to use the exact wording in the guides. At other times, you will probably need to change the language to fit your content and purpose.

Chapter 2

Guides for Reporting Statistical Results

1. Most _____ are from _____ .
2. A lot of / twelve of the _____ lived _____ .
3. The majority / _____ percent of the students speak _____ languages.

Guides for Thesis Statements

1. My classmates are similar in _____ ways.
2. My classmates differ in _____ , _____ , _____ , and _____ .
3. Despite many differences in their backgrounds, my classmates share _____ .

Appendices include a section on **MLA** and **APA formats**, which enable students to correctly document research papers in a variety of academic fields.

APPENDIX G DOCUMENTING SOURCES WITH MLA AND APA FORMATS

In academic classes, your instructors will ask you to document the sources of outside information your have used in your paper. There are two steps to this process.

1. Insert a short reference in the body of your paper. This is called an in-text citation. The purpose of an in-text citation is to refer the reader to the works-cited list at the end of your paper.
2. Prepare a complete list of your sources. This list is titled either Works Cited or References and appears as the last page of your paper.

The two most commonly used formats for documenting sources are those used by the Modern Language Association (MLA) and the American Psychological Association (APA). Each format specifies style guidelines for referring to authors with in-text citations, footnotes and endnotes, and the sources list.

The MLA (Modern Language Association) system is used primarily for documenting work within the liberal arts and humanities—literature, English, foreign languages, art, and so on. The APA (American Psychological Association) system is mainly used to document source within the social sciences—sociology, psychology, anthropology, economics, and political science, etc. The next few pages will show you only the basics of the MLA and APA styles of formal documentation. In addition, be aware that each format has differences in punctuation rules which are too numerous to be dealt with here. Consult the *MLA Handbook for Writers of Research Papers* and the *Publication Manual of the American Psychological Association* for more detailed information. You can find these books and others like them in the reference area of any library.

THE BASICS OF MLA FORMAT

In papers using the MLA system, the name of the author typically introduces a quotation, paraphrase, or summary, and the page number of the source (if there is one) follows in parentheses before the period.

In-Text Citations

In-text citations give only enough information to allow the reader to find the full reference in the list of works cited at the end of your paper. Here are some guidelines.

ONE AUTHOR

Use the last name of the author and a page number (or numbers, if the borrowed information appears on more than one page). Use no punctuation.

(Clinton 17)

TWO OR MORE AUTHORS

If there are two or three authors, give all the names. If there are four or more, use the first author's name and the Latin abbreviation *et al.* ("and others") followed by a period.

(Bamberger and Yaeger 62)

(Singleton et al. 345)

CHAPTER 1

EXPOSITORY ESSAYS

OBJECTIVES

To write academic texts, you need to master certain skills.

In this chapter, you will learn to:

- Analyze an expository essay
- Examine the elements of a well-structured essay
- Identify context and grammar clues for correct article use
- Follow and practice the steps in the writing process
- Write, revise, and edit an essay based on personal experience

No two writers work in the same way. What is your writing style?

In many of your courses, you will be asked to write various types of academic papers, from relatively short essays to long papers based on research. Each chapter of this book will teach you the writing and research skills necessary to produce these academic papers, beginning with the essay and ending with the research paper. These skills include finding information through research, evaluating the information, and incorporating it into your essays. For the moment, however, this chapter will focus on the structure of the essay and the process of writing it.

An **essay** is an organized discussion of a topic in a series of paragraphs. It contains three main parts: an **introduction** (an introductory paragraph), a **body** (usually at least two, but often more, supporting paragraphs), and a **conclusion** (a concluding paragraph).

The introduction performs several roles. It attracts readers' interest. It establishes the essay's specific topic and states the writer's position or **claim** about that topic in a **thesis statement**. It may also provide a preview of the body of the essay.

Each body paragraph of an essay supports and develops a subtopic of the thesis statement. The paragraph states its **controlling idea**, or the writer's area of focus, in a **topic sentence**. The remaining sentences support the topic sentence with facts, details, and explanations, which lead logically to the next paragraph. The conclusion, or the essay's last paragraph, may summarize main points, end with a question for the reader, or cite a memorable quotation. In any instance, however, it provides a strong ending to the essay.

ANALYZING THE MODEL

The writing model describes the different methods that writers use as they begin the writing process. The essay is *expository*; that is, it explains something.

Read the model. Then answer the questions.

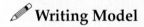 **Writing Model**

Explorers and Planners:
Ways to Discover and Organize Ideas

1   You are staring at a blank page or computer screen and encountering familiar questions: *How do I start? What do I have to say?* Everyone shares these problems, but they need not be serious obstacles. Since the average person can think ahead only seven words, plus or minus four, you probably do not begin a sentence knowing exactly how it will end, or exactly what the next sentence will say. Therefore, it is almost impossible to anticipate[1] the exact content of an entire paper. Although some experienced writers approach their first drafts with clearly organized plans, you may

---

[1] **anticipate:** meet someone or experience something without planning to

not be one of them. Your thinking may be disorganized, but that is to be expected. The beginning stage of writing is a time to discover your ideas and plan how to present them over subsequent[2] drafts, and there is more than one effective way to discover and plan: through freewriting, brainstorming, clustering, and outlining.

2   Of course, no two writers work in the same way. Everyone's ultimate[3] goal is to produce a clear, convincing, and engaging piece of writing. However, the process of arriving at that goal differs from person to person, and often from task to task. On the one hand are the planners. They carefully consider the structure and content of their ideas before writing them down. Then they revise their work only once or twice. On the other hand are the discoverers, which means almost everyone else. They compose messy first drafts, sometimes with unrelated ideas, which they progressively clean up and reshape through multiple revisions. One such discoverer was the Nobel Prize winning author Isaac Bashevis Singer. When asked how he went about composing his stories, he replied, "There's no plan, no formula. I may revise something twice or a thousand times."[4]

3   Whether writers are planners, discoverers, or a bit of both, their process of revision begins after the first draft. Then they can examine what they have said, see what ideas are emerging[5] or incomplete, and decide which to discard, replace, expand, or refine. They may change their minds and wording two, three, or a dozen times until the ideas and language are clear and concise. A writer's mind is filled with an ocean of ideas awaiting the chance to flow out. The task is to open the floodgates and channel the flow onto the page or screen.

4   One method that discoverers use for getting started is freewriting. It involves writing down words as fast as possible without concern for exact phrasing, grammar, or spelling. The work is uncensored and perhaps illogical, but the main goal is merely to keep writing. This process often leads to new discoveries and insights. Much, or even all, of freewriting may not end up in the final draft, but writers can highlight the parts worth keeping and then do a second, more focused, freewriting. By that point they can turn to planning their essay.

5   Another method discoverers often employ is brainstorming, or listing ideas. They jot down their thoughts in whatever order they occur. After that initial step, they highlight the most important ideas, cross out the irrelevant ones, and reorganize whatever remains. They may even do a second, more focused and detailed brainstorming list. This list shapes the first draft of the paper.

(continued on next page)

---

[2] **subsequent:** coming after or following something else
[3] **ultimate:** final, most important
[4] This exchange took place between the author and Mr. Singer at a banquet honoring him.
[5] **emerging:** appearing or coming from out of nowhere

6   Planners work more systematically than discoverers and organize their ideas from the very beginning. One way they generate and organize ideas is through a different version of brainstorming, called clustering. It starts with drawing a circle in the middle of a page and writing a word or phrase inside the circle. That idea should lead to related ideas, each circled and then linked to the first circle by a line or branch. More circles and branches follow until they form "clusters" of ideas. Planners can then examine the clusters, decide which to keep or discard, and begin a second, more focused, cluster diagram.

7   Finally, of course, planners can rely on an outline. One of the most efficient of these devices is the topic sentence outline. It begins with a statement of the essay's thesis. Then it includes the topic sentences of the body paragraphs and their supporting details. Not only does this type of outline help structure the essay, but it also provides a preliminary[6] set of topic sentences for the first draft.

8   Of course, many writers mix these methods or choose different ones, depending on the project. In fact, no matter what method writers choose for getting started, they must keep in mind that each one is merely a way to begin the writing process. Revision, redrafting, editing, and proofreading will follow. *Efficiency* is the key word in writing. Why stare at a blank page and waste your time? Why attempt to write a perfect first draft when you know full well that you are going to revise it later? Try the approaches that have proved so valuable in helping writers, whether they are discoverers or planners.

---

[6] **preliminary:** something that is done first

Questions about the Model

1. In what ways does the writer try to attract readers' interest in the introduction?

2. In Paragraph 1, which sentence is the thesis statement? Circle it in the writing model.

3. What two types of writers are introduced in Paragraph 2? Underline them in the writing model.

4. How many methods for beginning to write does the author describe? What are they?

5. Where are the topic sentences that introduce each method? Underline them in the writing model.

6. Why does the author quote the famous writer, Isaac Bashevis Singer?

7. In the concluding paragraph, the author asks, "Why stare at a blank page . . .". Which sentence from the introductory paragraph does this question echo? Why do you think the author includes this question?

✎ Noticing Vocabulary: Negative Prefixes

Good writers use a rich and varied vocabulary. Paying attention to, and learning more about, words will help you become a better writer, too. Notice that the writing model contains adjectives with **negative prefixes**. Prefixes are word parts that can be added to the beginning of a base word (that is, a full word to which a prefix is attached).* They change a base word's meaning, but not its part of speech.

The prefixes *dis-, un-, il-, im-, in-,* and *ir-* can mean "not" or "without." Adding these negative prefixes to an adjective usually creates another adjective with the opposite meaning.

| PRACTICE 1 | Forming Negative Adjectives |

Ⓐ Look at the writing model again. Find and underline adjectives that begin with the negative prefixes *dis-, il-, im-, in-,* and *ir-*.

Ⓑ Choose the adjective from Part A that best completes each sentence.

1. When two things are not connected to each other in any way, they are ____unrelated____.

2. When something cannot be done, it is an _____ task.

3. When something has no clear structure, it is _____.

4. When something is not finished, it is _____.

5. When an idea does not relate to the topic being discussed, it is

   _____.

6. When an idea makes no sense, it is _____.

7. When ideas have not been censored, they are _____.

---

* A base word can also take a **suffix**, a word part that is added to the end of the base word. Examples include the suffixes *-able, -ful,* and *-less.* Thus the base word *suit* and the suffix *-able* becomes *suitable,* and the base word *hope + -ful* or *-less* becomes *hopeful* or *hopeless.*

A well-organized essay helps readers understand how all its parts fit together in a logical whole. The thesis statement, topic sentences, and conclusion play a central role in that organization.

A CLEAR THESIS STATEMENT

Every essay addresses a broad general topic, such as *writing*. A **thesis statement**, however, is a full sentence that narrows the topic specifically to what the essay is about, such as *the beginning stage of writing*. It also makes clear the writer's position on or **claim** about that topic. Often the thesis statement gives a preview of the subdivisions or subtopics to be developed in the body of the essay. Look at the thesis statement from the writing model as an example.

┌─────── THE SPECIFIC TOPIC ───────┐ ┌──────────────────── THE WRITER'S CLAIM ────────────────────┐
The beginning stage of writing is a time to discover your ideas and plan how to present them, and there is more than one effective way to discover and plan:

┌──────── THE PREVIEW OF THE BODY ────────┐
through freewriting, brainstorming, clustering, and outlining.

PRACTICE 2   **Narrowing Thesis Statements**

Each thesis statement is too broad. Make each one more specific. Be sure to add a phrase that previews the subtopic that might follow in the body.

1. Learning a new language is not easy. *Mastering the pronunciation of a new language can be challenging for several reasons.*

2. My family has some interesting people. _____

3. School requires hard work. _____

4. The Internet is useful. _____

5. A college education is important. _____

6. I write best under the right conditions. _____

TOPIC SENTENCES

Just as a thesis statement introduces the specific topic of an essay, a **topic sentence** at or near the beginning of a paragraph introduces the topic of a paragraph, or what it is about. A topic sentence also establishes the **controlling idea** in the paragraph. Although controlling ideas sometimes are implied rather than stated directly, most are stated clearly in a topic sentence. Likewise, a controlling idea may be expressed as a **claim** that the writer makes about something. The remainder of the paragraph then explains, supports, or expands on the claim.

In general, there are three types of claims, as illustrated by the writing model.

- A claim that something is or was true:

    Of course, no two writers work in the same way.

    The remainder of the paragraph supports or explains the claim that writers differ in the way they work. Note, however, that this is only a *claim* that something is or was true. That is why it usually needs support, explanation, or, perhaps, proof. For example, *Elephants can fly* is also a claim that something is true, but its information is not factual.

- A claim that something is good, better, or worse:

    One of the most efficient of these devices is the topic sentence outline.

    The words "most efficient" establish value or worth. The remainder of the paragraph supports or explains the writer's claim that the outline is efficient.

- A claim that makes recommendations, suggestions, or demands for some action:

    No matter what method writers choose for getting started, they *must keep in mind* that each one is merely a way to begin the writing process.

    The rest of the paragraph supports the claim by explaining why it is important or useful.

PRACTICE 3   Generating Topic Sentences

Complete each topic sentence by adding a controlling idea expressed as a claim.

1. In addition to money, a part-time job can provide _valuable experience in time management and self-discipline._

2. Speaking more than one language equips someone _____

3. The relationship between teacher and student differs _____

(continued on next page)

4. A good way to begin any writing assignment is _____

_____

5. Computers are often essential tools in writing because _____

_____

6. Most professions value _____

_____

A STRONG CONCLUSION

The final or **concluding paragraph** of an essay often summarizes or rephrases the essay's thesis statement. Because the conclusion is usually a summary, it should *never* add new ideas or information. The paragraph often concludes with a phrase that echoes the language in the opening paragraph, as in the first and last paragraphs of the writing model. Depending on the content of the essay, the concluding paragraph might also end with a memorable quotation, or a call to action or recommendation of what the reader should do.

| PRACTICE 4 | **Evaluating Conclusions** |

Work with a partner. Choose the best conclusion from each pair of sentences and label it *best*.

1. ___*best*___ **a.** In short, the only solution to getting writing done is to write, write, and write.

_____ **b.** Try not to postpone writing an assignment.

2. _____ **a.** Another thing to consider is your audience.

_____ **b.** Always try to anticipate your audience's questions.

3. _____ **a.** Writing is a continual process of drafting and revision that stops only when the paper is due.

_____ **b.** Writing involves a lot of revision if it is going to be any good.

4. _____ **a.** Will you spend the time to do it well? If not, then you may be wasting your reader's time.

_____ **b.** Writing requires time.

5. _____ **a.** "Writing," says one well-known author, "is thinking."

_____ **b.** Writing demands constant thought.

6. _____ **a.** As I said earlier, keep all these things in mind.

_____ **b.** In sum, effective writing requires planning, drafting, and revision.

Of course, even the best-structured essay will not be clear if it contains frequent grammatical errors. One of the most common of these errors is using articles incorrectly. Articles give information about a noun or noun phrase by telling the reader whether that noun is indefinite or definite. Articles entered English long ago simply as different pronunciations of the words *one* ("an") and *that* ("the"). In other words, *a/an* is **indefinite** (not specific), but *the* is **definite** (specific).

USING ARTICLES

Articles appear before a noun, an adjective, or before an adverb, adjective, and noun combination.

NOUN	ADJ NOUN	ADV ADJ NOUN
A bird	A blue bird	A really beautiful bird

Use *a/an* to communicate new or unfamiliar information; use *the* to refer to information that you have mentioned earlier or that you expect the reader to be aware of.

Use of *A/An*

The indefinite articles *a/an* precede only **singular count nouns**; that is, nouns that can be counted, such as *chair*, *car*, or *bird*. These articles mean "one of many"; they do not specify a particular one, but mean that there is more than one choice. Therefore, these nouns are indefinite. *A* precedes words that begin with a consonant sound; *an* precedes words that begin with a vowel sound.

RULES	EXAMPLES
1. Use *a/an* when you don't have a specific person, place, or thing in mind.	Buy a notebook. (There are many notebooks available.) An introduction to an essay should attract an audience's attention. (There are many possible introductions, claims, and audiences.)
2. Use *a/an* when the person, place, or thing is unfamiliar to the reader. For example, when the noun appears for the first time.	You are staring at a blank page. Finally, of course, planners can rely on an outline.
3. Use *a/an* when you mean "one."	I may revise something twice or a thousand times. You will have an hour to write your paper.

Use of *The*

The definite article *the* precedes any specific singular or plural count noun as well as a specific noncount noun such as *furniture*, *traffic*, or *water*.

Rules	Examples
1. Use *the* when a noun is mentioned for the second time. (The reader already knows what is being discussed.)	It starts with drawing a *circle* and writing a word or phrase inside the *circle*.
2. Use *the* when the noun names a unique person, place, or thing. (There is only one possible choice.)	Revision begins after starting the first draft. The spring semester begins in April. Submit your essay to the instructor.
3. Use *the* when a phrase or dependent clause makes a noun specific.	The novels of Isaac Bashevis Singer . . . . . . the ideas that someone explores before beginning to write

---

PRACTICE 5   Choosing the Correct Article

Circle the article that best completes each sentence.

1. When I write (a / *an* / the) essay, I like to plan it first.

2. I begin by choosing (a / an / the) topic.

3. Then I write any ideas I have about (a / an / the) topic.

4. After that, I choose (a / an / the) best ideas and use them to write a thesis statement.

5. I make sure that my thesis statement includes (a / an / the) topic and (a / an / the) claim.

6. Then I use (a / an / the) thesis statement to create (a / an / the) outline.

7. I use (a / an / the) outline to write (a / an / the) first draft.

8. Finally, I edit and revise (a / an / the) draft and hand it in to (a / an / the) instructor.

No Article (Zero Article)

When a noncount noun or a plural count noun is referring to something in general, then do not place an article before it. This is often called the zero article.

RULES	EXAMPLES
1. Do not use an article when a count noun represents a general group, not one of many.	. . . often from **task** to **task** (The singular nouns are general) . . . an ocean of **ideas** (The plural noun indicates a general group.) Discoverers compose messy **first drafts**. (The plural noun indicates a general group, even though an adjective precedes it).
2. Do not use an article when a noncount noun represents a general category.	**Grammar** is important to **clarity** in **writing**. (All three nouns cannot be counted and indicate general groups.)

PRACTICE 6   **Adding Articles**

Complete the paragraph by adding the correct article. If no article is needed, write Ø. For some, there may be more than one correct answer.

_____ writing process begins with discovering

1.

_____ ideas. _____ methods of _____

2.   3.   4.

discovery include _____ freewriting, brainstorming, and

5.

clustering. Many people try one or more of these approaches. After

_____ writer has captured his ideas on _____ paper,

6.   7.

he or she can begin to draft _____ essay. _____

8.   9.

first draft is only _____ beginning step in composing, however.

10.

_____ essay will go through many more stages before it is

11.

finished. _____ stages of writing include _____

12.   13.

revising, editing, and proofreading. _____ final result should be

14.

clear and error free.

See Appendix C on page 203 for more information on articles.

As the writing model on pages 2–4 makes clear, composing an essay is a process. It consists of a series of steps. The process may include as many as seven steps, which are *recursive*; that is, they recur, or go back and forth. For example, a writer may be working on Step 3 and feel the need to go back to Step 1 to explore a new thought.

You will be following these steps as you complete the writing assignments in each chapter of this book, so it is important that you learn how each one works.

STEP 1: Explore your topic, audience, and purpose.

In this first step, let your mind explore ideas. Thoughts will occur to you while walking the dog, traveling to work, or doing the dishes. Capture those thoughts by making notes on whatever you can: napkins, scraps of paper, or even the back of your hand. Eventually you should focus your exploration more systematically on your topic, audience, and purpose.

Choosing Your Topic

Choose a topic that you know and care about. Then you will have something interesting to say, and you will say it clearly and confidently.

College assignments sometimes give you freedom to choose a topic. Often, though, you must select and then narrow your topic from a general one that your teacher has chosen. For example, if your teacher asks you to write an essay about cultural practices, you might narrow that topic by describing one specific custom in your family (or community).

PRACTICE 7	Narrowing a Topic

These essay topics are too general. Narrow each topic to a specific one that could be developed in a short essay.

1. my job

    my career as a pharmacist after graduating from college

2. a trip to the U.S.

    _____

3. education in another country

    _____

4. customs in another country

    _____

5. my academic goals

    _____

6. my first job

    _____

Addressing Your Audience

The less that your audience knows about your topic, the more you must define terms and provide basic background information. You probably would not need to define terms if you write for your instructors. For example, you would not tell your history teacher who fought in World War II. However, when you write for an audience with little knowledge of history, you might need to name the countries involved in the war.

Similar concerns apply to writing outside of school—in business, professional, and other communication. How much does the intended audience know about the topic, and what do you need to tell them?

Determining Your Purpose

Another important point to consider is the purpose of your essay. Is your goal to inform, to persuade, or to entertain—or maybe to do all three? If you are writing an expository essay about learning to speak another language, for instance, you are providing information. However, you might also include some amusing examples of errors that you or others have made when first learning another language.

STEP 2: Prewrite to get ideas.

As the writing model on pages 2–4 indicates, the second step of the writing process involves generating ideas and then organizing them on paper or on the computer screen.

Freewriting

One technique mentioned in the writing model is freewriting. Freewriting can be based on a topic (a focused freewrite), or the writer can simply write whatever topics come to mind. Here is an example:

> Freewriting. Let the words flow out without thinking about grammar and spelling. Maybe some of the ideas will not be usable later. But at least the ideas will be on the page for the writer to see. Experiment, you can always come back to sentences later & cross out the ones that do not fit. Write fast as if you were speaking to someone.

Once you have captured your ideas, you can select from and arrange them. Circle or highlight the best parts and perhaps do a second freewriting. This time, focus more narrowly on your topic and add more details.

Do three five-minute freewritings on whatever comes to your mind. Follow the instructions.

1. Set a timer for five minutes and then write continuously. Do not pause to revise or edit your work, and do not worry if you digress.

2. Read each of the freewritings. Then return to one freewriting in which an interesting idea has started to emerge.

3. Do another five-minute freewriting that focuses on that idea.

Brainstorming

The writing model on pages 2–4 also introduced you to brainstorming, or listing thoughts as they occur to you. Here is an example:

Writing on a computer

fast as you can type

easy to revise by deleting, cutting, and pasting

setting margins

setting line spacing

using spell and grammar checker

online thesaurus

handicap if you cannot type fast

don't have to worry about bad handwriting

danger with spell checker: selects different words from the ones
   you intend

essay looks different on the screen from the way it looks on
   the page

danger in not saving your work

different fonts and font sizes

Notice that a controlling idea of *advantages vs. disadvantages* emerges from this list, but the list is not yet organized. Therefore, the next step in the process is to rearrange the items. Number or highlight them, cross out the ones that do not belong, and then rewrite the list.

Writing on a computer

1. don't have to worry about bad handwriting

2. easy to revise by deleting, cutting, and pasting

3. using spell and grammar checker

Brainstorming about Language

Brainstorm ways in which another language such as Chinese differs from English. List ideas in whatever order they occur to you. Then reorder the list as explained on page 14.

Clustering

The model also mentioned clustering, which helps you organize your ideas as you brainstorm. Here is a short example of clustering based on the model. The central idea, "discoverers," is placed in the middle of the page, and the supporting ideas branch out from it. The central idea and the branches with their ideas form clusters.

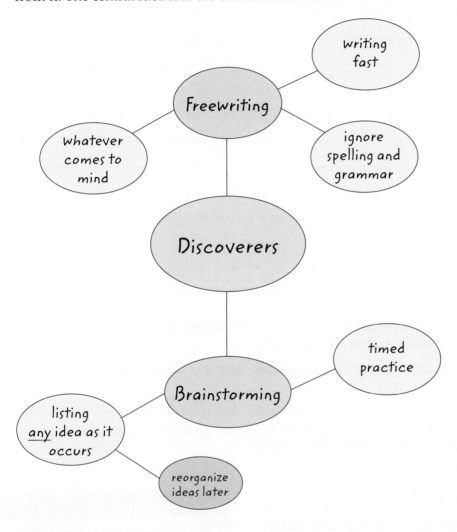

Creating a Cluster Diagram

Make a cluster diagram. Begin by writing the name of your favorite activity in the middle of a piece of paper. Then branch out to other circles with categories and branch out from them.

STEP 3: Organize your ideas.

Once you have gathered your ideas, then it is time to organize them.

Outlining

Outlining is often the best way to proceed with a plan. It allows you to list the essay's thesis statement, the topic sentences of the body paragraphs, and the supporting information for each topic sentence. A popular type of outline is one that features the thesis and topic sentences. Here is how a typical one is structured:

THESIS STATEMENT: _____

_____

   I. **Topic Sentence:** _____
      A. Support: _____
      B. Support: _____
  II. **Topic Sentence:** _____
      A. Support: _____
      B. Support: _____
 III. **Topic Sentence:** _____
      A. Support: _____
      B. Support: _____

TRY IT OUT! On a separate sheet of paper, turn your brainstorming list or clustering diagram into a formal outline. Follow the instructions.

1. Gather your information, deciding what to omit or include (you can add new ideas at this point).

2. Then organize the information into an outline. It should include a preliminary thesis statement, at least three major headings for the topic sentences, and subheadings for the supporting information.

STEP 4: Write the first draft.

You are now ready to begin the first draft, but do not try to be "perfect" at this point. No one gets it right on the first try. New ideas will come to you later, and you may discover a better way to arrange them.

Writing Tip

Composing your first draft on the computer has many advantages. You can move around material by using the "cut" and "paste" commands. You can use the spelling and grammar checker when editing (but don't depend on it to correct all your mistakes!).

STEP 5: Revise the draft.

Revision is different from editing. Revision involves changing, removing, adding, or shifting around material. It is the time to reexamine your work to see if it is clear, logically organized, and complete. Editing involves checking the paper at the end of the writing process to correct any errors in spelling or grammar, and to make some small changes.

Revision begins by reading your first draft carefully. Study its organization, word choice, and details. Make notes for changes in the margins and above the lines. Rearrange sections, say sentences differently, substitute words, or write whole new sections. Then make a clean copy before going any further.

Predicting

Readers do not merely receive information; they actively attempt to find meaning for themselves. They predict what will follow from your opening sentences, although they may adjust their predictions as they read on. As the writer, you can benefit from predicting, too. Here is how. Read the first couple of sentences in a paragraph. Then stop and think about what your readers would expect to follow in the remainder of the paragraph. Determine if the rest of the paragraph satisfies those predictions. Make notes on what to add, remove, or shift to satisfy those expectations. Predicting is especially helpful in peer review, when you exchange papers with others and offer suggestions for revision and improvement.

STEP 6: Edit and proofread.

You want people to judge your ideas, not your mistakes. Therefore, edit your work carefully. Have you marked all the revisions you intend to make, or are there others you see? Proofread your draft, or check for misspelled words, grammatical errors, incomplete sentences, and incorrect punctuation. Read the paper more than once, and perhaps read it aloud. Be sure to mark on your draft all the changes you wish to make. Use the correction symbols, such as the ones from Appendix H pages 221–223, to guide you in noting corrections.

STEP 7: Write a new draft.

Write a new draft, incorporating all your changes. Read your work another time, proofreading it carefully to be sure you are satisfied with it. Copy it over, or print it out again if you need to.

🖊 Applying Vocabulary: Using Negative Prefixes

Before you begin your writing assignment, review the information you learned about forming negative adjectives with negative prefixes on page 5.

| PRACTICE 11 | Writing Sentences with Negative Adjectives |

Write sentences about your experiences with writing. Use an adjective with a different negative prefix in each sentence.

1. *im-* _I thought it would be impossible to write a sonnet, but I succeeded._
   _____

2. *il-* _____
   _____

3. *ir-* _____
   _____

4. *dis-* _____
   _____

5. *im-* _____
   _____

6. *in-* _____
   _____

7. *un-* _____
   _____

WRITING ASSIGNMENT

Your assignment for this chapter is to write a five-paragraph expository or personal essay in which you discuss your earlier experiences with writing. When and where did you do it? What kind of papers did you write, what was their length, and how much did you revise them?

Remember, in a personal essay you describe your own experiences and express your own opinions. You use first person pronouns, such as *I*, *me*, and *mine* to refer to yourself. Follow the steps in the writing process.

Explore

STEP 1: Explore your topic, audience, and purpose.

- Think about your earlier writing experiences. Which ones mattered most to you? Narrow the topic to a specific one.
- Who will be your likely readers?
- Decide on your purpose. Do you want to use your personal experiences to inform, persuade, or entertain readers—or to do all three?

 Prewrite

STEP 2: Prewrite to get ideas.

- Do a freewrite on your topic or brainstorm a list of ideas. Circle ones that interest you.
- Use your freewrite, list, or both to create a clustering diagram.

 **Organize**

STEP 3: Organize your ideas.

- Write a preliminary thesis statement.
- Prepare an outline.

Write

STEP 4: Write the first draft.

- Include an introduction, body paragraphs, and a conclusion.
- Do not try to make it "perfect." Expect to revise it later.

 Revise

STEP 5: Revise the draft.

- Exchange papers with a partner, and give each other feedback on your papers. Use the Chapter 1 Peer Review on page 225 to guide your feedback.
- Carefully consider your partner's feedback. If you agree with it, revise your paper by marking the changes on the first draft.

Proofread

STEP 6: Edit and proofread.

- Use the Chapter 1 Writer's Self-Check on page 226 to help you find and correct errors in grammar, mechanics, and sentence structure.

Write

STEP 7: Write a new draft.

- Revise the draft, incorporating all the changes you made earlier.
- Proofread the draft so that it is error free.
- Make sure the draft is legible and follows the format your instructor has provided.
- Hand in the essay to your instructor.

EXPANSION

 ## TIMED WRITING

To succeed in academic writing, you often need to write quickly. For example, sometimes you have to write a paragraph in class or for a test, and you might have only 30 minutes to do so.

In this expansion, you will write the first paragraph of a personal essay in class. You will have 30 minutes. To complete the expansion, you will need to budget your time accordingly. Follow this procedure.

1. Carefully read the writing prompt below (or the prompt your teacher assigns). Make sure you understand the question or task. (5 minutes)

2. Review the model on pages 2–4 if you need to. Brainstorm to get ideas. Then make a quick outline to organize your ideas, and include a thesis statement. (5 minutes)

3. Write the first paragraph. Be sure to include a title, thesis statement, topic sentences for body paragraphs, and a conclusion. (10 minutes)

4. Revise your paragraph to be sure your ideas are clear and well organized. (5 minutes)

5. Edit and proofread to correct mistakes. (5 minutes)

6. Give your paper to your instructor.

Prompt: Write the opening paragraph of a five-paragraph personal essay describing your typical writing practices. Are you a discoverer or a planner? What do you typically do at the beginning, middle, and end of the writing process?

 ## COMPLETE THE PERSONAL ESSAY

After your teacher returns the opening paragraph, complete the essay at home. Make sure that each body paragraph develops a single controlling idea that supports the thesis statement. The concluding paragraph should summarize the body paragraphs or restate the thesis of the opening paragraph in different words.

CHAPTER 2

CLASSIFICATION ESSAYS

To write academic texts, you need to master certain skills.

In this chapter, you will learn to:

- Analyze a classification essay

- Classify information based on observations, notes, and surveys

- Use transition signals to write with unity and coherence

- Identify context and grammar clues for the use of quantifiers

- Write, edit, and revise an essay that classifies people's behavior

For the Amish, life has remained unchanged for more than 300 years.

In order to organize information, you instinctively classify all that surrounds you into categories. This is especially true during the writing process in which you must sort through and organize your ideas so you can present them clearly. For example, you begin by selecting a specific topic from a general set of categories. You do the same in choosing a purpose and audience for your essay. After generating ideas, you reverse the process by creating the categories. You formulate a preliminary thesis statement and establish the categories to support it. You develop each of these categories in paragraphs centered on a topic sentence. Classification is vital to good writing no matter what your subject is; however, it is essential when the subject relates to the social sciences.

The social sciences include sociology, psychology, anthropology, economics, and political science. A core principle in the social sciences is the attempt to observe and classify human behavior scientifically. Even if you are not studying in one of these fields, you should still become accustomed to making and reporting observations and research objectively; that is, without bias. Reliance on facts establishes the basis for almost all academic writing. The claims you make in your writing must be supported by facts, logical reasons, and references from trusted sources.

As you can see then, a **classification** essay is one that places information into categories, each based on a specific criterion or standard. This chapter will focus on classifying one type of information: observed behavior.

ANALYZING THE MODEL

The writing model describes the behavior of an unusual group of people in the United States.

Read the model. Then answer the questions.

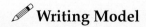 **Writing Model**

The Amish: An Intimate Society

1   One of the best examples of a unique self-contained community in the United States is the Old Order Amish, members of a religious group that broke away from the Swiss Mennonite church in the 1600s and settled in Pennsylvania around 1727. Most of today's 225,000 Old Order Amish live in just three states: Pennsylvania, Ohio, and Indiana. However, in the search for cheaper farmland, they have also moved to Arkansas, Colorado, Kentucky, Mississippi, Missouri, Nebraska, and West Virginia. About 10 percent live in Lancaster County, Pennsylvania. The Amish, who believe in large families, have doubled their population in less than two decades. Their traditions, practices, and other beliefs set them apart from those of the general culture found in cities, suburbs, and even in rural America.

2   Although just sixty-five miles from Philadelphia, "Amish Country" in Lancaster County seems to be a world away. For example, because Amish farmers use horses instead of tractors, most of their farms are only one hundred acres (40.47 hectares) or less. Five million tourists who pass through Lancaster County each year see the rolling green pastures, white farmhouses, simple barns, horse-drawn

buggies, and clotheslines hung with modest, dark-colored clothing in a style unchanged for 300 years. This scene conveys a sense of peace and innocence reminiscent[1] of a much earlier time.

3   Observers note that Amish life is based on separation from the world and obedience to their religion's teachings and leaders. Religion and discipline are the glue that holds the Amish together. The rejection of worldly concerns provides the foundation for such Amish values as humility, faithfulness, thrift, tradition, communal goals, joy of work, a slow-paced life, and trust in divine providence.

4   Observers also indicate that the Amish village government and community traditions revolve around shared values, which have been largely lost to industrialized society. The Amish make their decisions for the community in weekly meetings. There, by consensus, they follow a set of rules, or *Ordnugh*, to guide their behavior. Brotherly love and the welfare of the community are the most important values. In times of birth, sickness, and death, neighbors pitch in with the chores. In these ways, they maintain the bonds of intimate community.

5   Observers further stress the importance of other ties that hold the Amish together, including language (a dialect of German known as Pennsylvania Dutch). The family is the center of Amish life. Nearly all Amish marry, and divorce is forbidden. All major events take place in the home, including weddings, births, funerals, and church services. Amish children attend church schools, but only until the age of 13. (In 1972, the United States Supreme Court ruled that Amish parents had the right to take their children out of school after the eighth grade.) To go to school beyond the eighth grade would expose them to values and "worldly concerns." The Amish believe this exposure would create a conflict between the children and the community. They also believe that violence is bad, even personal self-defense. Therefore, they register as conscientious objectors[2] during times of war. They pay no Social Security taxes, and they receive no government benefits.

(continued on next page)

---

[1] **reminiscent:** reminding you of something in the past
[2] **conscientious objectors:** people who refuse to fight in a war because of religious or moral beliefs

6   The Amish cannot resist all change, of course. A special threat has come from urban outward growth, which has driven up the price of farmland. Unable to afford farms, about half of the men now work at other jobs. The Amish believe that when a husband works away from home, all aspects of life change, from the marital relationship to the care of the children. They also believe that if a man receives a paycheck, he will think that his work is of more value than his wife's. Because *Gemeinschaft*, or intimate society, is essential to maintain the Amish way of life, they worry about the men who have begun to work for non-Amish businesses. These men are being exposed to the outside world, and some are even using modern technology, such as cell phones and computers, in their jobs.

7   Nevertheless, observers indicate that the Amish adapt to change in ways least threatening to their basic values. Many of those who no longer farm try to work in farm-related businesses or in woodcrafts, and they go to great lengths to avoid leaving home. This continual adjustment allows the community to stay intact.

8   Despite living in a highly materialistic and secular culture, the Amish are preserving their values and traditions. Perhaps the most poignant[3] illustration of how the Amish differ from the dominant culture is this: When in 2006 a man shot several Amish girls at a one-room school, the Amish community established charitable funds not only for the family of the dead children, but also for the family of the killer.

Source: Essay adapted from Henslin, James M. *Sociology, A Down-to-Earth Approach*.

---

[3] **poignant:** having strong feelings, especially of sadness or pity

Questions about the Model

1. What is the purpose of this essay?

2. In Paragraph 1, what is the thesis statement, which is repeated in different words at the end of the paragraph? What claim does the thesis statement make about the Amish? Underline it.

3. Which categories, practices, or beliefs are discussed in Paragraph 2?

4. Paragraph 3 discusses the category of Amish values. What is the foundation of these values?

5. Which aspect of Amish life does Paragraph 4 describe?

6. What seems to be the writer's attitude toward the Amish? Does he criticize them, does he approve of them, or does his attitude seem objective? What evidence from the essay supports your opinion?

7. In your own words, list the categories of classification in the essay.

Noticing Vocabulary: Collocations

Many of the phrases in the model are **collocations**. A collocation is a group of two or more words that are often used together. They may be a verb and a noun, such as *draw a conclusion*; a verb and a preposition, such as *pass through*; an adverb and an adjective, such as *highly unusual*; or a noun and a noun, such as *a word of advice*. Collocations can be challenging because many of them are not logical or easy to guess the meaning of. For example, *heavy rain* is a natural collocation, but not *thick, dense,* or *deep rain*. Therefore, it is important to learn collocations bit by bit (that last phrase is also a collocation).

PRACTICE 1   Finding and Completing Collocations

Ⓐ Look at the writing model on pages 22–24 and find the word or words that complete each collocation. The word form may be different than it is in the model.

1. set _____*them*_____ _____*apart*_____ (*paragraph 1*)

2. believe _____ (*paragraph 1*)

3. pass _____ (*paragraph 2*)

4. _____ _____ buggies (*paragraph 2*)

5. revolve _____ (*paragraph 4*)

6. pitch _____ (*paragraph 4*)

7. _____ place (*paragraph 5*)

8. drive _____ (*paragraph 6*)

9. way _____ _____ (*paragraph 6*)

10. go to _____ _____ (*paragraph 7*)

Ⓑ Use the correct collocation from Part A to complete each sentence.

1. Amish people _____ the value of hard work.

2. Please visit us if you _____ town.

3. Amish life _____ _____ the importance of the family.

4. Many people _____ to help rebuild the school after it was damaged by the storm.

5. The _____ _____ _____ differs from society to society.

A classification essay must present its information in categories, with each one based on a specific **criterion**, or standard. For example, if you were writing about chairs, you might base one category on the criterion *type of material*. Then you could create a subcategory called *wood* and another subcategory called *steel*, and examine the characteristics of wood and steel chairs. This principle of forming categories and subcategories according to sets of criteria (the plural form of *criterion*) will help you to logically organize the information for your classification essay.

Like all essays, a classification essay includes an introductory paragraph, body paragraphs, and a concluding paragraph. A diagram of this type of organization, with examples from the writing model, looks like this:

Introductory Paragraph

The opening paragraph states the thesis and criterion used for classification.

Thesis: "One of the best examples of a unique self-contained community in the United States is the Old Order Amish . . . "

Criterion: "Their traditions, practices, and other beliefs set them apart from those of the general culture found in cities, suburbs, and even in rural America."

Body Paragraphs

Each body paragraph is devoted to a single category that supports the claims from the introduction.

Paragraph 2: A way of life unchanged for centuries

Paragraph 3: Special beliefs and values

Paragraph 4: Distinctive village government and community traditions

Paragraph 5: Other ties that set the Amish apart

Paragraph 6: Threats to Amish culture and way of life

Paragraph 7: The Amish's adaptation to change

Concluding Paragraph

The final paragraph restates the thesis in different words: "Despite living in a highly materialistic and secular culture, the Amish are preserving their values and traditions."

INTRODUCTORY PARAGRAPH

The introductory paragraph of a classification essay states its thesis. It also introduces the categories it will discuss and usually includes the specific criterion that the categories are based on. For example, in the writing model on pages 22–24, the thesis statement in the first paragraph maintains that the Amish are a unique self-contained community. Then it provides the criterion by classifying the practices and beliefs that make them unique.

BODY PARAGRAPHS

Each body paragraph in a classification essay examines a single category. The topic sentence often presents the topic and controlling idea of the paragraph. The rest of the paragraph supports the topic sentence with details that define the category.

For example, in the model, the observations of the Amish are grouped into five categories, and each is explained in a separate paragraph. These categories do not overlap, for each focuses on one aspect of Amish life.

Development of the Categories

Claims made in the topic sentences address the categories, as well as how these claims are supported, as shown in the examples.

PARAGRAPH 2

TOPIC SENTENCE Although just sixty-five miles from Philadelphia, "Amish Country" in Lancaster County seems to be a world away.

SUPPORT Examples that cite the size and appearance of the farms and the type of clothing worn by the Amish.

PARAGRAPH 3

TOPIC SENTENCE Observers note that Amish life is based on separation from the world and obedience to their religion's teachings and leaders.

SUPPORT Reference to how the Amish reject "worldly concerns" and stress humility and other values.

PARAGRAPH 4

TOPIC SENTENCE Observers also indicate that the Amish village government and community traditions revolve around shared values.

SUPPORT Description of shared decision-making in weekly meetings and support for neighbors "in times of birth, sickness, and death."

PARAGRAPH 5

TOPIC SENTENCE Observers further stress the importance of other ties that hold the Amish together.

SUPPORT Explanation of the importance of family, the role of church schools, the avoidance of "worldly concerns," and the rejection of violence in all forms, including military service.

PARAGRAPH 6

TOPIC SENTENCE The Amish cannot resist all change, of course.

SUPPORT Explanation of the "threat" that results from their not being able to farm and the necessity of men working outside the community. Further explanation of how this change threatens the equality of relationship between men and women.

(continued on next page)

TOPIC SENTENCE   Nevertheless, observers indicate that the Amish adapt to change in ways least threatening to their basic values.

SUPPORT   Short explanation of the men's attempt to work in farm-related businesses.

CONCLUDING PARAGRAPH

The final paragraph will probably restate the thesis in different words. The paragraph may also conclude with a memorable quotation or example. In the writing model, how the Amish gave charitable funds to the families of both the victims and the killer provides an extremely powerful example of the ways that the Amish are different from people in mainstream society.

ESTABLISHING UNITY AND COHERENCE

Each paragraph in a well-developed essay should display both unity and coherence. A paragraph with **unity** develops a single idea and links it to the rest of the paper; a paragraph with **coherence** flows logically from one sentence to the next.

UNITY

All the sentences in a paragraph must discuss just one main idea, stated in the topic sentence from the beginning to the end. Therefore, when you revise your paragraphs, look carefully at each supporting sentence and ask yourself these questions:

- Does it continue to support the topic sentence?
- Does the last sentence of a paragraph relate in some way to the first sentence?

COHERENCE

The ideas must also be coherent; that is, the logical relationships between sentences and paragraphs in the whole essay must be clear, and the movement from one sentence to the next must be smooth. You can achieve coherence in several ways through the use of transition signals, pronouns, and synonyms. Chapter 5 will discuss synonyms in greater detail.

Transition signals allow sentences to smoothly flow from one to another by alerting your reader to how the ideas in the new sentence or paragraph logically relate to those in the previous sentence.

Using Transition Signals to Introduce Ideas

RULES	EXAMPLES
1. Use these transition signals when you want to introduce additional ideas.	additionally another first, second, third furthermore in addition moreover yet (or still) another
2. Use these transition signals when you want to introduce a contrast.	by contrast despite however in spite of nevertheless on the one hand/on the other hand
3. Use these transition signals when you want to introduce examples.	for example for instance specifically to illustrate
4. Use these transition signals when you want to introduce further explanations.	in other words to put it another way
5. Use these transition signals when you want to introduce reasons.	because of due to
6. Use these transition signals when you want to introduce results.	as a consequence as a result consequently therefore thus

You can also use demonstratives to maintain coherence in your writing. Add the pronouns *this*, *that*, *these*, or *those* before nouns that refer back to an idea or ideas, or a noun or nouns, repeated from the previous sentence. Look at these examples from the writing model.

. . . the rolling green pastures, white farmhouses, simple barns, horse-drawn buggies, and clotheslines hung with modest, dark-colored clothing. . . . **This scene** conveys a sense of peace and innocence . . .

In times of birth, sickness, and death, neighbors pitch in with the chores. In **these ways**, they maintain the bonds of intimate community.

(continued on next page)

By using synonyms or expressions that have a similar meaning, you can restate your points without continually repeating nouns and phrases, which might make your sentences feel repetitive.

. . . the Amish **adapt to change** in ways least threatening to their basic values. . . . This **continual adjustment** allows the community to stay intact.

PRACTICE 2 **Establishing Coherence with Transitions**

Circle the transition signal that best indicates the logical relationship between the sentences.

1. The family provides us with the basic foundations of how to live. Later we develop friends who provide us with intimacy and a sense of belonging. *(Therefore / For example / On the other hand)*, sociologists call these two groups primary groups.

2. Group leaders tend to represent the values of the group. Leaders, *(also / consequently / however)*, tend to be more talkative and express self-confidence.

3. The size of a group influences our attitudes and behavior. *(For example / As a result / Nevertheless)*, in a group of perhaps four to six, people are willing to help each other. *(Furthermore / However / For example)*, in a very large group, people feel less responsible for each other.

4. The group you associate with will influence the way you view yourself. If you want to become a corporate executive, you might dress more formally and try to improve your vocabulary. *(Nevertheless / On the other hand / To put it another way)*, if you want to become a rock musician, you might grow your hair long, get tattoos and body piercings, and wear torn jeans.

5. Wanting to become a corporate executive might appeal to many people. *(Additionally / However / Despite this)*, for an Amish man that goal might cause a great deal of emotional discomfort.

Writing Tip

Academic writing is usually more formal than other forms of communication. Avoid using informal quantifiers such as *lots of*, *a lot of*, and *a little bit* in an academic paper. Instead, maintain the formal tone by using the quantifiers that appear in the charts.

In Chapter 1, you looked at how to use articles correctly. Another common grammatical trouble spot is the correct use of words or phrases that express quantities (how many or how much). These expressions are known as quantity expressions or **quantifiers**.

USING QUANTIFIERS

Quantifiers are words or phrases that precede a noun, or a pronoun that replaces it, and indicate a number or amount. Often, choosing the right quantifier can be complicated. In order to do so, you need to ask yourself a few questions:

- Does it precede a count or noncount noun?
- If it is a count noun, is that noun singular or plural?
- Are you writing in a formal or informal style?

With Count Nouns

RULES	EXAMPLES
1. Use *a few*, *many*, and *a number of* only with count nouns.	a few men many farms a number of people
2. Use *one*, *every*, and *each* with singular count nouns.	One person works on the farm. Every farmer is hard working.
3. Use *a couple of*, *both*, *a few*, *few*, *all*, *a large number of*, *several*, *many*, and *most* with plural count nouns. **Note:** Be especially careful about using *a few* and *few*: *A few* means a small number, while *few* means almost none.	The Amish have doubled their population in a couple of decades. Both boys and girls attend school until they are thirteen. Few Amish live outside their community. Most children go to school for eight years. Many of them do not continue into high school.

With Noncount Nouns

RULES	EXAMPLES
1. Use *a little*, *little*, *much*, *a great deal of*, *the majority of*, *the rest of* with noncount nouns. **Note:** Be especially careful about using *a little* and *little*: *A little* means a small amount, but *little* means almost none.	A little work is done in factories. A great deal of work is done on the farm. The majority of the Amish population lives in three states.
2. Use *an amount of* only with noncount nouns.	A great amount of time was spent discussing the new plans.

A Circle the quantifier that best completes each sentence.

1. (Much /(Many)) of the Amish live in Lancaster County, Pennsylvania.

2. They expect (many of / much of) the children to work on the farms.

3. The Amish have (fewer / less) disagreements than most groups because they decide almost everything by consensus.

4. There is (little / a little) crime in the Amish community because of the strong values that its members share.

5. Many Amish have (a great number / a great amount) of children.

6. Because the family is the center of the Amish community, (few / a few) events take place outside the home.

7. While (most / most of the) people have ambitions to gain wealth and success, the Amish are thrifty and humble.

8. Only (few / a few) of the Amish do not marry.

B Complete each sentence with information about your family, people living in your current community, or your hometown. Use the word or phrase in parentheses preceded by a quantifier. Use a different quantifier in each sentence.

1. In my hometown, (children) _most of the children attend public school until_ _they are eighteen years old._

2. (very young children) _____

_____

3. (women aged thirty-five or older) _____

_____

4. (men) _____

_____

5. When the weather is nice, (people) _____

_____

6. During the summer, (time is spent) _____

_____

7. Recently, (controversy about) _____

_____

8. (elderly people) _____

_____

PREPARATION FOR WRITING

During (and probably after) your college career, much of what you write will involve doing research. In the sciences and social sciences, research is central to the curriculum. In other fields, it may involve discovering how to interpret a piece of literature or a theory about economics, or investigating causes or effects in a specific situation. Outside of college, doing research may help you determine best business practices or how to improve a product. While much of this may require consulting print sources or the Internet, not all of it will. Some of it also may be based on your own investigation.

For instance, one way to generate information for a classification essay is through making your own observations. You take notes on what you discover about the people or things you have chosen to observe. Then you organize the notes, classify them into categories, and draw conclusions from them. These conclusions are objective; they report only on facts, but do not offer any opinions. Sociology, the scientific study of human and social behavior, provides a good example of academic writing based on first-hand observation and classification. The model and material in this chapter are taken from that field.

PLANNING, OBSERVING, AND NOTE TAKING

In order to observe people and classify their behavior, it is best to start with a plan in mind. After choosing a group of people to observe, follow the instructions.

Planning an Observation

1. Decide on the categories to examine, and then make a chart of those categories, such as the age of the participants, their manner of dress, their native language, and so on.

2. Write brief notes to remind yourself of what you see and hear, even using abbreviations or your own code words. Remember to focus on what people are actually doing, not on your interpretations of what they are doing. For example, you can claim that people are talking loudly. However, you cannot claim that they are rude, which is an interpretation or judgment. Try to be objective in your observations.

3. Complete your chart. List the details you have observed that fit in each category. For example, the category *dress of the participants* could include 1) very informal (T-shirts, torn jeans, shorts, and so on); 2) casual (slacks and long-sleeve shirt or blouse); 3) businesslike or formal (jackets and ties, or suits).

4. Review your notes to see if, based on your observations, you should create or eliminate categories or subcategories within the categories.

(A) Complete the chart by observing your classmates. Write the number of classmates who match each category.

APPROXIMATE AGE	GENDER	MANNER OF DRESS
Under 30 years old _____	Male _____	Very informal _____
Perhaps 30–45 _____	Female _____	Casual _____
Perhaps older than 45 _____		Formal _____ (such as suits)
		Traditional in a culture _____ (such as headscarves)

(B) On a separate sheet of paper, write a paragraph that reports your findings. Cite actual numbers for each category, or use quantifiers.

EXAMPLE

> The general manner of dress of the seventeen people in my class is either very casual or casual. Most of the men and more than half of the women are wearing jeans. A few of the men in jeans also have on white T-shirts, or T-shirts with the names of sports teams or players on them. Most, however, wear short-sleeve knit shirts or long-sleeve cotton shirts. Some of the women in jeans are wearing T-shirts with the brand names of the manufacturers.

CONDUCTING SURVEYS AND ADMINISTERING QUESTIONNAIRES

Not all information gathered about people comes from merely observing behavior. Sociologists, for example, also collect information about people through surveys or questionnaires by asking people to answer questions in specific categories. The results can then be used to report on people's backgrounds, age, opinions, beliefs, eating habits, or anything that the research focuses on.

Working with a Survey

A Copy the chart on a separate sheet of paper. Complete the chart by conducting a survey of all your classmates. If necessary, walk around the room to ensure that you speak to everyone.

Survey Chart

Criteria	Responses	Numbers with Same Response
1. Places People Are from Originally:	China	2
	Mexico	4
2. Birthplace (City, Town, or Village):		
3. Number of Siblings		
4. First Language		
5. Number of Languages Spoken		

Total Number Surveyed: _____

B On the same sheet of paper, write two sentences reporting on the information you have gathered for each category. You may make general statements, cite statistics, or do both.

Writing Tip

You can conduct a survey most efficiently on computers. The most popular online program for creating surveys is SurveyMonkey®, but there are competitors, including apps for smart phones and tablets.

PRACTICE 6 **Writing a Thesis Statement**

Using your sentences from Practice 5B, write a thesis statement for a classification essay. Indicate how similar or dissimilar your classmates are and introduce the categories that the body of the essay will discuss.

For writing guides to help you with a classification thesis, see Appendix A on page 189.

Using your sentences from Practice 5B and your thesis statement from Practice 6 on page 35, complete the plan for a classification essay.

Thesis Statement for Introductory Paragraph: _____

_____

_____

Paragraph 1:

Topic Sentence: _____

_____

Supporting Information/Examples: _____

_____

_____

_____

_____

Paragraph 2:

Topic Sentence: _____

_____

Supporting Information/Examples: _____

_____

_____

_____

_____

Paragraph 3:

Topic Sentence: _____

_____

Supporting Information/Examples: _____

_____

_____

_____

_____

✎ Applying Vocabulary: Using Collocations

As you work to improve the level of your academic vocabulary, it is important to include collocations that occur in formal academic writing. Before you begin your writing assignment, review the collocations you learned about on page 25.

<table>
<tr><td>PRACTICE 7</td><td>Writing Collocations</td></tr>
</table>

Use the collocations to write a sentence about your family traditions.

1. believe in _____

_____

2. base something on _____

_____

3. go to great lengths _____

_____

4. take place _____

_____

5. revolve around _____

_____

WRITING ASSIGNMENT

In your assignment for this chapter, you will become a "sociologist" and conduct a survey of the behavior of friends, relatives, coworkers, or classmates. Your teacher may choose to have you work in a group to prepare the questions and categories for the survey. You will write a five paragraph classification essay based on the information you have gathered. Follow the steps in the writing process.

POSSIBLE TOPICS

- Commuting habits to and from work or school (such as methods of transportation, number of daily trips, and time spent traveling)
- Eating practices (number of meals and snacks each day, typical diet, and number of meals spent with family members or others)
- Frequency and type of exercise (how often, how long, with or without weights or special equipment)
- Employment outside or in the home (types of occupations, number of hours at work, physical labor or other type of labor)

STEP 1: Explore your topic, audience, and purpose.

- Choose your topic from the list on page 37. Prior to your observation, brainstorm a list of categories for the survey that you think will be important.

- Decide who will be your likely readers, or the readers that you imagine would find your essay most useful or interesting.

- Consider your purpose: Are you informing your audience by providing information they do not have? Are you interpreting the behavior of the people you observe in an interesting way? Or are you describing the categories in an amusing way?

 STEP 2: Gather your information and prewrite.

- Conduct the survey and record the results.

- If you can, note specific examples that would support generalizations in each category.

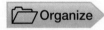 **STEP 3: Organize your ideas.**

- Write a preliminary thesis statement.

- Prepare an outline with topic sentences for the body paragraphs and supporting details and examples.

 STEP 4: Write the first draft.

- Write an essay to report on the survey you have conducted.

- In the introductory paragraph, indicate which group you have surveyed and what general conclusions you can draw about their behavior—but do not make any judgments.

- In the body of the essay, present your findings in each of the categories you have created, along with examples or further explanation.

- Conclude the essay with a brief summary or return to the main idea in the introductory paragraph.

 STEP 5: Revise the draft.

- Exchange papers with a partner, and give each other feedback on your papers. Use the Chapter 2 Peer Review on page 227 to guide your feedback.

- Carefully consider your partner's feedback. If you agree with it, revise your paper by marking the changes on the first draft.

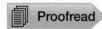 **STEP 6: Edit and proofread.**

- Use the Chapter 2 Writer's Self-Check on page 228 to help you edit and proofread your paper.

- Are the sentences clear and complete?

- Are quantifiers used correctly?

STEP 7: Write a new draft.

- Revise the draft, incorporating all the changes you made earlier.
- Proofread the draft so that it is error free.
- Make sure the draft is legible and follows the format your instructor has provided.
- Hand in the essay to your instructor.

SELF-ASSESSMENT

In this chapter, you learned to:

- ○ Analyze a classification essay
- ○ Classify information based on observations, notes, and surveys
- ○ Use transition signals to write with unity and coherence
- ○ Identify context and grammar clues for the use of quantifiers
- ○ Write, edit, and revise an essay that classifies people's behavior

Which ones can you do well? Mark them ✓

Which ones do you need to practice more? Mark them ⊘

EXPANSION

 TIMED WRITING

In this expansion, you will write the introduction and one body paragraph based on the survey you conducted and planned in Practices 4–6 on pages 34–35. Review these materials and bring them to class. You will have 50 minutes. To complete the expansion, you will need to budget your time accordingly. Follow this procedure.

1. Review the model on pages 22–24 if you need to. Review your outline so you have a clear idea how to organize your ideas and include a thesis statement. (5 minutes)

2. Write the two paragraphs. Be sure to include a title, thesis statement, and topic sentence for the body paragraph. (20 minutes)

3. Revise the paragraphs so your ideas are clear, and the paragraphs are unified and well organized. (15 minutes)

4. Check your paragraphs for errors. Correct any mistakes. (10 minutes)

5. Give your paper to your instructor.

Be a "sociologist" and observe the behavior of people in one of the following circumstances. Then write a classification essay about the group of people you have chosen to observe. Your essay should be at least five paragraphs long.

- Commuters on a bus or train
- Students in the college cafeteria or student lounge
- Children in a park
- Parents at a children's soccer game or other children's sporting event
- Several children (perhaps your own) playing together
- People at a party

Follow these guidelines in preparing to write, revise, and edit the essay:

1. Do your observation and take notes.

2. Limit your observation to no more than 15–20 minutes, unless you find that not enough is happening during that time period.

3. Try not to call attention to yourself as you take notes, and write quickly, abbreviating or using code words to represent observations.

4. Note specific examples that would support generalizations in each category. Write a preliminary thesis statement.

5. Prepare an outline with topic sentences for the body paragraphs and supporting details and examples.

6. In the introductory paragraph, indicate the group you have observed, where you observed them, and what general conclusions you can draw about their behavior— but do not make any judgments.

7. In the body of the essay, present your findings in each of the categories, along with examples or further explanation.

8. Conclude the essay with a brief summary, or return to the main idea in the introductory paragraph.

CHAPTER 3

PROCESS ESSAYS

OBJECTIVES

To write academic texts, you need to master certain skills.

In this chapter, you will learn to:

- Analyze a process essay

- Identify, plan, and organize the steps of process analysis

- Recognize and correct common sentence problems such as

  ○ Run-on sentences

  ○ Comma-spliced sentences

  ○ Choppy sentences

  ○ Stringy sentences

- Identify main ideas for writing a summary or abstract

- Write, edit, and revise an essay detailing an experiment

A scientist at work in a laboratory

In the previous chapter, you looked at the observation and classification of behavior. In this chapter, you will focus on analyzing a process. A **process essay** either describes a process or provides instructions for how to do something. In other words, it is a step-by-step explanation of how something works, or how to perform a task. Such an explanation is especially important in describing scientific experiments and summarizing their results. However, process analysis also applies to many other kinds of explanations or instructions. For example, you might describe the digestive process, the rotation of the moon around the earth, or the way a computer communicates with a laser printer. More simply, you might explain how to make chocolate chip cookies, how to connect the surround sound equipment to accompany a new flat screen television, or how to get from the airport to your home. However, this chapter will concentrate on the process essay as it relates to academic writing about science and medicine.

ANALYZING THE MODEL

The model essay describes the process of conducting a scientific experiment.

Read the model. Then answer the questions.

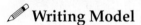 Writing Model

What Scientists Do

1   Human beings are curious. They constantly search for explanations: Why did something happen? How did it happen? They guess at answers to their questions and try to determine if their guesses are correct. In this way, whether they know it or not, they are taking the first step down the road of what scientists refer to as the scientific method. The next steps involve conducting experiments to determine if their guesses are correct, arriving at conclusions, and writing them down in a report. Those actions can take place in a laboratory or in the field. The process of investigation does not stop there, however. Other scientists usually repeat these experiments to verify the results, or conduct further experiments. Their goal is often to answer questions raised by the findings of the original experiments. The scientific method therefore creates a continual, self-correcting cycle of investigation and analysis involving six steps.

2   An example from biology illustrates this process. It would begin with a common sense idea or observation: regular exercise seems to help prevent heart disease and heart attacks. However, can we be sure that the observation is correct? The first step in the scientific method therefore poses a question that an experiment might answer: "Can regular exercise help prevent coronary[1] disease and heart attacks?" Then, scientists could proceed to the second step in the scientific method. They would state a

---

[1] **coronary:** relating to the heart

prediction, or hypothesis, that experiments or observations either verify or disprove. In this case, the hypothesis would be that regular exercise helps prevent heart disease and heart attacks.

3   The third step requires setting up a controlled experiment to test the hypothesis using animals instead of humans, in this case laboratory mice. As with all experiments, there would be two categories to examine: an experimental group and a control group. These groups are identical in every way except one: the experimental group includes a variable[2] to test—regular exercise—for its effect on coronary disease and heart attacks. Scientists would begin by selecting perhaps 100 specially bred laboratory mice of the same age and with the same genetics. The mice would all have an inherited susceptibility to coronary heart disease or heart attacks. The scientists assign half of the mice to the experimental group and the other half to the control group.

4   Having established the control and experimental groups, the researchers would now move on to the fourth step: conducting the experiment. First, they would have to assign a length of time for the experiment, for example, 120 days. They would also assemble all the materials needed to conduct the experiment: cages, food, water, and tools for monitoring the activities of the mice. They would keep all the conditions for both groups the same: diet, temperature, humidity, waking and sleeping cycles, water availability, and safety from harmful bacteria. However, the cages of the experimental group would be equipped with exercise wheels, while the cages of the control group would not. Then each week the researchers would gather data from the exercise wheels to ensure that the mice in the experimental group had been exercising.

5   At the end of the specified time period, the scientists could move on to the fifth step, analyzing the results. Suppose that the statistics produced by the experiment showed that 25 mice in the control group had heart attacks or developed coronary disease—one half of the total in the group. On the other hand, the disease rate for the mice in the experimental group turned out to be dramatically lower. Only 18 of them exhibited signs of heart disease or had heart attacks, or 36% of the total. In addition, the mice in the experimental group weighed an average of 10% less than the mice in the control group.

(continued on next page)

---

[2] **variable:** something that is different

6   The data would not prove the original hypothesis, but once the results had been written up and published—the sixth step in the experiment—the findings would form the basis for repeating the experiment and conducting further experiments. For example, the data might suggest other phenomena to investigate, such as whether the exercise or the weight loss from the exercise caused a decrease in heart disease. Did both contribute to the decrease? Was the weight loss simply an unanticipated result of the experiment?

7   These questions might lead to further experimentation. Other scientists could now conduct a series of related experiments. They might work first with mice, then with larger animals, and, if these revealed similar results, finally with human subjects. The findings of the scientists might vary, but the ongoing experimenting and dialogue would continue, following the same widely agreed upon principles of and steps in the scientific method.

Source: Kalizeka, C.J. and David Pearson. *Using the Scientific Method to Solve Mysteries.*

Questions about the Model

1. Who is the likely audience for this essay—scientists or nonscientists?

2. What is the thesis statement of the introduction? Circle it.

3. How many steps in the scientific method does the essay explain? Underline the topic sentences that identify these steps.

4. In Paragraph 4, what is the function of the phrase, "Having established the control and experimental groups"?

5. The example reports on two findings, one based on the hypothesis and the other not stated in the hypothesis. What kind of experiment would you expect scientists to conduct based on the unpredicted finding?

6. Could you actually conduct the experiment based on the essay's explanation? Why or why not?

Noticing Vocabulary: Irregular Plurals from Latin and Greek

Chapter 2 explained that the plural of the word *criterion* is *criteria*. This is because the word comes from Greek, which has retained its original plural forms for some words. Likewise some words that come from Latin have irregular plural endings; they do not add -*s* endings to the singular form. These words can be placed into four categories, which include many words used in scientific writing.

PRACTICE 1   Singular and Plural Forms of Irregular Nouns

Ⓐ Look at the writing model again. Find irregular nouns for each category in the chart. The beginnings of each word have been included to help you.

CATEGORY 1: NOUNS FROM LATIN	
Singular (-*um*) Ending	**Plural (-*a*) Ending**
medium	media
1. _____	bac_____
2. _____	dat_____
CATEGORY 2: NOUNS FROM GREEK	
Singular (-*is*) Ending	**Plural (-*es*) Ending**
thesis	theses
1. ana_____	
2. hyp_____	_____
3. bas_____	_____
CATEGORY 3: NOUNS FROM GREEK	
Singular (-*on*) Ending	**Plural (-*a*) Ending**
criterion	criteria
1. _____	phe_____
CATEGORY 4: SINGULAR NOUNS FROM GREEK WITH NO PLURAL FORM	
Singular (-*ics*) ending	
mathematics	
1. gen_____	
2. sta_____	

Ⓑ Complete the chart with the singular or plural form of each noun, where possible.

A typical process essay usually contains the same elements you have seen in the previous chapters: It consists of an introductory paragraph, body paragraphs, and a concluding paragraph. The content, however, is organized into a specific pattern. A diagram of the organization of a process essay with examples from the writing model looks like this:

Introductory Paragraph

The opening paragraph names the process under discussion, identifies the purpose of the essay, and provides a transition to the body paragraphs.

Process: the scientific method

Purpose: to explain each step of the scientific method to the reader

Transition: introduces the six steps that will appear in the body

↓

Body Paragraphs

The body paragraphs present every step of the process under discussion in sequential (chronological) order, providing a clear explanation of each.

Step one: Begin with a common sense idea or observation.

Step two: State a hypothesis to verify or disprove.

Step three: Set up controlled experiment groups.

Step four: Conduct the experiment and gather data.

Step five: Analyze the results.

Step six: Write up and publish the findings.

↓

Concluding Paragraph

The final paragraph summarizes the process and underscores the importance of the process by placing it in a larger context.

INTRODUCTORY PARAGRAPH

The introduction of a process essay should contain a thesis statement that names the process under discussion and indicates the structure of the body paragraphs. The introduction should also indicate whether the purpose of the essay is **informational** (giving the reader information about the process) or **instructional** (instructing the reader on how to perform the process). The thesis statement from the writing model names the process, indicates the informational purpose of the essay, and sets up the sequential structure of the body paragraphs by informing us that there are six steps.

The scientific method therefore creates a continual, self-correcting cycle of investigation and analysis involving six steps.

It is possible, however, that your readers may not be very interested in the topic of your essay. Another function of the introductory paragraph is to attract the readers' interest. This can be done in several ways, such as by asking questions or explaining how the process relates to the readers' lives, as in this example from the writing model:

> Human beings are curious. They constantly search for explanations: Why did something happen? How did it happen? They guess at answers to their questions and try to determine if their guesses are correct.

BODY PARAGRAPHS

The body paragraphs guide the reader step-by-step through the process. Each step is presented in sequential order; that is, moving from first to last. The amount of information included in each step depends on what the readers already know about the process. For instance, an explanation of the scientific method for students in a first-year biology class would likely define key terms such as *hypothesis*, *control group*, and *variable* as they are introduced; these would not be explained for readers in the science profession. Likewise, an explanation of how to set up a surround sound system would list the parts needed before it proceeds with the instructions on assembling those parts.

Purpose

The purpose of the essay affects how you address the reader. Informational explanations of how something works, for example, are most often written in the third person: "The third step requires setting up a controlled experiment to test the hypothesis. . . ." In contrast, instructional explanations generally address the audience directly in the second person: "First, you stir the mixture thoroughly before adding milk," or they imply *you* in sentences by using imperatives: "[You] Stir the mixture thoroughly before adding milk."*

CONCLUDING PARAGRAPH

The conclusion either summarizes the process or indicates its implications in a larger context. The model essay, for example, states that scientific experimentation follows well-established principles and leads to ongoing further experimentation.

> The findings of the scientists might vary, but ongoing experimenting and dialogue would continue, following the same widely agreed upon principles of and steps in the scientific method.

---

*Remember that person is divided into three categories with singular and plural forms: first person (*I*, *we*), second person (*you*, *both singular and plural*), and third person (*he, she, it, they*).

OUTLINING

As mentioned in Chapter 1, preparing an outline allows you to list the essay's thesis statement, the topic sentences of the body paragraphs, and the supporting information for each topic sentence.

An outline of a process essay looks like this:

I. **Introduction and thesis statement**
   A. Attracting the interest of your audience
   B. Naming the process
   C. Stating the goal of the essay: to help readers either *understand* or *perform* the process
II. **Body: Steps in the process**
   A. Step one: explanation and examples
   B. Step two: explanation and examples
   C. Step three, and so on
III. **Conclusion**
   A. Restatement of the goal of the process, or
   B. Summary of the process, or
   C. Statement of its role within a larger context

PRACTICE 2   Outlining the Model

Look at the writing model on pages 42–44. Use the information to complete the outline.

I. **Introduction and thesis:** _To explain the scientific method through a specific example_

   A. Naming the process: _Repeated experiments to determine if exercise prevents coronary heart disease or heart attacks_

   B. The goal of the essay: _____

II. **Steps in the process**
   A. _____
      Explanation/Examples: _____

   B. _____
      Explanation/Examples: _____

   C. _____
      Explanation/Examples: _____

D. _____

    Explanation/Examples: _____

    _____

E. _____

    Explanation/Examples: _____

    _____

F. _____

    Explanation/Examples: _____

    _____

III. Conclusion

    A. _____

    _____

    B. _____

    _____

SENTENCE STRUCTURE

In order to ensure that your essays are clear, you must be mindful of their sentence structure. Clear sentence structure depends on establishing where each sentence ends and the next one begins. When editing your work, you must locate and eliminate two common errors: **run-on sentences** and **comma-spliced sentences**.

RUN-ON AND COMMA-SPLICED SENTENCES

You probably know that every sentence must have an independent clause, which is a group of words containing a subject and verb that makes a complete statement. You probably also know that many sentences contain two independent clauses. Sometimes a semicolon joins the two clauses.

Far more often, however, a comma and a coordinating conjunction come between them. The seven coordinating conjunctions are _for_, _and_, _nor_, _but_, _or_, _yet_, and _so_. The first letters of the conjunctions spell the words _fan boys_, which is a good way to remember them. The comma separates or creates a pause between the clauses. The conjunction joins them and shows their logical relationship. If either the comma or the coordinating conjunction is omitted, or if they both are, common errors occur.

In a run-on sentence, nothing comes between the independent clauses.

    RUN-ON   Topic sentences are important they introduce the controlling idea of a paragraph.

In a comma-spliced sentence, only a comma comes between the clauses, but the conjunction is missing. In English, commas separate structures; they do not join them.

COMMA-SPLICED   Topic sentences are important, they introduce the controlling idea of a paragraph.

If you find any run-on or comma-spliced sentences when editing your work, you can correct them in several ways. How you correct these errors depends on the logical relationship you wish to establish between the clauses.

Correcting Run-On and Comma-Spliced Sentences

RULES	EXAMPLES
1. Insert a coordinating conjunction, or both a comma and coordinating conjunction between the two clauses, depending on what is missing.	Topic sentences are important, for they introduce the controlling idea of a paragraph.
2. Make the less important clause into a **dependent clause*** by beginning it with a **subordinating conjunction**. Most subordinating conjunctions refer to time relationships: *while, when, whenever, as, until, since, before, after,* or *as soon as.* Others establish different logical relationships: *because, if, unless,* and *although.*	Topic sentences are important because they introduce the controlling idea of a paragraph.
3. Rewrite one of the clauses so that it begins with *that, which,* or *who.*	Topic sentences, which introduce the controlling idea of a paragraph, are important.
4. End the first statement with a period.	Topic sentences are important. They introduce the controlling idea of a paragraph.
5. Join the two clauses with a semicolon.	Topic sentences are important; they introduce the controlling idea of a paragraph.

---

* You may recall that a dependent clause contains both a subject and a verb, but cannot be a sentence by itself. It must be attached to an independent clause.

PRACTICE 3   Correcting Run-ons and Comma Splices

Ⓐ Label each sentence *RO* (run-on), *CS* (comma-spliced), or *C* (correct).

_____ 1. The scientific method involves six steps each is important.

_____ 2. One group in an experiment includes a variable, the other is called the control group.

_____ 3. They must be alike in every other way, otherwise, the results of the experiment will not be valid.

_____ 4. The researchers establish a timeline for the experiment, they then gather data every week from each group.

_____ 5. Data from the experiment are carefully analyzed to determine if the hypothesis is correct or incorrect.

_____ 6. After the data are analyzed, they might suggest other points to investigate.

_____ 7. The results of the experiment are often published, then other scientists can conduct further experiments.

_____ 8. In scientific journals, each article is often preceded by a short summary, which is called an abstract.

B On a separate sheet of paper, correct and rewrite the sentences with errors. More than one correction is possible. Try to vary your use of conjunctions and punctuation.

> **Writing Tip**
>
> One way to determine whether a word is a conjunction (which joins two clauses) or a transitional word (which explains their logical relationship) is to try changing the position of words in the second clause. Transitional, or explaining, words can be moved to other locations, while conjunctions cannot. For example:
>
> . . . *however*, it does not join them.
>
> . . . it does not join them, *however*. (The explaining word can be moved.)
>
> . . . *but* it does not join them. (The conjunction cannot be moved.)

CHOPPY AND STRINGY SENTENCES

In a sense, two opposites of run-on and comma-spliced sentences are choppy and stringy sentences.

Choppy Sentences

In English, a good writer uses a variety of sentence types that vary in length. A single short sentence can be effective in emphasizing a point, especially after several long sentences, as in this example:

> Because of efforts by First Lady Michelle Obama to encourage better eating habits and changes in the school lunch requirements from the United States Department of Agriculture, the food served in schools is more nutritious and healthier than ever. Schools are offering fruit drinks in place of sugar-sweetened sodas, vegetables instead of potato chips or French fries, and sliced turkey instead of hamburgers.
>
> Kids, however, aren't happy.

The sixty-three words of the first two sentences are followed by one sentence of just four words, set off in a separate paragraph for dramatic effect.

However, continually using too many short simple sentences is considered poor style because it interrupts the flow of the text. This overuse of short sentences is referred to as **choppy sentences**. Each choppy sentence contains only one idea, so it cannot express complex thoughts; therefore, a series of choppy sentences may sound childish and even annoying:

> My sentences are short. They are simple. Each contains only one idea. They cannot express complex thoughts. They sound immature. I had better stop. You will be glad to finish reading this.

You can correct choppy sentences easily by combining two or more into a single compound or complex sentence through the use of coordination or subordination.

If the sentences express equal ideas, use coordinators to combine them.

CHOPPY My sentences are short. They are simple.

IMPROVED My sentences are short **and** simple.

If the sentences express unequal ideas, use subordinators to combine them.

CHOPPY They sound immature. They can't express complex thoughts.

IMPROVED They sound immature **because** they can't express complex thoughts.

PRACTICE 4   **Combining Choppy Sentences**

Improve the choppy sentences by combining them. If the ideas are equally important, write a compound sentence. If the ideas are unequal, write a complex sentence.

1. Many scientists work in a laboratory. They also work in the field.

   Combined: <u>Scientists work in a laboratory, but they also work in the field.</u>

   _____

2. Many American children eat unhealthy food. They do not get enough exercise.

   Combined: _____

   _____

3. Many children won't eat healthy food. They don't like the way it tastes.

   Combined: _____

   _____

4. People watch too much television. They spend too much time on computers and cell phones. They don't get enough exercise. *Combined:* _____

   _____

5. Too many Americans get diabetes. Too many Americans die of heart attacks. These may be related to their diets. They may also be related to lack of exercise.

Combined: _____

_____

_____

6. People have stressful lives. They tend to overeat. They do not get enough exercise.

They smoke. They develop heart disease. *Combined:* _____

_____

_____

Stringy Sentences

Whereas a choppy sentence is too short, a **stringy sentence** is too long. It contains too many clauses, usually connected by *and, so, but,* or *because*. It sounds like a long rambling monologue in which too many ideas are expressed in an unorganized manner with no clear relationship between the ideas, unlike mature, carefully edited writing. To correct a stringy sentence, divide it into logical thought groups by rephrasing parts of it, or recombining the clauses through subordination.

STRINGY SENTENCE I write like I talk, so I string together too many ideas in the same sentence, **and** I don't use subordination, **but** this has to stop **because** I need to write in a more academic style.

IMPROVED **Because** I write like I talk, I string together too many ideas in the same sentence without subordination. **However,** this practice must stop **so that** I can develop a more academic writing style.

PRACTICE 5   **Improve Stringy Sentences**

Revise and rewrite each stringy sentence.

1. Children don't like the food in school cafeterias, so they go to vending machines to buy candy and potato chips, but they get hungry later because the junk food doesn't fill them up.

Revised: *Because kids don't like the food in school cafeterias, they buy candy or*

potato chips at vending machines. However, this junk food is not filling, so the

children are soon hungry again.

(continued on next page)

2. The United States has the highest rate of obesity in the world, and more and more children are becoming obese, and they are developing diseases such as diabetes because they are consuming too much sugar and starch.

Revised: _____

_____

_____

3. Many people eat too much, and they watch too much television, and they don't get enough exercise, so they tend to get fat.

Revised: _____

_____

_____

4. In many poor neighborhoods in the United States, there aren't a lot of supermarkets, and food is expensive, so people tend to buy junk food and candy at the corner store, and these practices lead to obesity.

Revised: _____

_____

_____

5. Exercise plays an important role in staying healthy, so people should try to walk, run, or do some sort of physical activity every day for at least twenty minutes, but it's better to work out for longer than that if your schedule allows you to.

Revised: _____

_____

_____

6. Heart disease is the most deadly illness in the United States, and it results from a narrowing of the small blood vessels that connect to the heart, which happens when a waxy material called plaque builds up in them and sticks to their lining, and this condition is also known as hardening of the arteries.

Revised: _____

_____

_____

As you have seen in Chapters 1 and 2, every essay you write must be clearly organized, and that is especially true when you are explaining a process. If you omit a step in the explanation, your reader may be lost. For instance, imagine a poor friend trying to drive to your home from the airport, who has ended up on the other side of town because you left out a key instruction. Likewise, if you forget to mention some of the materials needed to assemble a stereo sound system, your friend may have to return to the appliance store to buy missing parts. Indeed, a careless explanation of some processes (in laboratory science, for example) can, in fact, lead to danger or harm.

PRACTICE 6   **Generating and Organizing Steps in Process Analysis**

A Brainstorm a list of steps for each thesis statement. Number the steps in a logical order.

B Work with a partner or in a small group. Compare your lists and decide on the best set of steps. Write your revised lists below.

1. *Thesis Statement:* There are _____ steps involved in registering for classes at this institution.

_____

_____

_____

_____

_____

Revised List:

_____

_____

_____

_____

_____

_____

(continued on next page)

2. *Thesis Statement:* The best way to study for an important examination involves

_____ steps.

_____

_____

_____

_____

_____

Revised List:

_____

_____

_____

_____

_____

MAKING TRANSITIONS BETWEEN STEPS IN A PROCESS

In Chapter 2, you studied how transitions establish unity and coherence in a classification essay. Here is a list of transition signals that will be useful in introducing the steps in a process essay. Note that some of the transition signals are followed by a comma but others are not.

Transition Signals to Explain Steps in a Process

RULES	EXAMPLES	
1. Use these transition signals when you want to introduce the beginning of a process.	First, The first step	To begin,
2. Use these transition signals when you want to demonstrate the continuation of a process.	Next, Afterward, Second, third, and so on	Then The next step
3. Use these transition signals when you want to introduce the end of a process.	Finally, The final step	Last,

For more information on using transitions, see Appendix B on page 200.

Adding Transitions

Rewrite the sentences into two paragraphs. Add transitions and combine sentences as needed to establish unity and coherence.

PARAGRAPH 1

To determine your resting pulse rate (the number of times your heart beats per minute), rest one arm on a flat surface.

Place two fingertips from your other hand over the artery just below your wrist.

Look at your watch for fifteen seconds.

Count the number of beats you feel.

Multiply that number by four to get the number of beats per minute.

Record it on a piece of paper.

_____

_____

_____

_____

_____

_____

PARAGRAPH 2

Determine your pulse rate after activity.

Jog in place for five minutes if you are in good health. Retake your pulse rate and again record it on a piece of paper.

In two-minute intervals, retake your pulse rate until it returns to the resting rate. Record the total time elapsed.

The shorter the recovery time, the better your cardiac condition is.

_____

_____

_____

_____

_____

_____

> _For writing guides to help you describe a process, see Appendix A, page 190._

When preparing an analysis of a process, it can be useful to summarize the steps involved. Of course, a **summary**, a short restatement of the thesis and main supporting points of a longer work, plays an important role in any kind of writing. The length of a summary usually depends on the length of the original material. A summary of a single paragraph may require only one sentence, whereas a summary of an article or essay may need a short paragraph, and a summary of a longer article or essay may call for a longer paragraph.*

A specialized kind of one-paragraph summary, called an **abstract**, often precedes reports published in professional journals. Abstracts provide a quick way for biologists, teachers, doctors, lawyers, and so on to determine the content of a report or article before deciding whether or not to read further. An abstract of a research report contains the extent, purpose, results, and conclusions that can be drawn from the research. An abstract of an article on literature usually contains the thesis, background, and conclusion of the story, novel, poem, or play.

In later chapters of this book, you will write summaries of essays, articles, or books, based on your own research.

PROCEDURE FOR SUMMARIZING AN ARTICLE

Here is a useful method for writing the summary of an article with many people or facts.

1. Make sure you understand the specifics of the topic. Read the title and subtitle of the original, for they often state or indicate the topic. Then read the whole work. As you read, decide what the author's position on the topic is, and what are the most important points made by the author. Underline or highlight these points. Look for the topic sentences of each paragraph (underline or highlight these as well), and pay special attention to their controlling ideas and claims. Take note of the introductory and concluding paragraphs of the work. Also, underline or highlight frequently repeated key words or phrases, as they probably represent main ideas of the work.

2. On a separate sheet of paper, organize the information in a chart. Include the title and author of the work (if these are provided), and write its thesis statement in your own words. Then present the main supporting points. You can write the controlling idea of each paragraph and some important supporting details in your chart:

PARAGRAPH	CONTROLLING IDEA	SUPPORT
Paragraph 1	Title, author, and thesis	
Paragraph 2	Controlling idea or claim	(Optional) Some supporting details
Paragraph 3	Central claim or point	(Optional) Some supporting details
And so on . . .		

---

*The length also depends on your goal in writing the summary. One type of summary, called a précis, is a single sentence that provides only the main idea of a piece of writing, a play, a movie, a novel, or a speech. A second type of summary, a synopsis, provides the outline of the plot of a novel or play. A synopsis gives the reader or viewer some background information before reading or viewing the performance.

3. Write the summary in your own words. Be objective: report only what the original has to say, and do not state any of your opinions or feelings.

4. Read over your summary and revise it, if necessary. Is it clear? Is it all in your own words, as it should be?

Writing Tip

Before you make the chart, do not look at the material you are going to summarize. Instead, list as many ideas as you can from memory. Then go back to it, see if you have omitted any ideas, and list these without looking at the material. Repeat this process as often as necessary until you have included all the important points.

PRACTICE 8   **Preparing to Write an Abstract**

Read the article. Underline the thesis statement and the topic sentences.

What Is a Heart Attack?

Everyone has heard the term "heart attack," but what exactly is it, and how does it happen? In order to answer these questions, we must first understand some basic physiology of the system that drives the heart. The heart is a muscle responsible for pumping the blood throughout the body. When the heart expands and contracts, blood flows out, carrying oxygen that is essential to the functioning of every muscle. However, since the heart is also a muscle, it too requires a steady supply of blood to its tissues, or the muscle will weaken or die (*World Book* 138).

Oxygen is delivered to the heart through blood vessels called the coronary arteries. Fat, calcium, and dead cells can form a waxy substance called plaque, which sticks to the interior of the arteries. This buildup results in either a narrowing or blockage of the arteries. If the arteries narrow too much, a clot can form, which decreases or shuts off the blood entering the heart. The result is a myocardial infarction or coronary thrombosis—in other words, a heart attack ("Coronary" and *Britannica* 465). However, not all clots affect the heart; a clot can travel to the brain and cause a stroke, which destroys part of the brain.

The main cause of the buildup of plaque is a substance called cholesterol, a waxy substance produced by the liver. Cholesterol cannot travel through the bloodstream by itself, but instead must combine with two types of proteins that carry it along. The first, high density protein or HDL—often called "good cholesterol"—actually removes cholesterol from the veins and arteries and returns it back to the liver, where it can be processed for distribution to the body. The second, low density protein or LDL—often called "bad cholesterol"—tends to stick to the walls of the veins and arteries and thus restricts or blocks the flow of blood (*World Book* 138). Although high amounts of LDL in the bloodstream may be hereditary, a healthy diet and exercise (along with certain kinds of drugs called statins) can lower its presence. Most people these days know that the other contributors to heart disease are obesity, smoking, and excessive consumption of alcohol.

Sources:
1. Crawford, M.H. (2012) "Heart." *World Book Encyclopedia.*
2. Coronary Artery Disease: The ABCs of CAD. American Heart Association.
3. "Myocardial Infarction." *Encyclopedia Britannica.*

Write a one-paragraph abstract of "What Is a Heart Attack?" and then compare your summary with a partner's. Use a chart to help you. The beginning of the summary is provided for you as an example.

According to "What Is a Heart Attack?", a heart attack is caused by a lack of oxygen reaching the heart muscle.

_____

_____

_____

_____

_____

_____

_____

✐ Applying Vocabulary: Using Irregular Plurals from Latin and Greek

Before you begin your writing assignment, review the irregular nouns you learned about on page 45. The assignment involves writing an essay about science, so you may include some of these nouns in your paper.

PRACTICE 9   **Selecting Singular and Plural Irregular Nouns**

Review the irregular nouns from Latin or Greek in Practice 1. Then complete each of the following sentences with the appropriate singular or plural noun.

1. The first step in the scientific method begins with the observation of a series of

   _____, or events.

2. A prediction that scientists test in an experiment is called a _____.

3. Scientists establish both a control and a variable group so that they have a

   _____ for comparing the results.

4. After the experiment is over, the scientists gather the _____.

5. The next step is to conduct one or more _____ of the information.

6. They may classify the information they receive using several _____.

WRITING ASSIGNMENT

In your assignment for this chapter, you will write a process essay that explains the steps in an imaginary experiment and reports on its results. Because you will not gather real data from your experiment, you will have to invent it. Your audience will be your classmates and instructor, not scientists. Assume that the essay you compose in the writing assignment is going to be published in a professional journal. Choose one of the topics and follow the steps in the writing process.

TOPICS

- Does a vegetarian diet cause tooth decay?
- Is water from one source safer to drink than water from another source?
- What brand of paper towels soaks up the most water?
- What cola is sweeter in a blind taste test?
- Does eating candy in a dark movie theater reduce the number of calories consumed?

 STEP 1: Explore your topic, audience, and purpose.

- Brainstorm a list to explore your topic.
- Review the brainstorming list.
- Can you add more details, explanations, or examples? Should you eliminate any that are not relevant or important?
- Consider the audience for the essay. Who would be most interested in the essay's content? What would you expect them to do with the information?

 STEP 2: Prewrite to get ideas.

- List any materials needed to complete the process. For example, if you choose to explain the steps in registering for classes, list the locations a student would need to know about.
- Freewrite to generate more ideas; let the words flow quickly as if you were speaking to the audience. Do not stop to revise, but underline sections you want to return to.

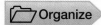 **STEP 3: Organize your ideas.**

- Now do the cutting and pasting from your freewriting.
- Then write a preliminary thesis statement.
- Prepare an outline of the steps involved to ensure that your organization makes sense.

STEP 4: Write the first draft.

- Include a thesis statement in the introduction that outlines or introduces the steps in the process.
- Discuss each step in a separate body paragraph. Use transitions to establish coherence.
- Conclude with a short summary of the process.

STEP 5: Revise the draft.

- Exchange papers with a partner, and give each other feedback on your papers. Use the Chapter 3 Peer Review on page 229 to guide your feedback.
- Carefully consider your partner's feedback. If you agree with it, revise your paper by marking the changes on the first draft.

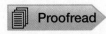

STEP 6: Edit and proofread.

- Use the Chapter 3 Writer's Self-Check on page 230 to help you find and correct errors in grammar, mechanics, and sentence structure.

STEP 7: Write a new draft.

- Rewrite the draft, incorporating all the changes you made earlier.
- Proofread the draft so that it is error free. Are the sentences clear and complete? Are there no run-on or comma-spliced sentences? Are the irregular nouns used correctly?
- Make sure the draft is legible and follows the format your instructor has provided.
- Then examine your essay carefully and write a one-paragraph abstract of its contents.
- Hand in the essay and the abstract to your instructor.

EXPANSION

TIMED WRITING

In this expansion, you will write a one-paragraph summary of the writing model on pages 42–44. Your summary should not be more than five or six sentences. You will have 35 minutes. To complete the expansion, you will need to budget your time accordingly. Follow this procedure.

1. Reread the model essay and underline the main ideas. Look especially at the thesis statements and topic sentences. (10 minutes)

2. Make a quick outline to organize your ideas. (5 minutes)

3. Write a draft of the paragraph. Be sure to include a thesis statement and a good concluding sentence. (10 minutes)

4. Revise your paragraph to be sure your ideas are clear and well organized. (5 minutes)

5. Check your paragraph for errors. Correct any mistakes. (5 minutes)

6. Give your paper to your instructor.

WRITE A SCIENTIFIC PROCESS ESSAY

Return to the brainstorming lists you developed in Practice 6 on page 55. Choose one as the subject for a process essay. Make sure your introduction names the process and includes the goal of the essay, such as helping the reader understand the process or perform the process. In the body paragraphs, be sure to include all the steps in the process in sequential order. Write at least five paragraphs.

After you have finished the essay, write a two- or three-sentence abstract of the experiment and its results.

CHAPTER 4

CAUSE / EFFECT ESSAYS

OBJECTIVES

To write academic texts, you need to master certain skills.

In this chapter, you will learn to:

- Analyze two cause / effect essays

- Distinguish between cause and effect

- Plan an essay using chain or block organization

- Recognize and use parallel structures to create symmetry

- Incorporate quotations, statistics, and examples to support claims

- Write, revise, and edit an essay about a historical event

John F. Kennedy: an Irish-American president of the United States of America.

Much of your thinking each day naturally focuses on analyzing events: you want to understand why something happened. Why, for example, do you have a sore throat? Why does your car not start? Likewise, you want to understand the results of some action or event. If you take some medicine, will it cure your sore throat? If you charge the battery, will the car start? These are the functions of causal analysis, which examines causes and effects.

A *cause* is a reason something happened or is happening, while an *effect* is the change that results from something happening. In academic and professional pursuits, cause / effect generally applies to examinations of social behavior, scientific investigation, and the study of historical events. A **cause / effect essay** is one that explores the causes and/or effects of an action, an event, or a series of occurrences. Many such things, however, have more than one cause or effect. For example, a virus may have caused that sore throat, but lack of sleep and too much stress may have lowered the resistance to the virus. Additionally, you cannot always be sure what causes something, nor can you predict with certainty what effects may result. In discussing causes or effects, therefore, you may use qualifying words such as *probable*, *possible*, and *likely*. You might also qualify your claims with data that show percentages, ratios, or trends. Although cause / effect analysis can apply to any subject matter, this chapter will focus on cause / effect analysis as it relates to history.

ANALYZING THE MODELS

The model essays explore a number of causes that led to a final result or effect. The first essay traces a series of causes, in which one leads to another. The second examines a group of effects occurring at approximately the same time.

Read the models. Then answer the questions.

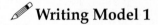 **Writing Model 1**

THE IRISH POTATO FAMINE

1   Throughout much of its history, the United States has welcomed immigrants to its shores. People have come because of opportunity, political liberty, and religious freedom. Others have come because of oppression and poverty in their native countries. There is no greater example of the latter reason for immigration than the Irish who fled to this country during the Great Potato Famine of 1845 through 1851. They came because of their failed crops and their resulting starvation, the loss of their homes and possessions to their indifferent landlords, and the ineffectiveness of the English and Irish governments to help them survive.

2   The conditions under which the majority of the eight million Irish lived were shocking. "There never was," the Duke of Wellington wrote, "a country in which poverty existed to the extent it exists in Ireland." A census in 1841 reported, "Nearly half of the rural population is living

(continued on next page)

in the lowest state." People were crammed inside one-room mud cabins without windows or furniture. Farmers slept with their pigs in filthy conditions. Homeless people put roofs over ditches or slept in tunnels they dug in the ground (Woodham-Smith 20).

3   All this misery could be traced to absentee[1] English and wealthy Irish landlords. An 1845 report stated that their property was merely "a source from which to extract as much money as possible." Landlords leased their land to others who divided it so they could collect more rent. The Irish tenants paid for the right to farm it and to put a cabin up on the property quickly. No money was exchanged, however. The payments were measured by the number of days the tenants worked (Woodham-Smith 20–21).

4   This arrangement depended "entirely and exclusively," on the potato (Woodham-Smith 35). It grew easily in the bad soil and was easy to cook. The potato was also perfect for feeding pigs, cattle, and chickens. The crop, however, would rot soon after harvesting and could not be stored between growing seasons (Woodham-Smith 35–36). By 1840, one-third of the Irish population depended entirely on the potato for food. It was, "a dependency that teetered[2] on the brink of starvation and created a time bomb that needed only the slightest spark to explode".

5   That spark exploded in 1845 when the potato crop was attacked by a fungus[3]. The leaseholders dug the potatoes up, only to find that they had turned into "a dark, gooey mess" (*The Great Hunger*). Six months later, the famine began. It continued and grew worse virtually every year until 1850.

6   At first, the British government tried to help by importing Indian corn from the United States. However, the corn made many people ill, and most tenants had to sell or pawn[4] all their possessions to pay for it. Then the government initiated a second plan: hiring the farm laborers to build roads and canals. By December of 1846, half a million men were breaking rocks up into pieces and shoveling dirt. At this point, however, some workers died of starvation before receiving their wages (Bloy).

7   The famine worsened in 1846 when disease struck the potato crop again. "A stranger," wrote a sub-inspector of police from County Cork, "would wonder how these wretched[5] beings find food. . . . They sleep in their rags and have pawned their bedding" (Woodham-Smith 92). Unfortunately, much of the food they found was the seed potatoes for next year's crop. As a result, when the 1847 harvest came in free of disease, it was too small to feed everyone. In 1848, the situation worsened as the blight[6] came back, destroying the entire crop.

---

[1] **absentee:** someone who lives a long way away from the property he or she rents to others
[2] **teetered:** stood or moved in an unsteady way as if going to fall
[3] **fungus:** a fast-growing mold
[4] **pawn:** leave something with another in exchange for borrowing money
[5] **wretched:** unhappy or poor
[6] **blight:** a plant disease in which parts of the plant dry up and die

8   By this time, even the landlords became desperate. They threw out half a million tenants who could not pay their rent through labor, and then burned their homes. Consequently, many went to live in poor houses. In 1847, however, all public work projects ended, and public poor houses were closed (*The Irish Famine*). Now with the tenants homeless and living in filth, typhoid fever, cholera[7], and dysentery[8] broke out, claiming more lives than starvation itself. An official estimate claimed that 750,000 people died from the famine and related causes, but the true number may have been twice as many (*Case-Studies*).

9   As a result, a million Irish poor fled the country, most of them heading by boat across the Atlantic. The conditions on these "coffin ships" were horrifying, and many people died during the journey. Of those who survived, the great majority went to Quebec and Montreal, Canada, but after arriving, over half walked across the border to the United States. They wanted no part of living in Canada, a British colony (Woodham-Smith 209).

10   The Irish viewed the rapidly growing United States as a land of opportunity. These poor immigrants showed up in rags, without money, education, or skill, but they had a small glimmer of hope[9]. Over the last nearly two centuries, that hope has been fully realized. The Irish population of the United States has more than doubled that of all of Ireland, and an Irish American was even elected to the most powerful position in the United States: John Fitzgerald Kennedy became the first Irish-American president in 1961.

Sources:
1. Bloy, Marjie. *The Irish Famine: 1845-9.*
2. Case-Studies: Irish potato famine (1845 to 1851).
3. Irish Potato Famine and Trade (History). Web. 10 May 1996.
4. Woodham-Smith, Cecil. *The Great Hunger.*

---

[7] **cholera:** a serious disease of the stomach and bowels caused by infected water or food
[8] **dysentery:** a serious disease of the bowels that leads to bleeding and passing more waste than normal
[9] **glimmer of hope:** a small sign of hope

(Questions on next page)

Questions about the Model

1. Which sentence in Paragraph 1 is the thesis statement of the essay? Underline it.

2. What important effect of the Irish potato famine does the concluding paragraph describe?

3. What chain of effects was created by the destruction of the potato crop over several years?

4. Which words or phrases signal or introduce each cause or effect? Circle them.

5. Why did the substitution of corn for potatoes fail?

6. Who does the author think is primarily responsible for the horrible conditions under which the Irish peasants lived? Why do you think so?

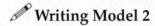 **Writing Model 2**

THE EXPLOSIVE GROWTH OF THE CITIES

By Mark C. Carnes and John A. Garraty

1   By the end of the nineteenth century, immigrants from southern and eastern Europe crowded into cities that were already heavily populated by native-born Americans. As a result, the cities suffered greatly from the effects of rapid growth. Sanitation, fire protection, and the paving of streets were inadequate. Housing was insufficient and overcrowded. Families fell apart, and crime grew out of control. Because of the extent of these problems, however, people eventually took steps to improve living conditions.

2   Sewer and water facilities could not keep pace with the rapidly increasing needs. By the 1890s, the tremendous growth of Chicago had put such a strain on the sanitation system that the Chicago River had become virtually an open sewer. The city's drinking water contained such a high concentration of germ-killing chemicals that it was almost undrinkable. In the 1880s, all the sewers of Baltimore emptied into the Back River Basin. According to the journalist H. L. Mencken, every summer smelled like "a billion polecats."[1] Fire protection became less and less adequate. Garbage piled up on the streets faster than workers could carry it away. The streets themselves crumbled beneath the pounding of heavy traffic. Urban growth proceeded with such speed that the cities laid out new streets much more rapidly than they could be paved. Chicago had more than 1,400 miles of dirt streets in 1890.

---

[1] **polecats:** skunks—small black and white animals that produce a very strong smell if they are attacked or afraid

3   The population explosion also placed a great strain on the housing supply. People poured into the great cities faster than houses and apartments could be built for them. As a result, the densely packed areas of the 1840s became unbearable. Greedy builders used every foot of space, squeezing out light and air in order to jam in a few additional family units.

4   Substandard living quarters aggravated[2] other evils such as the breakdown of family life, along with mental distress, crime, and juvenile delinquency.[3] The bloody New York riots of 1863, for example, were caused in part by the bitterness and frustration of thousands jammed together. A citizens' committee expressed amazement after visiting the slums "that so much misery, disease, and wretchedness can be huddled together and hidden."

5   Eventually, however, practical forces operated to bring about improvements. Once the relationship between polluted water and disease was fully understood, everyone saw the need for clean water and decent sewage systems. City dwellers of all classes resented the dirt, noise, and ugliness. In many communities, public-spirited groups formed societies to plant trees, clean up littered areas, and develop recreational facilities. When one city took on improvements, others tended to follow suit, prompted by local pride and competition between cities.

6   Gradually, the basic facilities of urban living were improved. Streets were paved, first with stones and wood blocks, and then with smoother, quieter asphalt. Gaslight, then electric arc lights, and finally Thomas Edison's incandescent lamps brightened the cities after dark. This illumination of the cities made law enforcement easier. It also stimulated nightlife and permitted factories and shops to operate after sunset. Life in the cities was far from ideal, but streetcars would take people quickly and inexpensively to work and back, and high-rise buildings would soon fill the horizons. The modern American city was forming throughout the East and Midwest.

Source: Adapted from Carnes, Mark C. and John A. Garraty. "American Society in the Industrial Age."

---

[2] **aggravated:** made a bad situation worse
[3] **delinquency:** illegal or unacceptable behavior, especially by young people

(Questions on next page)

Questions about the Model

1. According to the first paragraph, what led to the terrible living conditions of the cities? What was the final effect of these conditions?

2. What effects does the body of the essay focus on? How many are there?

3. What key effects are introduced in the final two paragraphs? Which sentences state them most directly? Underline them twice.

4. What specific measures were taken to address specific causes?

5. Quotations are included in both model essays. What purpose do they serve?

Noticing Vocabulary: Phrasal Verbs

The two writing models contain a number of **phrasal verbs**, which are special collocations. A phrasal verb combines a *verb* and one or two *particles* (short prepositions); together they have a meaning that is different from the verb alone. There are two types of phrasal verbs:

- A **separable phrasal verb** moves or changes the condition of its object. A noun object can come before or after the second word (the particle) of the phrasal verb.*

    The landlords *threw **the farmers** out*.

    The landlords *threw out **the farmers***.

    However, a pronoun object can come only before the particle.

    The landlords *threw **them** out*. (The verb moves the object.)

- An **inseparable phrasal verb** does not move or change the condition of the object. The object always follows the particle.

    Peasants *turned to **desperate measures***.

    Peasants *turned to **them***. (The object does not change or move.)

For more information about common separable and inseparable phrasal verbs, see Appendix D, page 206.

---

*Moving the noun object from one place to the other can also create an awkward sentence, especially when the particle ends the phrasal verb. For example: The cities *laid out **new roads*** (fine). The cities *laid **new roads** out* (awkward). Therefore, be careful in choosing the best word order.

Noticing Phrasal Verbs

Look at the writing models again and find the phrasal verbs. Using the context, label them *S* (separable) or *I* (inseparable).

MODEL 1

_____ **1.** put up *(paragraph 3)*

_____ **2.** depend on *(paragraph 4)*

_____ **3.** dig up *(paragraph 5)*

_____ **4.** turn into *(paragraph 5)*

_____ **5.** break up *(paragraph 6)*

_____ **6.** come in *(paragraph 7)*

_____ **7.** come back *(paragraph 7)*

_____ **8.** show up *(paragraph 10)*

MODEL 2

_____ **9.** fall apart *(paragraph 1)*

_____ **10.** pile up *(paragraph 2)*

_____ **11.** bring about *(paragraph 5)*

_____ **12.** take on *(paragraph 5)*

ORGANIZATION

Writing a cause / effect essay requires that you gather information and plan carefully. In some cases, it begins with research, such as finding and analyzing the possible causes of a historical event. In others, it starts with experimentation, such as noting the effects of a change in diet on laboratory mice. No matter what the case, however, you must address these two questions in planning your essay:

- Who will be reading my paper, and how much do they know about the subject matter?
- Am I examining more than one cause or effect? Are the causes or effects occurring at the same time, or does one lead to another?

The answer to the last question will help you decide on the structure of your essay.

An event may have more than one cause, and a cause may have more than one effect. Sometimes the causes occur one after another; in other words, in chain reaction. Writing Model 1 follows this pattern in examining the causes of the immigration of Irish peasants to the United States. At other times, all the causes or all the effects occur at about the same time. Writing Model 2 follows this pattern as it examines the effects of overcrowding in the cities.

The structure of a cause / effect essay can be organized in one of two ways: with **chain** organization, in which you examine causes or effects in a sequence, or with **block** organization, in which you examine the multiple causes or effects of some action or situation. This organization is appropriate when all the causes or effects are not in a sequence.

CHAIN ORGANIZATION

A chain organization examines causes and effects that are directly linked sequentially. In other words, one cause leads to an effect, which leads to another cause, and so on.

A diagram of this type of organization pattern, with examples from Writing Model 1, looks like this:

Introductory Paragraph

The opening paragraph states the effect and outlines the chain of events.

Effect: Irish peasants immigrating to the United States, because of a series of causes related to the Great Potato Famine

Chain of Events: failed crops, resulting starvation, the loss of their homes and possessions, and ineffective government response

↓

First Group of Body Paragraphs

The first body paragraphs examine causes, usually in chronological order.

Paragraphs 2 and 3: the extreme poverty of the rural Irish and terrible conditions in which they lived, farming land that they did not own

Paragraph 4: the reliance of the Irish on potatoes and the subsequent effect when the crop failed

↓

Final Group of Body Paragraphs

The final body paragraphs detail a step-by-step description of the cause / effect chain as support

Paragraphs 5 through 9: loss of possessions, enlistment on poorly designed public works projects, eviction from their homes, poor houses, disease, desperation, and passage to Canada

↓

Concluding Paragraph

The final paragraph states the conclusive effect.

Paragraph 10: coming to the United States and integrating into American society

---

BLOCK ORGANIZATION

Block organization, the structure of the second writing model, examines the multiple causes (or effects) of some action or situation when the causes or effects are *not* directly linked sequentially. A diagram of block organization, with examples from Writing Model 2, looks like this:

Introductory Paragraph

The opening paragraph introduces the topic, makes clear why it is important, and then provides a transition into an analysis of the causes or effects.

Thesis: cities suffered as a result of too rapid growth

Transition: the problems caused by this overgrowth were so widespread, steps for improvement had to be taken

↓

Body Paragraphs

The body paragraphs examine or suggest one possible or probable cause or effect, and provide information, data, or interpretation as support.

Paragraph 2: inadequate sanitation, water facilities, and fire protection

Paragraph 3: housing supply shortage

Paragraph 4: disease and disintegration of family life

↓

Concluding Paragraph(s)

The final paragraphs summarize the causes or effects discussed in the body paragraphs, and then state the consequences.

Paragraph 5: actions to provide cleaner water, make government more responsive, plant trees and clean up the cities, and illuminate the streets

---

Types of Support

As with any type of writing, you must support the claims in the body paragraphs of your cause/effect essay. Look again at the body paragraphs of the models. Note that each claim is supported by a survey, a set of statistics, one or more examples, a specific description, an explanation, or a quotation. You are already familiar with most of these types of support. Chapter 1 introduced you to explanations and examples. Chapter 2 taught you about conducting surveys, and briefly introduced you to statistics. Chapter 3 taught you how to summarize. And later in this chapter, you will learn more about using quotations.

> *For writing guides to help you introduce cause and effect, see Appendix A on page 190.*

Analyzing Paragraph Support

Look at Writing Model 1 on pages 65–67. Choose three body paragraphs to analyze. Identify the types of support used in each (*surveys*, *statistics*, *examples*, *specific descriptions*, *explanations*, or *quotations*), and include a two-to-four-word description of the content.

EXAMPLE

Paragraph ___2___ Types of support: __Quotation and statistics on number of__

__beds and chairs__

1. Paragraph _____ Types of support: _____

_____

2. Paragraph _____ Types of support: _____

_____

3. Paragraph _____ Types of support: _____

_____

Developing Paragraph Support

Underline the words or phrases that need to be explained or developed in each thesis statement. List examples of topics that might support the thesis.

1. The Thirteenth Amendment to the United States Constitution, which ended slavery in 1865, had <u>enormous consequences</u>.

   a. __freedom for large numbers of people__

   b. __need for former slaves to find employment__

   c. __need for former slave owners to find ways to run their plantations__

2. The invention of electricity led to dramatic changes in people's lives.

   a. _____

   b. _____

   c. _____

3. People immigrate to other countries for a number of reasons.

   a. _____

   b. _____

   c. _____

   d. _____

DISTINGUISHING BETWEEN CAUSE AND EFFECT

In order to ensure that your essay is clearly organized and flows logically, you should take care to avoid some of these potential problems with your analysis.

Confusing cause with effect

Although this may seem easy, separating cause from effect can be complicated. For example, was the poverty of the Irish peasants a *cause* of their starvation or an *effect* of their responding to the loss of the crops?

Confusing the sequence of events with their causes

If you woke up with a headache on a bright, sunny morning, did the sunshine cause your headache? If you were out in the rain and then developed a cold, did the rain cause the cold—or did lack of sleep, too much stress, or exposure to a virus cause it?

Oversimplifying complex causes and effects

Many effects have complex causes or possible causes; likewise, so do many causes have complex effects. Note that both model essays explore those complexities.

PRACTICE 4 **Identifying Causes or Effects**

Circle the cause and underline the effect in each statement.

1. Irish immigrants having few skills other than farming experienced great difficulty in finding a job in cities.

2. The rate of obesity in the United States has increased greatly in the past twenty years due to a number of factors.

3. The large numbers of people immigrating to the United States have increased the diversity of U.S. culture and society.

4. The emigration of Eastern Europeans in the beginning of the twentieth century was both an economic and a political necessity.

5. The Civil War in the United States was the result of a progressive series of events.

6. Global life expectancy has greatly increased thanks to improvements in sanitation and nutrition.

Transition Signals for Introducing Causes and Effects

As always, transition signals help establish unity and clarity in an essay. The list of expressions can help make the relationship between causes and effects clear.

RULES	EXAMPLES	
1. Use these transition signals to introduce *causes*.	a key factor because because of due to	one reason owing to since this occurred the first cause
2. Use these transition signals to introduce *effects*.	accordingly as a consequence as a result consequently	one outcome resulting in so the first effect
3. Use these transition signals to *qualify statements*.	could (have) may (have) might (have)	perhaps possibly probably

Short transition signals are valuable tools in a cause/effect essay. However, a clearly organized and gracefully written essay often benefits from whole sentences of transition.

For additional help using transitions, see Appendix B on page 200.

PRACTICE 5   **Adding Transitions**

Rewrite the passage, inserting transitions where needed.

People from all over the world immigrate to the United States. They search for better employment, or, for that matter, any job. Refugees from war and political oppression come here. People seek religious freedom or escape from persecution for their religious beliefs or practices. Other people wish to pursue a college education or post-graduate education at a university. A few happy people arrive in the country to marry an American citizen they have met abroad.

People from all over the world immigrate to the United States for a variety

of reasons.

SENTENCE STRUCTURE

One way to improve the clarity of your sentences is to keep items in a series consistent in grammatical form. This consistency is referred to as **parallelism**, like parallel lines in mathematics.

USING PARALLELISM

Clarity and maturity of style are the marks of effective writing. Parallelism, also called **parallel structure**, repeats items in a series using the same grammatical form so your ideas are symmetrical and clear. Look at these examples from the writing models at the beginning of the chapter.

PARALLEL INFINITIVES In many communities, public-spirited groups formed societies **to plant** trees, **clean up** littered areas, and **develop** recreational facilities. (Note that the repetition of *to* is not necessary.)

PARALLEL NOUNS City dwellers of all classes resented the **dirt**, **noise**, and **ugliness**. These poor immigrants arrived in rags, **without money**, **education**, or **skill**, but they had a small glimmer of hope.

PARALLEL SENTENCES Fire protection **became** less and less adequate. Garbage **piled up** on the streets. The streets themselves **crumbled** beneath the pounding of heavy traffic. (sentences in the identical pattern)

| PRACTICE 6 | **Identifying Parallel Structures** |

Underline the parallel structures in each passage.

1. They came because of their failed crops and their resulting starvation, the loss of their homes and possessions to their indifferent landlords, and the ineffectiveness of the English and Irish governments to help them survive.

2. Sanitation, fire protection, and the paving of streets were inadequate.

3. Substandard living quarters aggravated[1] other evils such as the breakdown of family life, along with mental distress, crime, and juvenile delinquency.

4. Residents of the city resented the crowds, smells, and pollution.

5. The city government began to build new housing, repair streets, and create public parks.

6. Streets were paved, first with stones and wood blocks, and then with smoother, quieter asphalt. Gaslights were used to brighten the cities after dark, which made law enforcement easier. Streetcars were introduced which took people quickly and inexpensively to work and back and cut back on traffic.

---

[1] **aggravated:** made a bad situation worse

Writing Parallel Structures

Complete each sentence with words or phrases that repeat the grammatical form of the italicized words. Look at the writing models on pages 65–69 as needed.

1. The rural Irish were *uneducated*, _poor, and hungry._

2. They *lived* in shacks, *shared living quarters*, and _____.

3. The potato served as food for the _____,

   _____, and _____.

4. The poor Irish became desperate, hoping *to find work*,

   _____, and _____.

5. The streets of the big cities in the U.S. were *dirty*, _____,

   and _____.

6. People began to *clean up* the cities, _____, and

   _____.

Writing Tip

One clue to identifying errors in parallelism is to circle every *and* in your first draft. The word *and* can join only structures that are grammatically equal. For example, "He is tall and thin," or "He is a husband and a father" are both logical. However, "He is tall and a father" is not!

Correcting Errors in Parallelism

Correct the errors in parallelism. Write your correction above the line. The italicized words provide hints as to which structures that follow them may be incorrect.

Controversy over immigrants and the language they speak is not new. Millions of Germans *moved* to the United States in the 1800s and bringing their language with them. They not only held their religious services in German, but they also opened private schools in which the teachers *taught* in German, published German-language newspapers, and speaking German *at* home, in stores, and also spoke it in taverns. Eventually all this changed.

The first generation of immigrants spoke German almost exclusively. The second generation assimilated, *speaking* English at home, but also would speak German when they visited their parents. For the most part, the third generation knew German only as "that language" that their grandparents used. Many other immigrants who came after the Germans have followed the same pattern: *the Japanese*, the Italians, Eastern Europeans, and there are many more.

PREPARATION FOR WRITING

The two writing models you read at the beginning of this chapter are based on research. Researching a topic can be interesting, even fun, once you know how to do it. The information you find will broaden your understanding of the topic and may even change some of your opinions on it.

CONDUCTING RESEARCH

Begin to research a topic by exploring what you already know. List any words or phrases related to the topic. Once you have your list, you can begin your research. With Internet searches, try to narrow broad terms so your search yields better results (for example, "elementary school curriculum in history" will lead you to more useful sources than simply "school" or "history"). You may want to expand your list later, based on what you discover.

Encyclopedias

An excellent place to get a basic understanding of a topic is in an encyclopedia at home or in a library. Among the most popular general encyclopedias are *The Encyclopedia Americana* and the *World Book Encyclopedia.* ** However, there are literally hundreds of encyclopedias, each for a specific field—from anthropology to zoology. An article in one of them can provide a broad picture of the main issues as well as key terms for further research. Make sure, however, that the encyclopedia you consult is current.

The Internet

The Internet has become the primary source of research, especially because it is as close by as your computer or one at your school (or even a public library). The best-known encyclopedia on the Internet is *Wikipedia*. However, some teachers do not allow students to use it because it is not written by experts. Therefore, check with your instructor on his or her policy.

The remaining chapters of this book will provide specific instruction on searching and documenting information from the Internet.

---

* At the time of this writing, these were still being published in bound book editions, but new editions may move to the Internet.

Research immigration trends on the Internet and use your findings to write a summary. Follow the instructions.

1. On an Internet search engine, type in "Immigration from" and add the name of the country in which your parents or ancestors were born. You should find many resources.

2. Select one and find a section that interests you.

3. Then write a one-paragraph summary of the section, beginning by identifying the source, such as "According to *Wikipedia*, . . ." or "James Smith writes in 'Guatemala: Economic Migrants Replace Political Refugees' . . ."

4. Include a quotation if it is appropriate.

QUOTING MATERIAL FROM OUTSIDE SOURCES

As you have seen in the models, an essay gains strength from the backing or support you provide for the claims in topic sentences. Quotations based on your research are a strong source of that support. A **quotation** is a word-for-word, comma-for-comma, exact copy of materials found in outside sources. Quotation marks (" ") signal to your readers that the materials are copied from a book, a magazine, or the Internet. You must identify the source, either prior to or following the quotation. Also after the quotation, you should either explain it or indicate its relationship to the topic idea of the paragraph. Note this pattern in the first example below.

Documenting the sources of quotations, paraphrases, and summaries is a complex issue, based on differing systems used in academic work. Later chapters in this book will show you how to do all this. However, at this point, observe these punctuation and capitalization rules for any quotations you use.

PUNCTUATING QUOTATIONS

Quotations can be punctuated in several ways, depending on the number of sentences quoted, and whether the source of the quote precedes, follows, or breaks up the quotation.

1. A phrase introducing the source appears before the quotation.

> A census in 1841 reported, "Nearly half of the rural population are living in the lowest state." People were crammed inside one-room mud cabins without windows or furniture.

Note that:

- the introductory phrase is followed by a comma
- a period, question mark, or exclamation point[1] goes inside the closing quotation marks
- the first word is capitalized because the quotation is a full sentence
- the sentence following the quotation explains, interprets, or adds information to the quotation

---

[1] In rare cases, question marks or exclamation points go outside the closing quotation marks if they are not part of the quotation, such as: Have you read the chapter in *The American Nation* entitled, "American Society in the Industrial Age"? (The chapter title is quoted.)

2. The first sentence makes a claim that the quotation supports. In this case, the source follows the quotation.

> Abraham Lincoln was regarded as a humble working man. *(Quotation supporting the claim)* "The middle-class country had got a middle-class President at last," wrote the famous author Ralph Waldo Emerson when Abraham Lincoln took office in 1861. *(Relevance to the topic idea)* Indeed, Lincoln greatly advanced the growth of the middle class when he authorized the building of the transcontinental railroad.

Note that a comma replaces a period at the end of the quotation; again, the sentence following the quotation explains, interprets, or adds information to the quotation.

3. Only a few words are quoted and incorporated into a paraphrase, so the punctuation differs again.

> In the 1880s, all the sewers of Baltimore emptied into the Back River Basin, and according to the journalist H. L. Mencken, every summer they smelled like "a billion polecats."

Note that the first word of the quotation is not capitalized; there is no comma before the quoted words.

4. The phrase identifying the source splits the quotation in two parts.

> The founding fathers of the United States were practical men. "The earth belongs to the living," wrote Thomas Jefferson, "not to the dead." Their Constitution and Bill of Rights put those practical concerns into law.

Note that a comma ends the first part of the quotation; a second comma precedes the second part.

5. In a long quotation (about four or more sentences), quotation marks are not even used.

> Jacob A. Riis, a reporter, captured the horror of the crowded conditions of poor immigrants in New York in his classic study of life in the slums, *How the Other Half Lives* (1890):
>
> > The metropolis is to lots of people like a lighted candle to the moth. It attracts them in swarms that come year after year with the vague idea that they can get along here if anywhere; that something is bound to turn up among so many. Nearly all are young men, unsettled in life, many—most of them, perhaps— fresh from good homes, beyond a doubt with honest hopes of getting a start in the city and making a way for themselves. Few of them have much money to waste while looking around, and the cheapness of the lodging offered is an object. Fewer still know anything about the city and its pitfalls.

Note that a colon follows the introduction of the source; the left and right margins of the long quotation are indented; the quotation does not have quotation marks.

Punctuating and Capitalizing Quotations

Add punctuation and capital letters to each quotation.

1. At his Inaugural Address in 1961, President John Fitzgerald Kennedy famously said, "Ask not what your country can do for you. Ask what you can do for your country."

2. During the Civil War, President Abraham Lincoln cautioned it is best not to swap horses while crossing the river

3. A house divided against itself cannot stand Lincoln also said

4. The ballot Lincoln added is much stronger than the bullet

5. Why should there not be a persistent confidence in the ultimate judgment of the people said Lincoln in his First Inaugural Address is there any better or equal hope in this world

6. Mark Twain, the famous American author, once wrote always do right this will gratify some people and astonish the rest

✏️ **Applying Vocabulary: Using Phrasal Verbs**

Before you begin your writing assignment, review the phrasal verbs you learned about on page 70.

Using Phrasal Verbs

Use the phrasal verbs in parentheses to write another sentence. Place the object of the phrasal verb where it fits best.

1. The Great Potato Famine caused terrible suffering. (led up to) _It led up to the_
   death of many people.

2. The famers borrowed money to feed their families. (pay back) _____

   _____

3. Each year, the crops were destroyed again, but the farmers did not completely lose hope. (wait for) _____

   _____

4. Finally, however, they became exceedingly weak and hungry. (gave up)

   _____

   _____

See Appendix D on page 206 for more examples of phrasal verbs.

5. They left Ireland for Canada and the United States. (start over) _____

_____

6. In the United States, they began new lives. (look for) _____

_____

WRITING ASSIGNMENT

Your assignment in this chapter is to write a cause/effect essay about a historical event. Choose a historical event that relates to you, your family, or others—either in another country or in the United States. Write an essay of at least five paragraphs that examines either the causes or the effects of the event. It need not be anything dramatic or political. It could, for example, relate to a festival, a tradition, or a celebration that has a long or interesting history.

Consult one source, either in the library or on the Internet, and use some of the information, including quotations, in your essay.

Develop the body paragraphs with explanations, examples, and even statistics that you find in your research. Do not, however, base your entire essay on what you learn from the source.

Include your personal knowledge of, or experience with, the event, or what you have learned from members of your family. Follow the steps in the writing process.

 Explore

STEP 1: Explore your topic, audience, and purpose.

- Examine what you know, and add to your knowledge about the subject by consulting one outside source. Take notes on what you find.
- Decide on your purpose. Do you want to inform or entertain your readers.

 Prewrite

STEP 2: Prewrite to get ideas.

- Freewrite, brainstorm, or do clustering to explore your ideas.

Writing Tip

Do a cluster diagram to help you generate and organize your paper. For *chain organization*, start at the top of the page and link the circles downward. Then add more circles to the sides to indicate supporting information. See the cluster diagram on page 15 for reference.

For *block organization*, start on the left side of the page and move across to the right. Then add more circles below to indicate supporting information.

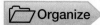 **Organize**

STEP 3: Organize your ideas.

- Write a preliminary thesis statement.
- Write an outline of the steps involved, based either on block or chain organization.

 Write

STEP 4: Write the first draft.

- Include an introduction, body paragraphs, and a conclusion.
- If you are analyzing the causes of an effect, state the effect in the first paragraph. Also state when and where it happened, and who was involved.
- Likewise, if you are analyzing effects, state the cause of the effects in the first paragraph.

 Revise

STEP 5: Revise the draft.

- Exchange papers with a partner, and give each other feedback on your papers. Use the Chapter 4 Peer Review on page 231 to guide your feedback.
- Carefully consider your partner's feedback. If you agree with it, revise your paper by marking the changes on the first draft.

 **Proofread**

STEP 6: Edit and proofread.

- Use the Chapter 4 Writer's Self-Check on page 232 to help you find and correct errors in grammar, mechanics, and sentence structure.

 Write

STEP 7: Write a new draft.

- Revise the draft, incorporating all the changes you made earlier.
- Proofread the draft so that it is error free.
- Make sure the draft is legible and follows the format your instructor has provided.
- Hand in the essay to your instructor.

EXPANSION

TIMED WRITING

In this expansion, you will write a one-paragraph summary of one of the writing models at the beginning of the chapter. Limit yourself to the main ideas of the model, but *do not include any of your opinions*. Incorporate at least one quotation from the model in your summary. You will have 30 minutes. To complete the expansion, you will need to budget your time accordingly. Follow this procedure.

1. Reread the writing model, underlining the topic sentences of each paragraph. (5 minutes)

2. Write a draft of the paragraph. Be sure to include a title and thesis statement. If possible, combine the ideas of topic sentences, and restate the ideas in your own words. (10 minutes)

3. Revise your paragraph to make sure that a) your ideas are clear and well organized, and b) you have not copied directly from the model. (10 minutes)

4. Check your paragraph for errors. Correct any mistakes. (5 minutes)

5. Hand in your paper to your instructor.

EXAMINING ALTERNATIVES

Write one or two paragraphs in which you suggest at least one possible action that the English government could have done differently to prevent the Irish from starvation during the Potato Famine. Explain how this action might have resulted in a different effect.

CHAPTER 5

EXTENDED DEFINITION ESSAYS

OBJECTIVES

To write academic texts, you need to master certain skills.

In this chapter, you will learn to:

- Analyze an essay that explores a definition

- Write definitions using synonyms, formal statements, and negation

- Use noun clauses and adjective clauses as subjects and objects

- Paraphrase ideas to avoid plagiarism

- Write, revise, and edit an essay defining a concept

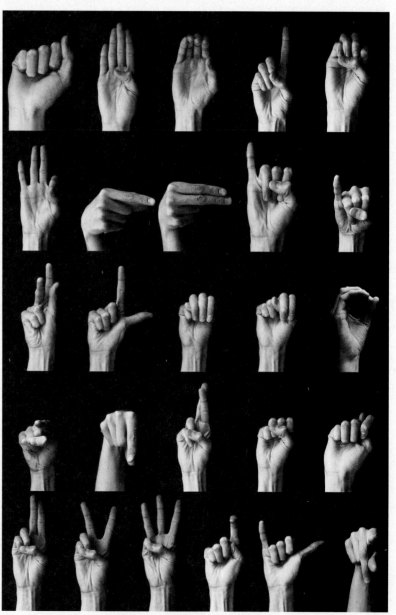

American Sign Language alphabet

Chapter 2 focused on classification. As you will see, **definition** also involves classification. Definition plays two roles in essays. The first and primary role devotes an entire essay to exploring the meaning of a word, phrase, or idea. The second and supporting role simply makes clear the meaning of an unfamiliar word or phrase in a paragraph of an essay. You will examine both roles in this chapter, but the emphasis will be on writing a fully developed essay of definition.

Where are definitions most likely to be needed? That depends on the audience for your essay, but most often you will need to define abstract terms such as "belief" or "honor," or scientific or technical terms. For example, in psychology, which the *Longman Advanced American Dictionary* defines as "the study of the mind and how it works," many terms may need to be defined. The writing model in this chapter is taken from the field of psychology, specifically, how the brain acquires language.

ANALYZING THE MODEL

The writing model explores an extended definition of *language*, developing and illustrating it through references to experts.

Read the model. Then answer the questions.

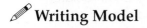 **Writing Model**

What Is Language?

1   We all speak it, and we all write it, but what exactly is it? The *Longman Advanced American Dictionary* defines *language* as "a system of communication by written or spoken words which is used by the people of a particular country or area." While this general definition is useful, it seems far too limited. It refers only to people in *one* country or area, not to *all* people everywhere. Furthermore, it does not explain the "system," and ignores the fact that words alone are only a partial element of language. The arrangement and form of words (and often other nonverbal signals) also convey meaning. Clearly, language is more complex than merely writing and speaking, and therefore, must involve a deeper set of processes operating in the human brain. What are these processes, and where do they come from?

(continued on next page)

2   In order to address these questions, we need a broader definition of language. According to Carole Wade and Carol Tavris, *language* is "a system of rules for combining elements that are essentially meaningless into utterances[1] that communicate meaning. The 'elements' are usually sounds, but they can also be gestures of American Sign Language (ASL) and other manual languages used by deaf and hearing-impaired people. Because of language, we can refer not only to the here and now, but also to past and future events,

A language class

and to things and people who are not present" (Wade, 2011). Thus, not only does language refer to these things and events, but also to abstract concepts that cannot be seen or heard, such as love, loyalty, democracy, and Einstein's general theory of relativity. These concepts exist only in our minds, so, in a sense, language makes them a part of our reality.

3   Such a reference to things, people, events, and abstract concepts occurs through the use of *symbols*. *Symbols* represent things, but they are *not* the things themselves. For example, we can see a picture of a chair and immediately recognize what the picture represents. Language, therefore, is a distinctly human ability to identify and shape our world. Animals make sounds that may reveal fear, anger, or other emotions, but (as far as we know) they cannot communicate abstract thoughts.

4   This broader definition is nonetheless limited, however, for it does not answer the question of how we acquire language. *Linguists*, specialists in the study and use of languages, have offered many explanations. For example, "[a]t one time, most psychologists assumed that children acquired language by imitating adults and paying attention when adults corrected their mistakes" (Wade, 2011). This belief was exploded by Noam Chomsky, "who argue[s] that language was far too complex to be learned bit by bit, as one might learn the list of world capitals" (Wade, 2011). Instead Chomsky believes that humans are born with the capacity to learn language because their brains are programmed with what he calls "a universal grammar." In an interview with John Gliedman, Chomsky defined the term as "the sum total of all the immutable[2] principles that heredity builds into the language organ. These principles cover grammar, speech sounds, and meaning. Put differently, universal grammar is the inherited genetic endowment[3] that makes it possible for us to speak and learn human languages" (1983). In short, humans are born with a set of rules for acquiring language that apply to any language they are exposed to.

---

[1] **utterances:** sounds
[2] **immutable:** unchanging
[3] **endowment:** gift

5   While most linguists and psychologists today agree with Chomsky's general idea, experts differ on how to explain the origin of universal grammar. Many believe that the ability to acquire a language is instinctual, like the untaught behavior of animals. Charles Darwin, the English naturalist famous for his theory of evolution, first expressed this theory in 1871. He argued that the language ability evolved over time:

> [M]an has an instinctive tendency to speak, as we see in the babble of our young children; whilst no child has an instinctive tendency to brew, bake, or write. Moreover, no philologist[4] now supposes that any language has been deliberately invented; it has been slowly and unconsciously developed by many steps (1874).

6   Stephen Pinker, a professor of psychology at Harvard University, has written several books that support Darwin's position. Pinker compares language to the human eye, saying that like the eye, language has an evolutionary adaptation (1994). Further proof that the ability to use language has evolved comes from our understanding of anatomy. The primary functions of the organs associated with producing oral language relate to eating and breathing, not speaking. Communicative ability in humans comes from an area of the brain called the cerebral cortex, where the elements of language are located. The brains of animals lack highly developed cortexes, so the sources of their sounds come from other areas of the brain that are largely associated with emotion (Pinker, 1994). The human brain is programmed to produce language.

7   What exactly is language, then, and where does it come from? The answer is that language represents and creates our reality through symbols. Human beings have evolved into speaking, writing, and signing creatures through a long process of evolution that makes us ready to acquire language at birth. Although languages differ greatly throughout the world, our brains possess a universal grammar that prepares us to communicate in any of them. Language is what makes us human.

Sources:
1. Chomsky, Noam. "Things No Amount of Learning Can Teach."
2. Darwin, C.E. *The Descent of Man*.
3. *Longman Advanced American Dictionary*.
4. Pinker, Stephen. *The Language Instinct*.
5. Wade, Carole and Carol Tavris (2011). *Psychology*.

---

[4] **philologist:** a person who studies language

(Questions on next page)

Questions about the Model

1. According to Paragraph 1, what are the problems with the dictionary definition that was quoted?

2. Where is the thesis of the essay introduced? Does the thesis introduce one main idea or two?

3. Which quoted sentence in Paragraph 2 provides a second definition of language? Underline it. Why does the quotation continue?

4. What other words or phrases are defined in the essay? Circle these words and underline the word or phrase that defines them.

5. Why does the essay contrast humans with animals?

6. How do the views of Chomsky differ from those of Darwin and Pinker? What conclusion does the essay draw about these contrasting views?

Noticing Vocabulary: Synonyms, 1

A *synonym* is a word with the same or nearly the same meaning as another word. For example, a synonym for *idea* is "thought," and synonyms for *gestures* are "movements" and "motions." Using synonyms provides variety of word choice and thus contributes to lively and sophisticated writing.

PRACTICE 1 **Finding Synonyms**

Look at the writing model again and find these words. Using the context to help you, supply a synonym for each word as it is used in the model. Use your dictionary as needed.

1. convey *(paragraph 1)* _____

2. impaired *(paragraph 2)* _____

3. concept *(paragraph 2)* _____

4. distinctly *(paragraph 3)* _____

5. acquire *(paragraph 4)* _____

6. capacity *(paragraph 4)* _____

7. immutable *(paragraph 4)* _____

8. origin *(paragraph 5)* _____

9. adaptation *(paragraph 6)* _____

10. evolution *(paragraph 7)* _____

In this chapter, you will focus on writing definitions. Statements and essays of definition often include two types of clauses: **noun clauses**, which can function as subjects or objects, and **adjective clauses** (also called relative clauses because the information they contain relates back to the nouns they describe).

NOUN CLAUSES

As its name indicates, a **noun clause** can function either as a subject or an object. There are three kinds of noun clauses:

- Clauses beginning with *that*
- Clauses beginning with a question word
- Clauses beginning with *if* or *whether*

The most commonly used clause typically begins with the word *that*. Compare these sentences:

SIMPLE NOUN SUBJECT Her speech was fascinating.

NOUN CLAUSE SUBJECT **That** she spoke without notes was amazing.

Compare these sentences. The first contains a simple noun object; the second contains a noun clause object:

SIMPLE NOUN OBJECT Many believe **the results**.

NOUN CLAUSE OBJECT Many believe that **the ability to acquire a language is instinctual**.

Other noun clauses begin with a question word, although the clause retains the word order of a statement:

BEGINNING OF STATEMENT	NOUN CLAUSE
He told me	**what** I should say.
	where I should say it.
	when I should say it.
	why I should say it.
	how I should say it.

And some noun clauses begin with *if* or *whether*, especially in indirect questions, which also retain the word order of a statement and end with a period.

BEGINNING OF STATEMENT	NOUN CLAUSE
He asked me	**if** I could speak Mandarin.
	whether I spoke Mandarin at home.

Complete each sentence with a noun clause.

1. I understand _what I must do_ .

2. I told you _____ .

3. My brother asked me _____ .

4. Do you know _____ ?

5. _____ was really clever.

6. _____ or not it is unimportant.

ADJECTIVE CLAUSES

An **adjective clause** follows the noun it describes, whether the noun is a subject or an object in a sentence. You can best understand adjective clauses if you think of two sentences that should be combined, as discussed in Chapter 3.

CHOPPY   Language is a system of combining elements and sounds.
         They communicate meaning.

IMPROVED Language is a system of combining elements and sounds
         that communicate meaning.

The adjective clause begins with a relative pronoun:

- *that* and *which* for things and ideas
- *who* or *whom* (and sometimes *that*) for people

Note: The possessive adjective *whose*, which describes a noun, can refer to people, things, or ideas.

Adjective clauses appear in two positions: following the main clause or inside the main clause, as in these examples:

FOLLOWING THE MAIN CLAUSE

Charles Darwin was the first *person* **who** claimed that language was instinctual.

Children seem to know instinctively the *rules* **that** determine the grammar of any language.

In 1859, Darwin published *On the Origin of Species*, **which** established the theory of evolution.

Irregular verbs are *verbs* **whose** endings do not include *-ed*.

However, adjective clauses can follow a noun that appears anywhere in a sentence, as in these examples.

INSIDE THE MAIN CLAUSE

Further *proof* **that** the ability to use language has evolved comes from our understanding of anatomy.

Charles Darwin, **who** proposed the theory of evolution, claimed that language must be instinctual.

Syntax, **which** means the arrangement of words in order to form sentences or phrases, is a key component of language.

Restrictive and Nonrestrictive Adjective Clauses

There are two types of adjective clauses: restrictive and nonrestrictive clauses (also called identifying and nonidentifying clauses). A **restrictive adjective clause** provides information necessary to identify the noun it describes.

I have three brothers. *My brother* **who** **lives in New York** is a research scientist.

A **nonrestrictive adjective clause** simply provides additional information, which is not necessary to identify the noun it describes. The noun is already identified in some other way, as in these examples.

My oldest brother, **who lives in New York,** is a research scientist.

Darwin, **who proposed the theory of evolution,** published his work in 1859.

His famous book, **which is still being read today,** changed the way we think about plants, animals, and humans.

Notes:
- Never use *that* to begin a nonrestrictive adjective clause.
- Never enclose a restrictive clause in commas.
- Always use commas with nonrestrictive clauses beginning with *who* or *which*.

Relative Pronouns as Objects

Look at the examples. Notice that the relative pronoun *whom* replaces the object pronoun *him* and moves to the beginning of the adjective clause.

Noam Chomsky is the man. Most people regard **him** as the father of modern linguistics.

Noam Chomsky is the man **whom** most people regard as the father of modern linguistics.

Here are more sentences in which the object pronoun begins an adjective clause:

A lesser-known Asian language is Mongolian, **which** only people in Mongolia and northern China speak.

However, English is the language **that** the largest numbers of people speak throughout the world, either as their first or second language.

Often you can omit the object pronoun from the sentence without affecting meaning:

> Noam Chomsky is the man **[whom]** most people regard as the father of modern linguistics.

> English is the language **[that]** the largest numbers of people speak throughout the world, either as their first or second language.

Other relative pronouns can replace *that* and *which* as objects, and can often be omitted:

> . . . the places **[where]** English is spoken.

> . . . the reasons **[why]** children learn language so easily.

> . . . the year **[when]** the book was published.

Additionally, you can omit both the relative pronoun *subject* + any form of the verb *be* in many sentences:

> English is the language **[that is]** spoken in the most countries either as a first or second language.

PRACTICE 3 **Combining Sentences to Create Adjective Clauses**

Using the appropriate relative pronoun or possessive adjective, combine the sentence pairs. Add commas as needed, and omit relative pronouns where possible. Some items have more than one possible answer.

1. An essay begins with an introduction. It states the thesis, or controlling idea.

   An essay begins with an introduction that states the thesis, or controlling idea.

   _____

2. You may define a term with a synonym. It has approximately the same meaning as the term.

   _____

   _____

3. One of the foremost authorities on language is Noam Chomsky. He argues that all languages have a universal grammar.

   _____

   _____

4. The world was shocked by the publication of *The Origin of Species*. It introduced the theory of evolution.

   _____

   _____

5. Linguistics demonstrates many similarities among languages. It is the scientific study of human language.

_____

_____

6. French, Italian, and Spanish have many similarities. Their shared ancestor is Latin.

_____

_____

7. Spanish is the most common language. People speak it throughout Central America, much of South America, the Caribbean, and, of course, Spain.

_____

_____

8. Aside from the United States, Canada, and Great Britain, India is the place. The largest numbers of people speak English as their first or second language there.

_____

_____

9. Humans' communicative ability comes from an area of the brain called the cerebral cortex. The elements of language are located in this area.

_____

_____

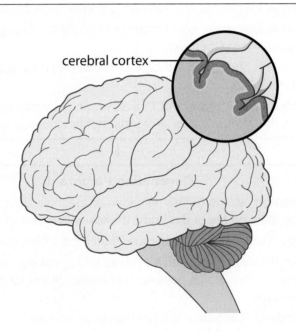

cerebral cortex

As its name indicates, a **definition essay** defines a term. If it merely defined the term, however, the essay might be only a sentence or perhaps a paragraph long. Although short definitions often play a supporting role in essays that pursue a different goal, a definition essay offers a complex discussion of the definition. It compares or contrasts one definition to others, and it examines and supports its claims throughout.

The organization of a definition essay, with examples from the writing model, looks like this.

Introductory Paragraph

The opening paragraph establishes the reason or need to define the term in question and may provide an initial definition. It sometimes begins with a question:

Question: We all speak it, and we all write it, but what exactly is it?

Definition: ". . . defines language as 'a system of communication by written or spoken words which is used by the people of a particular country or area.'"

Need: While this general definition is useful, it seems far too limited.

Thesis: ". . . language is more complex than merely writing and speaking, and therefore must involve a deeper set of processes operating in the human brain."

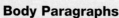

Body Paragraphs

The body paragraphs either expand on the definition by explaining and illustrating the main points, or they provide a different definition and then explain and illustrate its main points.

Paragraph 2: States a different definition and analyzes it further.

Paragraph 3: Introduces and defines the term *symbols*, and provides examples.

Paragraph 4: Discusses how language is acquired through heredity and cites the linguist Noam Chomsky.

Paragraph 5: Introduces the theory of Darwin: that language is instinctual, and quotes him.

Paragraph 6: Cites the work of Pinker, which generally supports Chomsky's and Darwin's theories, but also contends that language is partly learned.

Concluding Paragraph

The final paragraph returns to the main idea of the introductory paragraph and may summarize the main points of the body. It ends with a strong statement.

Main Idea: What exactly is language, then, and where does it come from?

Summary: "Human beings have evolved into speaking, writing, and signing creatures . . . our brains possess a universal grammar that prepares us to communicate . . ."

Strong Ending: "Language is what makes us human."

THREE WAYS TO DEFINE A TERM

The statement of definition itself is the critical element of the essay, and there are many ways to define a term. These include defining by synonym, by a formal statement of definition, and by negation—that is, by saying what a word does not mean.

Defining by Synonym

One of the most common methods of defining a term is to use a synonym to do so. As you recall from Noticing Vocabulary on page 90, a **synonym** has a similar meaning to the term being defined. The synonym and the term it defines must be the same part of speech—plural nouns, adjectives, and so on. Of course, the synonym must also be familiar to your reader.

Here are two ways to incorporate definitions by synonym into your writing.

RULES	EXAMPLES
1. Use a direct statement of meaning.	*Ambiguous* **means** "indefinite." The *spinal chord* **is** the "backbone."
2. Place a synonym in *apposition*, in which you enclose the defining information in commas or dashes. The word or phrase in apposition takes the same grammatical form as the word it defines. **Notes:** 1. In *apposition*, two noun phrases describing the same thing or person, appear one after the other. 2. The words "or" and "that is" often introduce the definition.	. . . It is not always easy to discriminate, or distinguish, between different sounds. . . . Neurons—that is, nerve cells—transmit signals throughout the central nervous system.

PRACTICE 4 Defining with Synonyms

A Look at the words in italics in each sentence. Circle the word or phrase in parentheses that is in apposition. Consult your dictionary as needed.

1. Much of what infants say sounds like *gibberish*, or (nonsense / a foreign language).

2. Language ability, according to Noam Chomsky, is *innate*, or (unnatural / instinctive).

3. Linguists debate whether language is a *consequence*, or (result / accident) of nature or nurture.

4. A number of languages share certain *commonalities*, that is (things that are shared / things that are ordinary).

5. One's *native tongue*, or (first language / nationality) may be part innate and part learned.

6. *Syntax*, or (grammar / sentence structure) differs among various languages.

B These terms appeared in the writing model on pages 87–89. On a separate sheet of paper, write definitions using one or more synonyms for each term.

1. instinctual   3. evolve   5. naturalist

2. acquire   4. heredity   6. babble

Using a Formal Statement of Definition

When a definition requires more information or explanation than a synonym can provide, you may need to provide a **formal statement of definition**. You may consult a dictionary for the formal definition, but be sure to inform your reader of the source and to quote the definition exactly as it appears in that source, as in this example.

The *Longman Advanced American Dictionary* defines *nurture* as "the education and care that you are given as a child, and the way it affects your later development and attitude."

Sometimes, however, you need to create your own formal definition, which includes two parts. The first places the term to be defined into a **classification** or **category**.

[TERM]	[CLASSIFICATION OR CATEGORY]
Clinical psychology	is a branch of psychology.
Syntax	means the arrangement of words.

The second part of the definition provides more specific information.

[TERM]	[CLASSIFICATION OR CATEGORY]	[DISTINGUISHING INFORMATION]
Clinical psychology	is a branch of psychology	that specializes in the diagnosis and treatment of mental illness and related issues.
Syntax	means the arrangement of words	in order to form sentences or phrases.

PRACTICE 5 **Completing a Formal Statement of Definition**

Complete each definition by adding its distinguishing characteristics to the underlined category. Use your dictionary as needed.

1. *American Sign Language* is a <u>way of communicating</u> that _consists of body_

    movements, hand motions, and facial expressions. _____.

2. *Evidence* is <u>information</u> that _____

    _____.

3. A *dialect* is a <u>form of communication</u> that _____

    _____.

4. A *sentence* is a <u>group of words</u> that _____

    _____.

5. *Grammar* is <u>a set of rules</u> that _____

_____.

6. *Instinct* is <u>a reaction</u> that _____

_____.

7. A *translator* is <u>a person</u> who _____

_____.

Definition by Negation

Since the verb *to define* means "to set limits," a good definition not only establishes what a word means, but it also determines what it does not mean. Here is an illustration of one such definition from the writing model.

> Symbols represent things, but they are **not** the things themselves.

The statement of negation may either precede or follow the formal statement of definition. Look at this example from the writing model.

DEFINITION — Language therefore is a distinctly human ability to identify and shape our world. Animals make sounds that may reveal fear, anger, or other emotions, but they **cannot** draw, they **cannot** write, and (as far as we know) they **cannot** communicate abstract thoughts.

DISTINGUISHING BY NEGATION

Potential Problems with Definitions

When you formulate your own definition, avoid some of these potential problems.

Making the category too broad

It is not enough to say that a *psychiatrist* is a "person," or even a "doctor." A psychiatrist is a *medical doctor*; many Ph.D.s are psychologists, but they are not psychiatrists.

Making the distinguishing information too vague

It is not enough to say that a psychiatrist treats mental illnesses; he or she studies, diagnoses, and treats mental illnesses as well as other mental disorders.

Making the definition circular

A circular definition repeats the term you are defining in a slightly different form. For example, *Psychiatry is a field of medicine practiced by a psychiatrist.* Clearly, if the reader doesn't know the first term, he or she will not understand the second. Give examples of what the practice of *psychiatry* involves.

> **Writing Tip**
>
> Always consult a dictionary after you have formulated your own definition. This way, if your definition contradicts that of the dictionary, you will be prepared to defend yours with logical reasons and solid evidence to support it.

Work with a partner or in a small group. Using synonyms, formal statements of definition, or negation, brainstorm possible definitions for these terms. Do not consult a dictionary until after you have written each definition.

1. An accent _____

_____

2. A dictionary _____

_____

3. An idiom _____

_____

EXPANDING ON A DEFINITION

You can make a term or concept more understandable if you expand on it by adding examples and explanations to the definition. For instance, look again at this paragraph from the writing model, which includes two definitions contrasted by distinctions by negation.

INTRODUCTION OF TERM — Such a reference to things, people, events, and abstract concepts occurs through the use of *symbols*. *Symbols* represent things, but they are *not* the things themselves. For example, we can see a picture of a chair and immediately recognize what the picture represents. Likewise, we can read or hear the word *chair* and recognize the mental picture it depicts. *Language*, therefore, is a distinctly human ability to identify and shape our world. Animals make sounds that may reveal fear, anger, or other emotions, but they cannot draw, they cannot write, and (as far as we know) they cannot communicate abstract thoughts.

DEFINITION

DISTINGUISHING BY NEGATION

DEFINITION

DISTINGUISHING BY NEGATION

FURTHER DEFINITION

The definitions introduce the concepts, and the material that follows gives them a more concrete meaning.

TRY IT OUT! Work with a partner or in a small group. Expand these definitions by providing one or more examples and an explanation.

1. *Slang* can be defined as "very informal words that are used by people who belong to a particular group, such as young people." For example, _____

_____

_____

_____

_____

2. The *Longman Advanced American Dictionary* defines the word *culture* as "the ideas, beliefs, and customs that are shared and accepted by people in a society."

_____

_____

_____

_____

_____

3. *Communication*, the process by which people exchange information, occurs in

many forms. _____

_____

_____

_____

_____

> For writing guides to help you introduce and support a definition, see Appendix A, page 191.

PREPARATION FOR WRITING

Previous chapters have shown you how to summarize and quote material to support and explain a claim. Another way to deal with source material is through paraphrasing.

PARAPHRASING MATERIAL FROM SOURCES

As the writing model demonstrates, much of the support for an extended definition comes from research. However, in using research material, you should not overly rely on quotations. If you do, your essay will seem more like a collection of what other people say rather than your own ideas. You should quote memorable or important statements from sources, but keep these quotations to a minimum. Instead, turn to **paraphrasing**, that is, restating another person's language in your own words and with your own sentence structure. A paraphrase differs from a summary, which provides the main information but not the details. Instead, the paraphrase includes all the main points of the original but in a simpler, shorter, and clearer way.

However, if the paraphrase is too similar to the original, it might be viewed as **plagiarism**, a serious matter of academic dishonesty, in which you intentionally (or even unintentionally) copy from someone else without quoting the language, or do not correctly acknowledge the source of the material.

Writing a Good Paraphrase

A good paraphrase:

- identifies the source of the original
- shows that you have fully understood the material
- differs enough from the original that it is clearly your own writing
- does not merely substitute synonyms for the words in the original sentence

Here is an example of a paraphrase from Wade and Tavris, whose work was discussed in the model:

ORIGINAL MATERIAL

> Learning explanations of language acquisition assume that children are rewarded for saying the right words and punished for making errors. But parents do not stop to correct every error in their children's speech, so long as they understand what the child is trying to say (Brown, Cazden & Bellugi, 1969). Indeed, parents often reward children for incorrect statements! A 2-year-old who says, "Want milk!" is likely to get it; most parents would not wait for a more grammatical (or polite) request.

PARAPHRASED MATERIAL

> Carole Wade and Carol Tavris say that children do not acquire language from parents praising their correct speech and punishing their errors. For example, if parents can understand a child's request for milk, even if it is ungrammatical, they will give the child the milk. In effect, say Wade and Tavris, the parents "reward the child for incorrect statements" (2011).

Note that the paraphrase identifies the source and restates its ideas without copying them. It also integrates a short quotation from the original when it borrows the exact language.

Writing Tip

To write a good paraphrase you will need to follow a process:

1. Read the original passage carefully more than once, underlining the main points in the passage.

2. Cover the material so you cannot refer to it.

3. To help you restate the material in your own words, imagine that you are explaining the material to a good friend.

4. Finally, compare the original to your restatement to see if it expresses the same meaning—without using the same phrases.

Compare these examples of a good and a bad paraphrase.

ORIGINAL PASSAGE FROM WADE AND TAVRIS

> Because of the way our species evolved, many abilities, tendencies, and characteristics are either present at birth in all human beings or develop rapidly as a child matures.

BADLY PARAPHRASED PASSAGE

> Carole Wade and Carol Tavris say that due to the way the human species evolved, a lot of its abilities, tendencies, and characteristics appear at birth or develop quite fast as a child gets older.

WELL-PARAPHRASED PASSAGE

> According to Carole Wade and Carol Tavris, human evolution has provided us with many abilities, potentials, and traits that we are born with or quickly develop.

Notice how the bad paraphrase repeats the sentence structure and includes most of the words of the original without quoting. By contrast, the sentence structure of this paraphrase is different, and only a few common words from the original are repeated.

Blending Paraphrase with Quotations

Sometimes while paraphrasing, you may find yourself unable to find good substitutes for some of the original language. Here is how to blend paraphrase and quotations. As you read over the original material, underline or highlight the short sections that 1) would be difficult to restate in your own words, or 2) would make a strong statement if quoted. Integrate these sections into your paraphrase by enclosing them in quotation marks without capitalizing the first word:

ORIGINAL

> Human language appears to be a unique phenomenon, without a significant analogue in the animal world (Noam Chomsky).

PARAPHRASE WITH QUOTATION

> Noam Chomsky maintains that the language of humans seems to be unique to our species, "without a significant analogue" among animals.

Integrating Quotes and Paraphrase

All integrated quotations must fit logically and grammatically into the paraphrase. However, not all the material you quote may be such a comfortable fit. You can make it fit in two ways:

- Change the form of a quoted word by inserting the change in brackets, like this example taken from the model:

  This belief was exploded by Noam Chomsky, "who argue[s] that language was far too complex to be learned bit by bit, as one might learn the list of world capitals." (The past tense -*ed* ending of the verb is changed to -*s*, in the present tense.)

- Mark omitted words from the middle of quotations, as in this paraphrased material from the model:

  A baby's ability to communicate "comes from an area of the brain . . . where the elements of language are located." (The omitted words, "called the cortex," are replaced by three dots, called *ellipsis*.)

PRACTICE 6   **Paraphrasing**

Paraphrase each of the passages. You may quote short parts of the original if necessary.

1. Original: *Animals, whom we have made our slaves, we do not like to consider our equal.* (Charles Darwin)

   Paraphrase: _Charles Darwin writes that because we have made animals into_

   "our slaves, we do not like to consider [them as] our equal."

2. Original: *It is not the strongest of the species that survives, nor the most intelligent that survives. It is the one that is the most adaptable to change.* (Charles Darwin)

   Paraphrase: _____

   _____

   _____

   _____

   _____

3. Original: *The newest research is showing that many properties of the brain are genetically organized, and don't depend on information coming in from the senses.* (Stephen Pinker)

   Paraphrase: _____

   _____

   _____

   _____

   _____

   _____

4. Original: *Most of the fundamental ideas of science are essentially simple, and may, as a rule, be expressed in a language comprehensible to everyone.* (Albert Einstein)

Paraphrase: _____

_____

_____

_____

5. Original: *Language is a process of free creation; its laws and principles are fixed, but the manner in which the principles of generation are used is free and infinitely varied.* (Noam Chomsky)

Paraphrase: _____

_____

_____

_____

_____

✎ Applying Vocabulary: Using Synonyms, 1

Before you begin your writing assignment, review the information you learned about synonyms on page 90.

PRACTICE 7   **Using Synonyms**

Paraphrase each sentence, substituting a synonym for the boldfaced word. Use your dictionaries as needed. You may integrate quotations into your paraphrase.

1. The order and form of words, as well as the words themselves, **communicate** meaning.

Word order, word forms, and the words themselves all convey meaning.

_____

2. Not only does language refer to these things and events, but also to abstract **notions**, such as love, loyalty, democracy, and Einstein's general theory of relativity.

_____

_____

3. Language therefore is a **specifically** human ability to identify and shape our world.

_____

_____

4. Chomsky believes that humans are born with the **capability** to learn language because their brains are programmed with a universal grammar.

_____

_____

5. While most linguists and psychologists today agree with Chomsky's general idea, experts differ in how to explain the **foundation** of universal grammar.

_____

_____

6. Pinker suggests that it is useful to think of language as an evolutionary **modification**.

_____

_____

WRITING ASSIGNMENT

Your assignment for this chapter is to write an essay that examines and illustrates an extended definition of a term from the box, or a term that your teacher suggests. Be sure to support your definition with examples and explanations. Follow the steps in the writing process.

communication	education	partnership
courage	friendship	wisdom

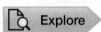 **Explore**

STEP 1: Explore your topic, audience, and purpose.

- Begin by examining your own ideas about the term you will define. If you can't think of a synonym or a good formal definition, look in a dictionary—or in several. A dictionary or encyclopedia might also provide useful and interesting historical origins of the term.
- If the dictionary definition does not express the meaning you intend, however, then develop your own definition. Discuss your ideas with your classmates.

 Prewrite

STEP 2: Prewrite to get ideas.

- Freewrite, brainstorm, or create cluster diagrams to explore your ideas further.
- Decide whether to define the term through a formal statement of definition, a definition by synonym, or a definition by negation (this may be especially useful if your definition is very different from one your readers might know).

Organize

STEP 3: Organize your ideas.

- Write an outline of the essay. In the first paragraph, introduce and/or define the term, and make clear why the reader would want to learn about it.
- Then draft the thesis statement. This sentence often includes the definition of a term, but not always. The most important function of the sentence is to make clear to readers why (or at least by what method) you are defining the term.

 Write

STEP 4: Write the first draft.

- Include an introduction, body paragraphs, and a conclusion.
- Develop and support your definition with examples, explanations, further definitions, and material from outside sources in the body of the essay.

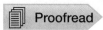 Revise

STEP 5: Revise the draft.

- Exchange papers with a partner, and give each other feedback on your papers. Use the Chapter 5 Peer Review on page 233 to guide your feedback.
- Carefully consider your partner's feedback. If you agree with it, revise your paper by marking the changes on your first draft.

 Proofread

STEP 6: Edit and proofread.

- Use the Chapter 5 Writer's Self-Check on page 234 to help you look for and correct errors in grammar, mechanics, and sentence structure.

 Write

STEP 7: Write a new draft.

- Revise the draft, incorporating all of your planned changes.
- Proofread the new draft so that it is error free.
- Make sure the draft is legible and follows the format your instructor has provided.
- Hand in the essay to your instructor.

EXPANSION

 ## TIMED WRITING

Write a paraphrase of Paragraph 6 on page 89 from the writing model. Perhaps include at least two short quotations in the paraphrase. You will have 35 minutes. To complete the expansion, you will need to budget your time accordingly. Follow this procedure.

1. Reread the paragraph from the model, and underline key phrases that you might quote in your paraphrase. (3 minutes)

2. Read the first sentence of the original, and then write a paraphrase without looking at it. Assume you are explaining the sentence to a friend. Repeat the same procedure with every sentence in the paragraph. (15 minutes)

3. Now revise your paraphrase. Include the name of the person you are paraphrasing, and incorporate a short quotation or two. (8 minutes)

4. Edit and proofread your work to make sure that a) your ideas are clear and b) you have not unintentionally plagiarized the original. (5 minutes)

5. Check your paragraph for errors. Correct any mistakes. (4 minutes)

6. Give your paper to your instructor.

 ## WRITING A DEFINITION

Write an essay of five or more paragraphs in which you define and illustrate a practice from your native country or culture. You might, for instance, write about a traditional practice that is involved in wedding ceremonies, holiday celebrations, or other special community or family events. Do some research on the history of the practice, or on how it differs from region to region or group to group. Define any terms unfamiliar to your readers.

CHAPTER 6

PROBLEM / SOLUTION ESSAYS

Bullying is a very serious problem in some schools.

Many of your intellectual and practical activities involve attempts to solve problems, from the simplest to the most complex. You often write about these problems in college assignments, in the workplace, in discussions of politics, and in other situations outside of school. Here are a few examples:

- why class sizes in an elementary school are so large, and how they can be lowered
- why a business is losing customers, and what steps it can take to regain them
- why the polar ice caps are melting, and what governments and industry can do about it

A **problem / solution essay** first identifies and analyzes a specific problem and then offers a possible solution or solutions.

While problem / solution writing applies to any topic, this chapter will focus on problems related to education. Elementary schools, high schools, colleges, and universities constantly attempt to solve problems related to a variety of issues. These issues include funding, class size, curriculum, student achievement, and student conduct. Finding their solutions requires careful analysis, research, and practical advice.

ANALYZING THE MODEL

The writing model examines the causes of a serious problem in schools in the United States and then offers a series of solutions.

Read the model. Then answer the questions.

✏️ **Writing Model**

BULLYING IN SCHOOLS IN THE UNITED STATES

1   School is a relatively safe place to be. Considering that more than 55 million students attend school each day, very few of them are victims of a violent act. Nevertheless, when bullying in schools occurs, it can be utterly devastating to its victims. In this case, the victims of bullying include not only the students who are bullied, but also those who do the bullying, and "innocent bystanders" who see it happening and do absolutely nothing to stop it. Although bullying continues to be a serious problem, teachers and school administrators can take a number of steps to prevent it or lessen its impact.

2   Bullying, often considered just "what kids do," has become a topic of concern. Bullying takes two forms: nonphysical and physical aggression. The first is "a type of emotional violence where individuals use relationships to harm others. Examples include exclusion from a group and rumor spreading" (*Ophelia Project*, 2005, p. 3). The second, physical aggression, includes shoving, tripping, and taking personal items. Both forms, however, share common traits. "Bullying is a weapon of people driven by the need for power. Bullying can be a single action—verbal, physical, or emotional—but it is always done to cause fear and to exert power" (White-Hooel, 2006, p. 30).

3   Almost everyone has been teased or called names at some point, and most people have teased others or have been guilty of name-calling. However, when teasing becomes repeated and cruel, and when its intent is to embarrass, hurt, or isolate someone, it becomes bullying. When rumors are intentionally spread in class (or over the Internet) to destroy the reputation of another, gossip becomes bullying. Most teachers can identify students who are obvious bullies. Teachers can also identify those who seem to be targets of name-calling and subtle forms of nonphysical aggression. A more difficult task is identifying potential cyberbullies and their victims and determining what to do once they identify those students.

4   What, then, can schools do? The Safe and Drug Free Schools Act includes bullying and harassment, and requires all schools receiving federal funds to not only respond to all instances of bullying, but also to actively prevent it. Additionally, school districts have been developing and requiring anti-bullying policies and programs. Books such as *Aggression and Bullying* (Guerin & Hennesy, 2002) and *Cyberbullying: Bullying in the Digital Age* (Kowalski, Limber & Agatson, 2012) shed light on the consequences of bullying for both the aggressor and the victim. Books like these and established anti-bullying programs reveal that many bullies were either bullied themselves at some point, or perhaps abused in some way by family members.

5   For teachers, dealing with most bullying situations is complex, especially because some teachers do not understand all the circumstances. They have not been trained to deal with the large amount of psychological information on bullying and its victims. Nevertheless, teachers can take some specific actions to help solve the problem of bullying in classrooms and schools. Here are some examples:

- Keep an eye out for bullying and take it seriously. When seeing a child harming or threatening another child either physically or verbally, the teacher should immediately stop it.

(continued on next page)

- Be an obvious presence. Early childhood and elementary teachers should supervise the playground. Middle and high school teachers should be highly visible and extremely attentive in the hallways, at lunchtime, at bus drop-off areas, at performances, sports events, and so on. Preventing an act of bullying is far more effective than responding to one.

- Bullying often comes from a lack of confidence, so do everything possible to help potential bullies develop genuine self-confidence. Likewise, strong self-esteem will also help victims of bullying to better withstand it and to get help. Maintain a strongly supportive atmosphere in the classroom that rewards students for good behavior and good work.

- Incorporate formal or informal lessons to help students understand that all forms of nonphysical and physical bullying are deeply harmful and absolutely unacceptable.

- Fully implement prescribed anti-bullying programs. Developmental psychologist Susan Limber, PhD, the associate director of the Institute on Family and Neighborhood Life at Clemson University in Clemson, S.C., says that the most effective strategies to stop bullying involve "the entire school as a community to change the climate of the school and the norms of behavior" (Crawford, 2002, p. 64).

- Follow up with appropriate and fair treatment for both the bully and victim of the bullying. Ensure that witnesses of bullying may safely report what they have seen. Assure them that their identities will not be revealed and that their complaints will be taken seriously. Furthermore, once a bully has been identified, the school should take steps to prevent further instances and not embarrass the student. These actions may include involving the school counselor or social worker. They may also include contacting the bully's parents and asking for their cooperation and support.

6   Research indicates that bullying may be the last significant stage before the bully or the victim turns to physical violence against other students. School remains a relatively safe place for children to be, and every teacher, staff member, and parent must work to maintain that atmosphere.

Source: Essay adapted from Powell, Sara Davis. *Your Introduction to Education.*

Questions about the Model

1. What problem is introduced in the essay's first paragraph? Who is affected by the problem?

2. What is the thesis statement of the essay? Underline it.

3. What types of behavior may be classified as bullying?

4. Which sentence in the third paragraph begins a transition between the problem and its possible solutions? Circle it.

5. What general steps have schools taken to help solve the problem?

6. What actions can individual teachers take to help solve the problem?

7. What phrase or idea from the introductory paragraph is repeated in the conclusion? Why?

✐ Noticing Vocabulary: Adverbial Intensifiers

You already know that *very* can precede adjectives or adverbs to intensify them. Other adverbial intensifiers, however, naturally precede certain adjectives, such as *utterly wrong* or *strongly determined*. They are another type of collocation. Note that these intensifiers, like almost all adverbs, end in *-ly*.

PRACTICE 1 Finding Adverbial Intensifiers

In addition to *very*, the writing model includes seven adverbial intensifiers. Find and write each along with the adjective it precedes. The beginning of each intensifier has been included to help you.

1. re_latively_ _safe_ *(paragraph 1)*

2. ut_____ _____ *(paragraph 1)*

3. hi_____ _____ *(paragraph 5, 2)*

4. ex_____ _____ *(paragraph 5, 2)*

5. st_____ _____ *(paragraph 5, 3)*

6. de_____ _____ *(paragraph 5, 4)*

7. ab_____ _____ *(paragraph 5, 4)*

As noted earlier, a problem / solution essay both identifies a problem and offers a solution. The problem is stated first and the solution stated afterward. A diagram of this organizational pattern, with examples from the writing model, looks like this:

Introductory Paragraph

The opening paragraph identifies and briefly illustrates the problem, and suggests or proposes a solution (which is the thesis).

Problem: ". . . bullying in schools can be utterly devastating to its victims."

Solution: ". . . teachers and school administrators can take a number of steps in order to prevent it or lessen its impact."

First Group of Body Paragraphs

The first body paragraphs analyze the nature and extent of the problem and provide statistics, quotes, and other data to support the analysis.

Paragraph 2: defines bullying with examples and quotations from experts

Paragraph 3: expands the definition of the term by explaining what it is not and giving more examples.

Transitional Body Paragraph

As its name indicates, this paragraph provides a smooth transition from the problem to the solution.

Paragraph 4: introduces the solution by asking what schools can do

---

Final Group of Body Paragraphs

Any remaining body paragraphs explain how the proposed solution responds to the problem, and provide examples, facts, and figures on why the proposed solution will (or might) work.

Paragraph 5: provides a list of specific actions teachers can take to avoid or solve the problem

---

Concluding Paragraph

The final paragraph returns to the main idea of the introductory paragraph and asks that someone carry out the suggested solution.

INTRODUCTORY PARAGRAPH

Your first paragraph not only names the problem, but also indicates why it is important. When possible, you should note how widespread the problem is and what effect it has on people or institutions. You then propose a solution, which is the thesis of your essay.

BODY PARAGRAPHS

In the body of the essay, a paragraph (or two) should explain the problem in more detail. Then a transitional statement should lead into the paragraphs that introduce and discuss a possible solution.

Explaining the Problem

Your readers must understand the nature of the problem. Therefore, you should establish why the problem is troubling, frustrating, or harmful. Support your claims with definitions (if necessary), logical reasons, facts and figures, and quotations from outside sources or interviews.

The second paragraph of the writing model lists two types of bullying—nonphysical and physical—and explains them. The explanation includes quotations from authorities as well as examples. Nonphysical aggression is "emotional violence" such as spreading rumors. Physical aggression includes shoving and tripping. They share a common trait, "to cause fear and to exert power."

Since not all readers may agree that the issue is a problem, try to anticipate their objections, then acknowledge them, and, finally, respond to them. For example, note how Paragraph 3 of the writing model anticipates a common argument: everyone has teased others or called them names. The paragraph then explains, however, that bullying is different in degree and intent. It means to "embarrass, hurt, or isolate someone" or "destroy the reputation of another."

Making a Transition

After defining and illustrating the problem, you should move on to exploring a solution or solutions. This shift in focus requires a transition, which goes beyond a single word or phrase such as "therefore" or "as a result." Sometimes it is merely a sentence, but other times the transition may be a full paragraph. Both forms occur in the writing model. The last sentence of Paragraph 3 starts the transition by stating that the issue revolves around what to do once teachers identify bullies. Paragraph 4 expands on the transition. It indicates that schools are making plans to address bullying as required by Federal law. It also cites books that help teachers understand the effects of bullying. Then Paragraph 5 introduces the six steps that form the solution.

See Appendix B on page 200 for a list of more transitional words and phrases.

Explaining the Solution

You should devote the remainder of the body to your solution(s) to the problem. Explain why you think they will or might work, and contrast them to other less effective or ineffective solutions.

Again, if possible, back up your claims with facts and figures, results of surveys, or quotes from authorities, similar to the quotation used in the writing model from the assistant director of an institute. You may also want to emphasize your main points by setting them off in a bulleted or numbered list, as in the writing model.

CONCLUDING PARAGRAPH

Your concluding paragraph should include a call to action, in which you ask your readers to become part of the solution or at least allow others to carry it out. In the writing model, this call to action appears in the last sentence of Paragraph 6 that states, "School remains a relatively safe place for children to be, and every teacher, staff member, and parent must work to maintain that atmosphere."

TRY IT OUT! Choose a topic and write an introductory paragraph for a problem / solution essay. Make sure to establish the problem, emphasize its importance, and propose a solution.

- Poor nutrition and its effects on learning
- Name-calling and teasing in school
- Large class sizes of 30 or more students
- Lack of arts education in elementary schools

GRAMMAR

Correct use of adverbials is especially important when writing a problem / solution essay. You need to describe the problem and the solution in some depth, which naturally involves the frequent use of adverbs.

FORMING ADVERBIAL PHRASES

Not all adverbs are single words; entire clauses can also function as adverbs. To review, an independent clause can be a sentence by itself. A dependent clause cannot stand alone as a sentence; instead, it must be attached to an independent clause.

One type of dependent clause takes on the role of an adverb; that is, it explains *when*, *where*, *how*, or *why* the action of the independent clause happens or happened. Most of these adverbial dependent clauses indicate time relationships, as in these examples:

Before the problem becomes too large, . . .

After the changes have taken place, . . .

When a child is the victim of bullying . . .

Other adverbial dependent clauses establish reasons or conditions relating to the independent clause.

Because bullies lack self-confidence, . . .

If bullies are identified quickly, . . .

Although bullying is a serious problem, . . .

Although adverbial dependent clauses are essential to expressing ideas, you should not overuse them. You can achieve greater sentence variety and a more mature style by changing some of these clauses into phrases—groups of two or more words.

ADVERBIAL CLAUSE **When a teacher sees a child harming or threatening another child either physically or verbally**, he or she should immediately stop it.

ADVERBIAL PHRASE **When seeing** a child harming or threatening another child either physically or verbally, the teacher should immediately stop it.

ADVERBIAL CLAUSE **After a school has identified a bully**, it should take steps to prevent further instances and not embarrass the student.

ADVERBIAL PHRASE **After identifying a bully**, the school should take steps to prevent further instances and not embarrass the student.

ADVERBIAL CLAUSE **Because bullies lack self-confidence**, they often benefit from attempts to build their self-esteem.

ADVERBIAL PHRASE **Lacking in self-confidence**, bullies often benefit from attempts to build their self-esteem.

ADVERBIAL CLAUSE **If bullies are identified quickly**, they may cease their harmful behavior.

ADVERBIAL PHRASE **If identified quickly**, bullies may cease their harmful behavior.

When the dependent clause changes to a phrase, notice that its subject shifts to the independent clause. If that subject is a noun, move it to the second clause. Otherwise, the sentence may not be clear.

UNCLEAR *If identified quickly*, **they** may cease their harmful behavior. (Who are they?)

CLEAR *If identified quickly*, **bullies** may cease their harmful behavior.

UNCLEAR *Lacking in self-confidence*, **they** often benefit from attempts to build their self-esteem.

CLEAR *Lacking in self-confidence*, **bullies** often benefit from attempts to build their self-esteem.

Change each adverbial clause into an adverbial phrase.

1. When teachers are observing students in the hallways, they must be highly attentive. _When observing students in the hallways, teachers must be highly attentive._

2. Unless bullying is reduced, it may cause great psychological or physical harm to some children. _____

3. Although bullying is frequently discussed, it is not always prevented in some schools. _____

4. If rules are consistent and fair, they should make most children comfortable in a school environment. _____

5. After it passed the Safe and Drug Free Schools Act, the government required most schools to actively prevent bullying. _____

6. While children are playing at recess, they may not push or shove each other. _____

7. When witnesses report on bullies, they need to know their identities won't be revealed. _____

8. Once clear policies have been established, they may reduce the frequency of bullying. _____

ELIMINATING DANGLING MODIFIERS

One danger in shortening clauses to phrases is accidentally creating dangling modifiers. Every modifier—that is, a word, phrase, or clause that functions as an adjective or adverb—must attach itself to the word or phrase it modifies or describes. A **dangling modifier**, however, does not attach itself to anything in the sentence. Most dangling modifiers begin a sentence, so readers expect the subject of the clause that follows to name the actor a modifier describes. If that actor is not named, the sentence is imprecise or unclear—or even humorous, as in these examples:

UNCLEAR Upon seeing an instance of bullying, it must be stopped at once. [No one sees the bullying in the sentence!]

CLEAR Upon seeing an instance of bullying, **a teacher** must stop it at once.

It is important to stop an instance of bullying the moment **a teacher sees it**.

UNCLEAR When teased or bullied, the results can be very hurtful. [The *results* are not teased or bullied; *people* are.]

CLEAR When teased or bullied, **people** can feel extremely hurt.

Teasing or bullying can be very hurtful to people.

Correcting dangling modifiers is easy to do, but noticing them is much harder, especially in your own writing. You must edit your papers carefully, asking, "Can this be misunderstood?" When spotting a dangling modifier, you can eliminate the problem in one of two ways:

- Name the actor as the subject of the sentence.
- Name the actor in the modifier.

PRACTICE 3   **Identifying and Correcting Dangling Modifiers**

Underline the dangling modifier in each of the following sentences. Then rewrite the sentence to eliminate the lack of clarity.

1. After spotting a bully in the playground, he must be prevented from continuing.

   After spotting a bully in the playground, someone must prevent him from continuing.

2. Though not easily prevented, teachers can try to lessen the effects of bullying.

   _____

   _____

3. Acknowledging the seriousness of the problem, the school buildings must be supervised constantly by teachers. _____

   _____

(continued on next page)

4. Teased or pushed, the results can be devastating to the victim.

_____

_____

5. Driven by the need for power, the victims suffer from bullies.

_____

_____

6. To help students develop self-confidence, they must be encouraged and praised by

their teachers. _____

_____

PREPARATION FOR WRITING

A strong essay supports its claims with explanations and examples, as well as with research material. In Chapters 4 and 5, you learned how to conduct basic research by using the library, magazines, and the Internet. You also learned how to quote and paraphrase material you find. Now you can move on to using material from several sources to back up a claim.

RESEARCHING A TOPIC IN MULTIPLE SOURCES

Before beginning your research, be sure to narrow your topic. With Internet searches, for example, a topic that is too broad will lead you to far too many sources. Therefore, start by listing any words or phrases related to the topic, and then select the ones that are likely to produce specific results. For example, "elementary school" will take you to more useful Internet sources than simply "school" or "education." "Bullying in elementary school" will produce even more specific results. You can then narrow (or expand) the list further, based on your initial findings.

PRACTICE 4　　**Finding Sources**

Use at least two search engines to find two or more "hits" (that is, websites) for each of the following key phrases. List the search engines you used and the titles of the websites you found.

Example: non-physical bullying

Google: "Bullying Harassment." www.bullyingstatistics.org./content/bullying-harrassment.html

Yahoo: Swart, Estelle and Judith Bredekamp. "Non-physical Bullying: exploring the perspective of Grade 5 girls. South Africa Journal of Education. Web.up.ac.za/sitefiles/file/47/bullying%20article.pdf

1. Inner-city education

   Search engines: _____

   _____

   Titles of websites: _____

   _____

   _____

2. Public high school completion rates

   Search engines: _____

   _____

   Titles of websites: _____

   _____

   _____

3. English language learner strategies

   Search engines: _____

   _____

   Titles of websites: _____

   _____

   _____

TRY IT OUT!   Consult an Internet source for information on one of these educational leaders. Then write an introductory paragraph for an essay explaining a problem or problems the person faced and solved. You will complete this essay in the Expansion activity on page 127.

John Dewey	Robert Maynard Hutchins
Maria Montessori	Mary McLeod Bethune
Benjamin Bloom	W. E. B. Du Bois

SYNTHESIZING MATERIAL FROM SOURCES

A good research-based essay uses material from several sources, not just one, in order to provide a stronger backing for claims. Often, however, these sources make similar points and should be **synthesized**, or blended together. Look for similarities (or differences) between the sources and include them in the same paragraph.

You must also explain the logical relationships between the sources. In your own words, and without referring to your sources, state the main point, or claim, that the sources support. Then cite the source material that agrees or disagrees with this claim. Paraphrase material whenever you can, but quote from it when the writer or speaker is a recognized authority or his or her phrasing is particularly strong.

There are two main ways that you can synthesize the information from different sources:

- indicate that the second source agrees with the first and perhaps expands on it in some way
- indicate that the two sources disagree, with or without your judging which one is right

Here is an example of the first method taken from the writing model on page 111.

> Bullying, often considered just "what kids do," has become a topic of concern. Bullying takes two forms: nonphysical and physical aggression. The first is "a type of emotional violence where individuals use relationships to harm others. Examples include exclusion from a group and rumor spreading" (*Ophelia Project*, 2005, p. 3). The second, physical aggression, includes shoving, tripping, and taking personal items. *Both forms, however, share common traits.* **(This sentence establishes the agreement between the sources.)** "Bullying is a weapon of people driven by the need for power. Bullying can be a single action—verbal, physical, or emotional—but it is always done to cause fear and to exert power" (White-Hooel, 2006, p. 30).

This next example, adapted from the *U.S. Department of Justice Office of Community Oriented Policing Services* blends several sources together to support the general claim of the opening sentence.

> Bullying is widespread not only in the United States, but also throughout much of the world. *Extensive studies in other countries during the 1980s and 1990s* **(This introduces the main areas of agreement among the sources.)** generally found that between 8 and 38 percent of students are bullied with some regularity, and that between five and nine percent of students bully others with some regularity. Chronic victims of bullying, bullied once a week or more, generally make up between 8 and 20 percent of the student population (Olweus, 1992; Rigby and Slee, 1999; Ortega and Lera, 2000; Salmivalli, 1999; Farrington 1993).

Here is an example of the second method of synthesis again from the *U.S. Department of Justice Office*. It begins with a general statement of possible disagreement and then contrasts several theories on the causes of bullying.

The reasons that people bully others are not entirely clear. Some researchers suggest that bullies have poor social skills and compensate by bullying. Others *(This introduces the contrast.)* suggest that bullies have keen insight into others' mental states and take advantage of that by picking on the emotionally less resilient (Smith and Brain, 2000). Along this line, there is some suggestion, currently being explored in research in the United States and elsewhere, that those who bully in the early grades are initially popular and considered leaders. However, by the third grade, the aggressive behavior is less well-regarded by peers, and those who become popular are those who do not bully. Some research also suggests that "[bullies] direct aggressive behavior at a variety of targets. As they learn the reactions of their peers, their pool of victims becomes increasingly smaller, and their choice of victims more consistent" (Harachi, Catalano and Hawkins, 1999). Thus, bullies ultimately focus on peers who become chronic victims due to how those peers respond to aggression.

Introducing Sources

Keep these points in mind as you introduce the sources:

> **Writing Tip**
>
> When you introduce different sources, try not to begin each sentence the same way. Use different verbs as well. Instead of repeating "says" each time, use "claims," "suggests," "maintains," "reports," "argues," and so on.

- Name the source. Chapters 8 and 9 and Appendix G will provide you with detailed instructions on how to do so, but for now you should simply indicate the author's name (if it is given) and the name of the publication.

- Decide on the order for presenting the sources. Which one should go first?

- If possible, introduce sources that agree in the same sentence. For example, "Thomas Wilson and Helen Cowan both believe that bullying in the schools can be controlled." Then you can paraphrase or quote each source.

- Refer to multiple sources in one sentence ("four people" or "several sources"). Then quote from or paraphrase one of the sources as an example.

- Explain or interpret a quotation from a source, showing its relationship to your claim.

- When sources disagree, include both sides in the same paragraph. Use transitions such as "On the other hand," "In contrast," "However," to show the contrast. With a complex issue, explain the relationship between the ideas in one or more full sentences.

For writing guides to help you introduce agreement and disagreement between sources, see Appendix A, page 192.

Look at the paragraph below from the writing model. Underline the sentence or phrase that synthesizes sources.

> [4] What, then, can schools do? The Safe and Drug Free Schools Act includes bullying and harassment, and requires all schools receiving federal funds to not only respond to all instances of bullying, but also to actively prevent it. Additionally, school districts have been developing and requiring anti-bullying policies and programs. Books such as *Aggression and Bullying* (Guerin & Hennesy, 2002) and *Cyberbullying: Bullying in the Digital Age* (Kowalski, Limber & Agatson, 2012) shed light on the consequences of bullying for both the aggressor and the victim. Books like these and established anti-bullying programs reveal that many bullies were either bullied themselves at some point or perhaps abused in some way by family members.

TRY IT OUT!   Work with a partner and find two articles on the Internet that deal with time spent on studying. Select a passage from each that agrees or disagrees. Then, on your own, write a paragraph in which you synthesize the two passages in a paraphrase of both.

✎ Applying Vocabulary: Using Adverbial Intensifiers

Adverbial intensifiers tend to fit somewhat with a particular adjective. Furthermore, they vary in their degree of intensity. For example, *relatively* is not as strong as *highly*, and *highly* is not as strong as *absolutely*. Before you begin your writing assignment, review the intensifiers you learned about on page 113.

PRACTICE 6 Writing Intensifiers

Using the list of intensifiers from Practice 1 on page 113, choose the one that is most appropriate in each sentence. Do not use the same word twice.

1. One child bullying another is _____ wrong and should be stopped.

2. Walking on railroad tracks is _____ dangerous.

3. After it was so hot yesterday, the weather today is _____ cool.

4. It is _____ unlikely that you will be struck by lightning.

5. I was _____ saddened to hear the bad news.

6. Living 1,000 years is _____ impossible.

WRITING ASSIGNMENT

Your assignment for this chapter is to write a problem / solution essay of five or more paragraphs about an issue related to education. Choose one of the topics and follow the steps in the writing process.

POSSIBLE TOPICS
- Poor nutrition and its effects on learning
- Junk food sold in school vending machines
- Television or video games and their effect on homework
- The length of the school year
- Transportation to and from school
- Arts and music education

 Explore **STEP 1: Explore your topic, audience, and purpose.**
- Begin by doing some research on your topic.
- Take notes on facts, figures, quotations, and the sources of your information. With print or Internet materials, include the title of the article, the author (if one is listed), and the place where the article was found.
- Decide on the audience for your paper—the person or people most concerned about the problem.

Prewrite

STEP 2: Prewrite to get ideas.

- Freewrite, brainstorm, or do clustering to explore your ideas.

 Organize

STEP 3: Organize your ideas.

- Draft a preliminary thesis statement
- Outline your paper.
- Introduce the problem, and indicate why it needs to be solved.
- Explain the problem and its specific implications.
- List the support for your claims.
- Introduce a (possible) solution or solutions to the problem.
- Include a call for action.

 Write

STEP 4: Write the first draft.

- Include an introduction, body paragraphs, and a conclusion.
- Introduce the problem and the solution in the first paragraph. Explore the problem specifically in the first body paragraph.
- Introduce and explain the solution in the remaining body paragraphs.
- Include a transition that introduces the solution.
- Support your claims with material that you synthesize from your research.

 Revise

STEP 5: Revise the draft.

- Exchange papers with a partner, and give each other feedback on your papers. Use the Chapter 6 Peer Review on page 235 to guide your feedback.
- Carefully consider your partner's feedback. If you agree with it, revise your paper by marking the changes on your first draft.

Proofread

STEP 6: Edit and proofread.

- Use the Chapter 6 Writer's Self-Check on page 236 to help you look for and correct errors in grammar, mechanics, and sentence structure.

Write

STEP 7: Write a new draft.

- Revise the draft, incorporating all the changes you want to make.
- Make sure the draft is legible and follows the format your instructor has provided.
- Proofread the draft so that it is error free.
- Hand in the essay to your instructor.

EXPANSION

TIMED WRITING

In this expansion, you will write a summary of the writing model. You will have 30 minutes. To complete the expansion in time, you will need to budget your time accordingly. Follow this procedure.

1. Review the writing model on pages 110–112. Make note of the claims in your own words and copy any quotations that are used to illustrate them. (10 minutes)

2. Write the paragraphs. Be sure to paraphrase the problem and solution(s) concisely in the thesis statement and end with a call to action. (10 minutes)

3. Revise your paragraphs to be sure they are clear and well organized. (5 minutes)

4. Check your paragraph for errors. Correct any mistakes. (5 minutes)

5. Give your paper to your instructor.

COMPLETE THE ESSAY

Return to the paragraph you wrote on an educational leader on page 121 and do further research. Then expand the paragraph into a full essay of at least five paragraphs. Make sure that the body paragraphs explain the nature and extent of the problem that this person encountered before introducing how he or she attempted to solve the problem. Be sure to provide supporting facts, figures, and quotes for your claims. The concluding paragraph should refer to the thesis of the opening paragraph and perhaps make a call for more action on solving the problem.

CHAPTER 7

SUMMARY / RESPONSE ESSAYS

OBJECTIVES

To write academic texts, you need to master certain skills.

In this chapter, you will learn to:

- Analyze a summary / response essay

- Distinguish between objective and subjective points of view

- Summarize an essay in an introductory paragraph

- Plan and write a response to the essay

- Use active and passive voice in appropriate contexts

- Write, edit, and revise an essay about culture

The United States: a mixture of cultures

Writing a summary and response essay plays an important role in college work. Throughout your academic career, you will be expected to produce summary and response writing in essay examinations and research papers. A **summary** demonstrates your understanding of a reading's main ideas. Then your **response** allows you to analyze it, compare or contrast it with other material you have studied, agree or disagree with its claims, or expand on the claims further.

Summary and response also plays an important role outside of the college classroom. In business correspondence and presentations, you may summarize the contents of a report, memo, discussion, or experiment before analyzing, comparing, or evaluating those results. In the field of medicine, doctors, nurses, and hospital personnel may summarize information from patients to evaluate the symptoms before responding by recommending treatment. Police officers write summaries of events in automobile accidents and then file a report. Lawyers summarize the facts of a case before making their arguments in response. People who write letters to public officials or newspaper editors often summarize an issue before stating their viewpoints on the matter. In this chapter, you will summarize and respond to issues related to cultural traditions and adaptations.

ANALYZING THE MODEL

The model essay summarizes and then responds to an article by Richard Rodriguez. The model is based on the assignment.

> *Assignment: Write an essay in which you summarize the article "An Education in Language" and then explain what you think Richard Rodriguez's parents might have done in order to maintain a close relationship with Richard as he learned English and succeeded in school.*

Read the model. Then answer the questions.

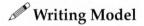 Writing Model

Did It Have to Happen?

1   Learning the language of an adopted country provides great benefits: It helps the child get an education, get accepted into society, and enjoy economic opportunities. Unfortunately, for some children these benefits come at a cost. They lose their closeness with their family because their parents still communicate by using their primary language. This loss can even lead to a child's feeling embarrassed because his or her parents keep their "old fashioned" or even "illiterate" ways. This happened to Richard Rodriguez, a famous author, journalist, and social commentator. In his article, "An Education in Language," he describes his experiences in learning English and leaving behind his "family language" of Spanish. While adapting to English-speaking culture, he

(continued on next page)

felt increasingly alienated from the warm and loving environment of his family. After he was able to communicate in this second language, he quickly "moved very far from the disadvantaged child" the school thought he was. However, he says, "This great public success was measured at home with a great sense of loss. We remained a loving family—[but] enormously different. No longer were we as close as we had been earlier." Although his mother and father "wanted for my brothers and me the chances they never had," they were ambivalent[1] about Richard's academic success. His father, "whose hands were calloused by a lifetime of work," claimed that "school work was not real work," yet he could not understand why Richard did not show off his own academic awards in his bedroom. His mother, a high school graduate who had been discouraged from becoming a typist, was proud of his achievements but could not fully understand them. He writes that, as a result, his departure for college "made only physically apparent the separation that had occurred long before."

2   Rodriguez's story raises two questions in my mind. Was his emotional separation from his parents just the result of assimilation? In other words, could the separation have been avoided? Or could his parents, he, or the school system have done more to allow him to feel both a proud Latino and American? Although there are no perfect answers to these questions, I believe that certain steps could have made the changes in Rodriquez's life easier.

3   For one thing, both his parents spoke English (although not perfectly), but they used only Spanish at home. They did not start speaking English to Richard until he entered school at the age of "nearly seven" after his teachers convinced them to do so. However, if they had chosen to speak both languages to Richard from birth, as my best friend's parents did, he might have felt more comfortable reconciling his use of Spanish, the intimate language of his family and culture, and English, the "public" language of the larger society. Instead, he admits, his inability to speak English, the public language, "kept me safely at home and made me a stranger in public. In school, I was terrified by the language of Gringos."[2] He could feel at home only in his Spanish-speaking environment. That feeling decreased, however, as he acquired English skills and achieved academic success in the larger society.

4   Second, since his parents spoke some English, they could have made more of an effort to expose Richard to both their native and adopted cultures from the time Richard was born. They could have read him books in both English and Spanish, sung him songs in both languages, and taken him to museums, libraries, and other public facilities. Yes, these efforts would have required them to learn more about the public culture themselves. However, they were not completely isolated from that public culture. Richard's mother had worked in two English-speaking jobs. Richard's father had "dressed in a dandy's wardrobe," attended Saturday operas, and even "used to watch polo matches on Sundays" upon his arrival in the United States. Clearly, he wanted to assimilate. Although Richard's parents had been disappointed in their hopes for advancement, his mother wanted her children to "get all the education [they] can." But, as the saying goes, education begins in the home. Instead, however, Richard confesses, "My teachers became the new figures of authority in my life. . . . It was their encouragement that mattered to me." He wanted to impress his teachers more than his parents. Richard felt ashamed of his parents and "then guilty of the shame."

5   Third, although his father was bitter about his hard life and personal disappointments, he did not have to show that bitterness to his children. Richard explains that his father had been a laborer since the age of eight, when he dropped out of school in Mexico. Certainly, his father had a right to be resentful. Nonetheless, because he made fun of higher education and "Gringos" this

---

[1] **ambivalent:** unsure whether you want or like something or not

[2] **Gringos:** Spanish slang for non-Spanish-speaking people, often from the United States

made Richard and his brothers feel distant from him emotionally. They were becoming part of the "Gringo" culture and began to see their father's attitude as a threat to their attempts to fit in.

6   Every immigrant or refugee child probably feels caught between the "inside" world of their families and the dominant "outside" culture. Richard's parents were loving and devoted. They certainly wanted their children to escape from what Rodriguez describes as a "socially disadvantaged" environment. Unfortunately, that escape often means leaving something behind and only the most thoughtful and understanding parents can help their children with the conflict they feel. Could Richard's parents have done better? Yes, they could have. The challenge would have been great, but if they had met it, Richard and his brothers might not have felt so estranged from their parents.

Source: The essay was a response to Rodriguez, Richard. "An Education in Language."

Questions about the Model

1. What is the thesis statement in Paragraph 1? Underline it.

2. What is the thesis of Paragraph 2? Circle it.

3. What, according to the author of the response, caused the separation between Richard Rodriguez and his parents?

4. How realistic are the suggestions in the response? Would they have prevented Richard from feeling alienated from his parents?

5. Have you or anyone you know encountered problems similar to the ones Rodriguez faced? If the answer is yes, briefly discuss them.

✎ Noticing Vocabulary: Words Related to Cultural Change

These words from the writing model can be useful in summarizing and responding to articles about differences in traditions and family relationships in various cultures.

PRACTICE 1   **Finding Meaning from Context**

These words have more than one meaning. Find them in the writing model. Then circle the word that best expresses the meaning of each word based on its context. Use a dictionary as needed.

1. primary *(paragraph 1)*   **a.** first   **b.** most important

2. assimilate *(paragraphs 2 & 4)*   **a.** conform   **b.** be similar

3. reconcile *(paragraph 3)*   **a.** merge   **b.** make peace with

4. intimate *(paragraph 3)*   **a.** private   **b.** confidential

5. acquire *(paragraph 3)*   **a.** learn   **b.** know

6. isolated *(paragraph 4)*   **a.** segregated   **b.** cut off

7. conflict *(paragraph 6)*   **a.** fight   **b.** tension

8. dominant *(paragraph 6)*   **a.** forceful   **b.** main

In a summary / response essay, the opening paragraph addresses the **summary**. The summary must be **objective**. That is, it must report only what you have read; it does not include your opinions or interpretations. Therefore, a well-written summary should never include the personal pronouns *I* or *me*. On the other hand, the **response**, which follows the summary, is **subjective** and consists of your interpretations of and opinions about the material summarized at the beginning of the essay.

A summary / response organization, with examples from the writing model, looks like this:

Introductory Paragraph

The summary appears in the opening paragraph(s). It identifies the author, topic, and title of the reading and states the main ideas, usually in the sequence of the original. The final sentence can restate the topic or transition into the response.

First Body Paragraph

The response appears in the remaining paragraphs. The first paragraph of the body transitions into the response and states the central claim of the reaction (thesis).

Transition: restates the author's name and recycles language from the previous paragraph

Thesis: states his belief that the author's life might have been easier if his parents had done things differently

Subsequent Body Paragraphs

Each subsequent body paragraph states a main supporting idea to your claim and supports it with examples, details, and explanations.

Paragraph 3: parents could have spoken English as well as Spanish at home

Paragraph 4: parents could have exposed the author to both Spanish-speaking and English-speaking cultures

Paragraph 5: his father need not have displayed his own bitterness toward "Gringo" culture

Concluding Paragraph

The last paragraph restates the central claim of the response.

Paragraph 6: If the Rodriguez parents had been more thoughtful, their relationship with their sons might have been better.

THE SUMMARY

The steps in writing a summary will be addressed later in this chapter. Meanwhile, recall what you learned about summarizing in Chapter 3. You must state the author's main idea and key points in your own words. Provide the author's name (if one is given) and the title of the material you are summarizing. Write the summary as a unified, coherent paragraph, beginning with a thesis statement that states the central idea of the material. Although the summary may include a few details, examples, or quotations, most of the specific information should be incorporated as support for the claims in the response.

THE RESPONSE

The remainder of the essay consists of a response to the summary, in which you develop and support your own thesis. The response should begin with a transition and a statement of your thesis, which can appear either at the end of the summary or in the paragraph immediately following the summary.

Your goal—and the main goal of the essay—is to present and develop an original, logical argument. Unlike the summary, a response is subjective; it expresses *your* interpretations, opinions, and arguments. For example, you may agree or disagree with one or more claims in the reading. You may now use the first-person personal pronouns *I*, *me*, *my*, or *mine*. For instance, in Paragraph 2 of the writing model, the author states his thesis in the first person, "… I believe that certain steps could have made the changes in Rodriquez's life easier."

You should expand on the main ideas in the reading by relating them to your own experiences, your knowledge of the subject matter, or other concepts or readings you have studied in the course. Throughout the response, you should support your claims with short quotations or paraphrases from the reading.

Read the excerpt from an article. Then with a partner or in a small group, list the key points that you would include in a summary.

Arranging a Marriage in India
Serenda Nanda

1   In India, almost all marriages are arranged. Even among the educated middle classes in modern, urban India, marriage is as much a concern of the families as it is of the individuals. So customary is the practice of arranged marriages that there is a special name for a marriage which is not arranged: It is called a "love match."

2   On my first field trip to India, I met many young men and women whose parents were in the process of "getting them married." In many cases, the bride and groom would not meet each other before the marriage. At most, they might meet for a brief conversation, and this meeting would take place only after their parents had decided that the match was suitable. Parents do not compel their children to marry a person who either marriage partner finds objectionable. But only after one match is refused will another be sought. . . .

3   The basic rule seems to be that a family's reputation is most important. It is understood that matches would be arranged only within the same caste and general social class, although some crossing of sub-castes is permissible if the class positions of the bride's and groom's families are similar. Although the dowry is now prohibited by law in India, extensive gift exchanges take place with every marriage. Even when the boy's family does not "make demands," every girl's family nevertheless feels the obligation to give the traditional gifts to the girl, to the boy, and to the boy's family. Particularly when the couple would be living in the joint family—that is, with the boy's parents and his married brothers and their families, as well as with unmarried siblings—which is still very common even among the urban, upper-middle class in India, the girl's parents are anxious to establish smooth relations between their family and that of the boy. Offering the proper gifts, even when not called "dowry," is often an important factor in influencing the relationship between the bride's and groom's families and perhaps, also, the treatment of the bride in her new home.

4   In a society where divorce is still a scandal and where, in fact, the divorce rate is exceedingly low, an arranged marriage is the beginning of a lifetime relationship not just between the bride and groom, but between their families as well. Thus, while a girl's looks are important, her character is even more so, for she is being judged as a prospective daughter-in-law as much as a prospective bride. Where she would be living in a joint family, as was the case with my friend, the girl's ability to get along harmoniously in a family is perhaps the single most important quality in assessing her suitability.

Source: Adapted and excerpted from: Nanda, Serenda. "Arranging a Marriage in India."

Key Points:

1. _____
   _____

2. _____
   _____

3. _____
   _____

4. _____
   _____

5. _____
   _____

6. _____
   _____

GRAMMAR

To write well in English, you should be clear and to the point. Your writing should be natural (but not too formal or informal) otherwise it may sound awkward. One common source of awkwardness is the inappropriate use of the passive voice, which often does not indicate who or what is performing the action of the verb.

USING PASSIVE AND ACTIVE VOICE APPROPRIATELY

There are two voices in English: **active**, in which the subject performs the action of the verb, and **passive**, in which the subject receives the action of the verb:

SUBJECT   VERB
Active voice: Many *people* in Latin America *speak* Spanish.

SUBJECT ┌— VERB —┐
Passive voice: *Spanish is spoken* throughout most of Latin America.

A passive voice verb includes some form of *to be* and the *past participle*. The verb can occur in any tense:

PRESENT TENSE   Foreign language **is taught** in many high schools.

PAST TENSE   The holiday **was celebrated** on Sunday.

FUTURE TENSE   Final grades **will be mailed** after the holidays.

PRESENT PERFECT TENSE   The distance from the earth to the moon **has been precisely calculated**.

Logical Uses of Passive Voice

To decide whether or not you want to use passive or active voice, think about what you wish to emphasize. The passive voice is logical and appropriate in some circumstances:

RULES	EXAMPLES
1. Use the passive voice when the action is more important than the person who performs it.	Spanish is spoken throughout most of Central America, South America, and most of the United States. *(The identities of the speakers are not important.)*
2. Use the passive voice when we do not know or care who performed the action.	My wallet was stolen! *(You do not know who stole the wallet.)*
3. Use the passive voice to describe processes.	The children are sent to school where they are taught only in English.
4. Use the passive voice to introduce formal evidence.	A distinction can be made between the intimate family culture and the public culture.

However, many statements in the passive voice result in problems. Because they do not specify who performs the action, the statements are unclear, or they sound awkward and unnatural. Compare these sentences in the passive and active voices:

PASSIVE VOICE The homework was finally completed at 3:00 A.M.
(Who completed it?)

Adding words to the passive voice to specify who performs the action not only makes the sentence longer, but also unnatural sounding:

PASSIVE VOICE The homework was completed by me at 3:00 A.M.
(This sounds awkward and uses more words than the active-voice statement.)

Instead, the sentence requires the active voice.

ACTIVE VOICE I completed my homework at 3:00 A.M.

PRACTICE 3 **Revising Passive Voice Sentences**

Rewrite each sentence using the active voice.

1. English is spoken in my home by my friend's parents.

   My friend's parents speak English at home.

2. The book was finished by me in a very short time.

   _____

3. The information has been received by our office.

   _____

4. Rodriguez's father's clothes were worn with great pride.

_____

5. Rodriguez's awards were barely acknowledged by his parents.

_____

6. His public success was measured by Rodriguez's parents "with a great sense of loss."

_____

PRACTICE 4 **Forming Passive and Active Voice Sentences**

Complete each sentence in the passive voice using the verb in parentheses.
Then rewrite the sentence in the active voice.

1. The news _was communicated_ to Rodriguez's parents by his teachers.
(communicate)

Rewritten: _Rodriguez's teachers communicated the news to his parents._

2. He _____ to be a slow learner by them. (perceive)

Rewritten: _____

_____

3. His roots eventually _____ as he assimilated. (abandon)

Rewritten: _____

_____

4. In many schools, bilingual education _____ by the local
school board. (require)

Rewritten: _____

_____

5. Richard _____ by his teachers at first. (discourage)

Rewritten: _____

_____

6. Aspects of both the family and public cultures _____ by
Richard's parents in their home. (address)

Rewritten: _____

_____

The two parts of the summary and response are closely linked. A reader may not accept the arguments of your response if the summary is inaccurate or incomplete. Therefore, you must take special care to ensure that your summary is accurate, clear, and concise. You must likewise construct a clear and well-supported response that addresses the issues raised in the summary.

WRITING THE OPENING SUMMARY

Follow this procedure to prepare your summary.

1. Preview the reading. Scanning the material before starting to read it will help you see its general organization and main ideas. In textbooks, look for chapter objectives or chapter-ending summaries. In long articles or chapters in a book, look for headings that identify central ideas. And in any work, look at the opening paragraph, the first sentences of body paragraphs, and the conclusion.

2. Read the selection carefully. Then read slowly, highlighting or underlining topic sentences and making notes in the margins. Do the same with supporting ideas. Reread difficult passages until you are sure that you understand them.

3. Take notes and plan. Return to the parts you have highlighted or underlined. Then jot down a list of the ideas you want to include. Focus on the main ideas, not on supporting details.

4. Organize your ideas. List or outline the main points in a clear and consistent arrangement. In most cases, you will follow the organization of the original, presenting the information in the same sequence.

5. Draft a thesis statement that captures the main point of the material you are summarizing.

6. Write the summary in the present tense since you are explaining what the material *says now*—as you read it—even though the author wrote in the past. Do not copy sentences or parts of sentences from the original. *Paraphrase* the material, and, if necessary, quote short phrases from the original. If you omit words when quoting, you can use ellipsis marks (. . .) to show where they are omitted.

7. Introduce your response in a transitional sentence, either at the end of the summary paragraph or in the first sentence of the second paragraph.

WRITING THE RESPONSE

Follow this procedure for planning and writing the response.

1. Review your earlier notes and formulate a thesis. Consider which ideas or arguments you wish to develop. You can use any of these questions to help you create your thesis:

   - Does a problem or issue described in this source still exist today? Why or why not?

   - Do you agree or disagree with the author's argument or claims? Why? How?

   - Does the author's argument persuade you to think about an issue in a new way? Why? How?

   - What are the causes of the event or problem the author discusses in his essay? What are the effects?

   - What solutions would you propose to address a problem the author raises in the essay?

   - Have you observed or read about real-life examples that illustrate the author's claims or themes?

   - Which of the author's ideas are important to know, and why? Or does the author ignore ideas that you think are important?

2. Outline your main points. Make a list or informal outline, deciding on the order for presenting your claims.

3. Draft and revise the response. Make each major claim in a separate paragraph. Explain your reasoning, provide evidence (which can include specific details or quotations from the reading), and cite examples from other sources, including personal experience.

Writing Tip

Remember that the work you are summarizing pursues a thesis; it makes a point. Phrases such as "Jane Doe *writes about* . . ." or "Jane Doe *says* . . ." do not indicate the point, but only announce the subject matter of the work. Therefore, select a verb that most accurately characterizes the author's intentions; for example, "Jane Doe *reports, asserts, contends, insists, concludes, maintains, states, argues, suggests,*" and so on.

For writing guides to help you introduce a summary and a response, see Appendix A, page 193.

Read this short excerpt from a sociology textbook. Write a two- or three-sentence summary of this short essay on the lines below. Be sure to include the author and title.

Material and Nonmaterial Culture
James Henslin

1   What is culture? The concept is sometimes easier to describe than to define. For example, suppose you meet a young woman from India who has just arrived in the United States. That her culture is different from yours is immediately evident. You first see it in her clothing, jewelry, makeup, and hairstyle. Next you hear it in her speech. It then becomes apparent by her gestures. Later, you might hear her express unfamiliar beliefs about relationships or what is valuable in life. All of these things are characteristics of culture—the language, beliefs, values, norms, behaviors, and even material objects that are passed from one generation to the next.

2   In northern Africa, I was surrounded by a culture quite different from mine. It was evident in everything I saw and heard. The material culture—such things as jewelry, art, buildings, weapons, machines, and even eating utensils, hairstyles, and clothing—provided a sharp contrast to what I was used to seeing. There is nothing inherently "natural" about material culture. That is, it is no more natural or unnatural to wear gowns on the street than it is to wear jeans.

3   I also found myself immersed in an unfamiliar nonmaterial culture, that is, a group's ways of thinking (its beliefs, values, and other assumptions about the world) and doing (its common patterns of behavior, including language, gestures, and other forms of interaction). North African assumptions that it is acceptable to stare at others in public and to push people aside to buy tickets are examples of nonmaterial culture. So are U.S. assumptions that it is wrong to do either of these things. Like material culture, neither custom is "right." People simply become comfortable with the customs they learn during childhood, and—as when I visited northern Africa—uncomfortable when their basic assumptions about life are challenged.

Source: Excerpted from Henslin, James M. *Sociology, A Down-to-Earth Approach.*

Summary: _____

_____

_____

_____

_____

Read this short essay. Write a thesis statement for a response in which you agree or disagree with the conclusion of the paragraph. Then list two points you would make in a response.

A Cultural Mosaic
Philip R. Popple and Leslie Leighninger

The presence of diverse racial, ethnic, and other distinct groups in society gives rise to various notions[1] about the proper relationship between individual groups and "the whole." Such notions emerge particularly in discussions of immigration, although they have relevance also to the situations of longtime residents (African Americans and American Indians) and of those belonging to categories such as the elderly or people with disabilities. A traditional version of "ideal group relations" in the United States is the idea of a melting pot, in which the cultures of all groups join to produce a new, distinctly American culture. In real life, this early twentieth-century idea of a "blended American" proved unrealistic. Newcomers were unwilling to give up all their traditions and customs, and, perhaps more significantly, the dominant society had a stake in maintaining its own identity. We like the reframing of the melting pot image proposed by historian Lawrence Levine. Levine argued that today's model of diversity "is not the American melting pot, but a cultural mosaic in which discrete ethnic groups persist and interact with other groups."

Source: Excerpted from Popple, Philip R. et al. *Social Work, Social Welfare, and American Society.*

---

[1] **notions:** ideas or theories

Thesis Statement: _____

_____

1. _____

2. _____

Here is another paragraph from Serenda Nanda's article on arranged marriages in India. Write a one-sentence summary of the paragraph and then one or two paragraphs in response. Do you agree with Nanda's viewpoint, or do you see some value in arranged marriages?

Six years later I returned to India to do fieldwork, this time among the middle class in Bombay, a modern, sophisticated city. From the experience of my earlier visit, I decided to include a study of arranged marriages in my project. By this time, I had met many Indian couples whose marriages had been arranged and who seemed very happy. Particularly in contrast to the fate of my married friends in the United States who were already in the process of divorce, the positive aspects of arranged marriages appeared to me to outweigh the negatives.

Applying Vocabulary: Using Words Related to Cultural Change

Before you begin your writing assignment, review what you learned about the words in Practice 1 on page 131.

Forming Different Parts of Speech

A Work in pairs or small groups. Fill in the appropriate word form for each. Use a dictionary as needed. As you work, look for recurring patterns.

VERB	NOUN	ADJECTIVE
1. acquire	_acquisition_	acquisitive
2. conflict	conflict	_____
3. reconcile	reconciliation	_____
4. assimilate	_____	assimilated
5. devote	_____	devoted
6. perceive	_____	perceived

B Change these nouns into verbs. Most, but not all, of the verbs will follow a consistent pattern. Consult your dictionary as needed.

NOUN	VERB
1. demonstration	_____
2. integration	_____
3. education	_____
4. definition	_____
5. invitation	_____
6. conversation	_____
7. evolution	_____
8. resolution	_____

C Choose the word form from Parts A and B that best completes each sentence.

1. When people get married, they pledge their complete _devotion_.

2. Young children learn to _____ in a second language more quickly than most adults.

3. The _____ of a new language can be very challenging.

4. A person who fits into a new culture is said to be _____.

5. When someone gets new eyeglasses, the person's visual _____ may improve.

6. When a person feels divided between one feeling and another, he is said to be

_____.

WRITING ASSIGNMENT

Your assignment for this chapter is to write a summary and response essay on a topic related to culture. Write an essay of at least five paragraphs on one of the topics below or one that your teacher suggests. Follow the steps in the writing process.

POSSIBLE TOPICS

- Cultural identity
- Cultural diversity
- Cultural differences
- Adapting to a new culture
- Cultural assimilation
- Cultural practices in education

 **STEP 1: Explore your topic, audience, and purpose.**

- Choose your topic from the list above.
- Research an Internet article on your topic.
- Read the article carefully, highlighting or taking notes of main points for your summary.
- Consider who might be interested in this article and a response; they are your audience.
- Consider what you wish to accomplish in your response; this is the thesis of your response.

 STEP 2: Prewrite to get ideas.

- Freewrite, brainstorm, or cluster to uncover your ideas.
- Draft a preliminary thesis statement for your response.
- Brainstorm examples from your personal experience or the experiences of others that support or refute the article's thesis or supporting points.

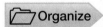 **STEP 3: Organize your ideas.**

- Select the ideas to include in the summary.
- Outline the response, listing each claim.
- Select passages that you will paraphrase or quote as support for your claims.

Write | **STEP 4: Write the first draft.**

- Summarize the article in the first paragraph. Be sure to include the title of the work and the author's name, a thesis, and the article's main points.
- Include a transition that introduces the response.
- Introduce and develop the response in the remaining body paragraphs.
- End with a return to the summary.

 Revise | **STEP 5: Revise the draft.**

- Exchange papers with a partner, and give each other feedback on your papers. Use the Chapter 7 Peer Review on page 237 to guide your feedback.
- Carefully consider your partner's feedback. If you agree with it, revise your paper by marking the changes on your first draft.

 Proofread | **STEP 6: Edit and proofread.**

- Use the Chapter 7 Writer's Self-Check on page 238 to help you look for and correct errors in grammar, mechanics, and sentence structure.

 **Write** | **STEP 7: Write a new draft.**

- Revise the draft, incorporating all the changes you want to make.
- Make sure the draft is legible and follows the format your instructor has provided.
- Proofread the draft so that it is error free.
- Hand in the essay to your instructor.

SELF-ASSESSMENT

In this chapter, you learned to:

○ Analyze a summary / response essay

○ Distinguish between objective and subjective points of view

○ Summarize an essay in an introductory paragraph

○ Plan and write a response to the essay

○ Use active and passive voice in appropriate contexts

○ Write, edit, and revise an essay about culture

Which ones can you do well? Mark them ✓

Which ones do you need to practice more? Mark them ✗

TIMED WRITING

Return to "A Cultural Mosaic" in Practice 6 on page 141. Now summarize and write a full response to the passage. You will have 45 minutes. To complete the expansion, you will need to budget your time accordingly. Follow this procedure.

1. Reread the passage, underlining or highlighting the statement of the main argument and key supporting points. (10 minutes)

2. Write a one-paragraph summary of the passage. State the main argument and key supporting ideas you have located. Omit any long examples and explanations. (10 minutes)

3. Then write a response, beginning with a smooth transition and a thesis statement. Make your position clear. Do you agree or disagree with the argument, or is your response mixed? Refer back to the article to support your claims. What in your own experience, or the experience of others you know, can you cite as backing for your claims? Cite examples. (15 minutes)

4. Revise and edit your work. Be sure your summary and thesis are clear. If you write by hand, you may make changes above the lines in the margins. (5 minutes)

5. Check your summary and response for errors. Correct any mistakes. (5 minutes)

6. Hand in your paper to your instructor.

RESEARCH AND RESPOND

Do an Internet search using the key words "bilingual education" or "bilingual immersion." Find a short article that argues either for or against one of these topics. Summarize the article and respond, using the same procedures you have followed in the chapter.

CHAPTER 8

ARGUMENTATIVE ESSAYS

OBJECTIVES

To write academic texts, you need to master certain skills.

In this chapter, you will learn to:

- Analyze two argumentative essays

- Examine the elements of a well-structured argument

- Structure an argument using block and point-by-point organization

- Use modals, phrasal modals, and the subjunctive mode

- Rebut counterarguments effectively

- Write, revise, and edit an essay on a controversial issue

Many people strongly oppose research on animals.

Controversy and, therefore, argument appear in almost every academic field: in discussions of new scientific research; in competing views on economic theory; in interpretations of art, literature, music, and movies; in debates about philosophy; concerns over best practices in education, and so on. Likewise, controversy and argument are widespread in everyday discussions of virtually every subject, from politics to business and sports, or any other subject you can think of.

An argument, however, is not a fight. Instead, an **argumentative essay** is an attempt to convince others that a particular point of view on a topic is or is not correct. Creating a sound argument is thus an essential skill both inside and outside of college or the university. While argumentative writing applies to any topic, the writing models will focus on controversy related to animal research and the costs of a college education.

ANALYZING THE MODELS

The first model essay presents an argument in favor of animal testing. The second model responds to arguments that a college degree is no longer a good investment.

Read the models. Then answer the questions.

Writing Model 1

A Scientist: I Am the Enemy
Ronald M. Kline M.D.

1   I am the enemy! One of those hated, cold-hearted physician-scientists involved in animal research. How strange, for I have never thought of myself as an evil person. I became a pediatrician because of my love for children and my desire to keep them healthy. During medical school and residency,[1] however, I saw many children die of leukemia,[2] prematurity,[3] and traumatic[4] injury—circumstances against which medicine has made tremendous progress, but still has far to go. More important, I also saw children, alive and healthy, thanks to advances in medical science such as infant respirators,[5] strong antibiotics, new surgical techniques, and the entire field of organ transplantation.[6] My desire to tip the scales in favor of healthy, happy children drew me to medical research.

(continued on next page)

---

[1] **residency:** the period in which a doctor continues training in a hospital after completing medical school
[2] **leukemia:** a type of cancer that affects the blood stream, often causing death
[3] **prematurity:** being born before the body's organs are developed enough to allow normal survival
[4] **traumatic:** seriously damaging
[5] **respirators:** devices to help people breathe
[6] **transplantation:** replacement of a body part, usually donated from another person

2   My accusers claim that I torture animals for the sole purpose of advancing my career. My experiments supposedly have no relevance to medicine and are easily replaced by computer simulation. Meanwhile, an apathetic public barely watches, convinced that the issue has no significance, and publicity-conscious politicians increasingly give way to the demands of the activists.

3   We in medical research have also been unacceptably apathetic. We have allowed the most extreme animal-rights protesters to seize the initiative and frame the issue as one of "animal fraud." We have been complacent in our belief that a knowledgeable public would sense the importance of animal research to the public health. Perhaps we have been mistaken in not responding to the emotional tone of the argument created by those sad posters of animals by waving equally sad posters of children dying of leukemia or cystic fibrosis.[7]

4   Much is made of the pain caused to these animals in the name of medical science. The animal-rights activists contend that this is evidence of our cruel and brutal nature. A more reasonable argument, however, can be advanced in our defense. Life is often cruel, both to animals and human beings. Teenagers get thrown from the back of a pickup truck and suffer severe head injuries. Toddlers, barely able to walk, find themselves at the bottom of a swimming pool while a parent checks the mail. Physicians hoping to alleviate the pain and suffering that these tragedies cause have but three choices: create an animal model of the injury or disease and use that model to understand the process and test new therapies, experiment on human beings—some experiments will succeed, most will fail—or finally, leave medical knowledge unchanged, hoping that accidental discoveries will lead us to the advances.

5   Some animal-rights activists would suggest a fourth choice, claiming that computer models can simulate animal experiments, thus making the actual experiments unnecessary. Computers can simulate, reasonably well, the effects of well-understood principles on complex systems, as in the application of the laws of physics to airplane and automobile design. However, when the principles themselves are in question, as is the case with the complex biological systems under study, computer modeling alone is of little value.

6   One of the terrifying effects of the effort to restrict the use of animals in medical research is that its impact will not be felt for many years and decades:[8] drugs that might have been discovered will not be; surgical techniques that might have been developed will not be; and fundamental biological processes that might have been understood will remain mysteries. There is the danger that self-serving political solutions will be found to satisfy a vocal minority, while the consequences of those decisions will not be apparent until long after the decisions are made and the decision-making forgotten.

---

[7] **cystic fibrosis:** a serious medical condition that makes breathing and eating difficult
[8] **decades:** groups of ten

7   Fortunately, most of us enjoy good health, and the tragedy of watching one's child die has become a rare experience. Yet our good fortune should not make us unappreciative of the health we enjoy or the advances that make it possible. Vaccines, antibiotics, insulin, and drugs to treat heart disease, hypertension,[9] and stroke are all based on animal research. Most complex surgical procedures, such as coronary-artery bypass and organ transplantation, are initially developed in animals. Presently undergoing animal studies are techniques to insert genes in humans in order to replace the defective ones found to be the cause of so much disease. These studies will effectively end if animal research is severely restricted.

8   In America today, death has become an event isolated from our daily existence—out of the sight and thoughts of most of us. As a doctor who has watched many children die, and their parents grieve, I am particularly angered by people capable of so much compassion for a dog or a cat, but with seemingly so little for a dying human being. These people seem so insulated from the reality of human life and death and what it means.

9   Make no mistake, however: I am not advocating the needlessly cruel treatment of animals. To the extent that the animal-rights movement has made us more aware of the needs of these animals and made us search harder for suitable alternatives, they have made a significant contribution. But if the more radical members of this movement are successful in limiting further research, their efforts will bring about a tragedy that will cost many lives. The real question is whether an apathetic majority can be aroused to protect its future against a vocal, but misdirected, minority.

Source: Adapted from Kline, Ronald M. "A Scientist: I Am the Enemy."

---

[9] **hypertension:** abnormally high blood pressure

Questions about the Model

1. Why does Dr. Kline state that he is "the enemy" in the first sentence? According to him, who thinks he is the enemy?

2. Who is the primary audience for this essay—animal rights advocates or people without strong opinions about laboratory experiments on animals?

3. Look at the first and second sentences of paragraphs 1 to 6. Whose arguments do they address—Dr. Kline's or those of animal rights advocates? Do the sentences that follow agree or disagree with the opening arguments?

4. In what way does Dr. Kline change his approach in paragraphs 6 to 9?

5. Does Dr. Kline agree with any of the arguments made by animal rights advocates? If so, where and why?

6. Can you find Dr. Kline's thesis in paragraph 9? Underline the statement.

The Value of a College Degree
Kathleen Porter

1   The rapidly rising cost of higher education is causing many to question the value of continuing education beyond high school. Many wonder whether the high cost of tuition, the cost of choosing college over full-time employment, and the accumulation of thousands of dollars of debt is, in the long run, worth the investment. The risk is especially large for low-income families who have a difficult time making ends meet without the additional burden of college tuition and fees.

2   In order to determine whether higher education is worth the investment, it is useful to examine what is known about the value of higher education and the rates of return on investment to both the individual and to society.

3   There is considerable support for the argument that the return on investment in higher education is high enough to justify the high cost of pursuing a college degree. Though the difference in earnings between college and high school graduates varies over time, college graduates, on average, earn more than high school graduates. According to the Census Bureau, over an adult's working life, high school graduates earn an average of $1.2 million; associate's degree holders earn about $1.6 million; and those with a bachelor's degree earn about $2.1 million (Day and Newburger, 2002). These statistics support the contention that, though the cost of higher education is significant, a college graduate's return on investment in his or her education is high enough to justify the cost.

4   While it is clear that investment in a college degree, especially for those students in the lowest income brackets, is a financial burden, the long-term benefits to individuals, as well as to society at large, appear to far outweigh the costs.

Source: Adapted from Porter, Kathleen. "The Value of a College Degree."

Questions about the Model

1. What is the purpose of Paragraph 1? How does it relate to Paragraph 2?

2. Which sentence in Paragraph 3 makes the central claim of the argument? What information supports this claim?

3. What conclusion does the argument draw?

4. Where do arguments against Kathleen Porter's position appear in her report?

✎ Noticing Vocabulary: Synonyms, 2

As you know, writers broaden their vocabulary through reading. When they encounter a new word, they may look it up in a dictionary. Other times, however, they can determine the meaning of a word from the context of the sentence in which it appears.

Defining Terms from Context

Look at Writing Model 1 on pages 147–149. Find the numbered words. Use the context to help you decide which synonym best defines each numbered word.

_____i_____ 1. apathetic *(paragraph 2)*   **a.** choice

_____ 2. initiative *(paragraph 3)*   **b.** imitate

_____ 3. complacent *(paragraph 3)*   **c.** treatment

_____ 4. alleviate *(paragraph 4)*   **d.** unworried

_____ 5. therapy *(paragraph 5)*   **e.** damaged

_____ 6. simulate *(paragraph 6)*   **f.** lessen

_____ 7. impact *(paragraph 6)*   **g.** effect

_____ 8. fundamental *(paragraph 6)*   **h.** basic

_____ 9. defective *(paragraph 7)*   **i.** unconcerned

_____ 10. alternative *(paragraph 9)*   **j.** advantage

GRAMMAR

An argument often requires that you make suggestions, recommendations, and even demands. These expressions usually include **modal verbs**, **phrasal modal verbs**, and the use of the **subjunctive mode**.

MODAL VERBS

Modal verbs express ability, possibility, probability, necessity, advice, and recommendations. A modal verb has only one form and is always followed by the base form of the verb.

RULES	EXAMPLES
1. Use *can* and *could* to express present and past ability.	We can find better treatments for leukemia. I became a researcher so I could help cure disease.
2. Use *should* to offer advice or make a recommendation.	We should consider better ways to conduct laboratory experiments.
3. Use *must* to express necessity. **Note:** the negative of *must* means it is **prohibited** to do something.	We must continue research using laboratory animals. We must not allow extremists to limit research. You must not kill these animals without a good reason for doing so!
4. Use *may, might,* and *could* to express probability or possibility.	The results may save lives. New discoveries might happen at any time. They could lead to improvements in treatment.

Writing Sentences with Modals

Use the modal verbs in parentheses to write another sentence.

1. Medical research on stem cells has led to important treatments of defective organs.

   (must) _We must make these treatments easily available._

   _____

2. We are not conducting enough research into the treatment of autism. (could)

   _____

   _____

3. College graduates earn more money over their lifetimes than high school

   graduates. (should) _____

   _____

4. There are several ways to help students afford the cost of a college education.

   (might) _____

   _____

5. A cure for all forms of cancer will certainly not occur soon. (may)

   _____

   _____

6. Computer simulations are useful in conducting some types of medical research.

   (might not) _____

   _____

7. There are several ways to get to school. (could) _____

   _____

8. Texting while driving has been proven to cause many accidents and even deaths.

   (must not) _____

   _____

PHRASAL MODALS

Another tool for making recommendations, suggestions, and demands is using a **phrasal modal** (or semi-auxiliary). A phrasal modal consists of two or more separate words and functions somewhat like a modal verb. It expresses ability, offers advice, makes recommendations, or discusses possibilities or probabilities. However, unlike a modal verb, which has one form, phrasal modals change according to person and aspect.

RULES	EXAMPLES
1. Use *be able to* + [the base form of the verb] for expressing achievement.	They have been able to make significant changes in research methods.
2. Use *be likely to* + [the base form of the verb] for expressing probability.	This change is likely to have profound effects.
3. Use *be going to* + [the base form of the verb] for expressing certainty with.	This change is going to benefit millions of people.
4. Use *have to* + [the base form of the verb] for expressing necessity. **Note:** The negative of *have to* means something is not necessary. It differs from *must not*, which means it is prohibited.	We have to conduct more research. We don't have to use animals in all experiments.
5. Use *had better* for expressing warning.	You had better be careful when working with dangerous chemicals.
6. Use *would rather* (without *to*) for expressing preference.	Most students would rather apply for a scholarship than take out a loan.

PRACTICE 3   Using Phrasal Modals

Choose five of the sentences you wrote in Practice 2 and rewrite them using phrasal modals.

1. _____

2. _____

3. _____

4. _____

5. _____

SUBJUNCTIVE MODE

One other structure commonly used when making suggestions, recommendations, and demands is the **subjunctive mode**. A statement in the subjunctive mode includes two clauses:

- the first clause includes a verb such as *suggest, propose, insist, recommend, request, require, stipulate, specify,* and *demand*
- the second clause begins with *that* and includes a short infinitive—irrespective of the time of the action

FIRST CLAUSE	SECOND CLAUSE
I suggest . . .	that computer simulations be used.
I recommend . . .	that he apply for a scholarship.
I request . . .	that experiments continue. (Note the implied future time.)
I demand (insist) . . .	that he stop immediately.
The college requires . . .	that each student complete two years of a foreign language.

| PRACTICE 4 | **Using the Subjunctive** |

Write a statement in the subjunctive after each of the following sentences. Use a different verb from the chart above in each statement.

1. Juan has only a high school degree. *I recommend that he get a college education.*

2. We are not doing enough research in cures for rare types of cancer.

   _____

   _____

3. This approach to the issue is clearly wrong. _____

   _____

4. The cost of a college education is too expensive. _____

   _____

5. The instructor will not accept handwritten essays. _____

   _____

6. We cannot allow industry to pollute the environment. _____

   _____

An argumentative essay is somewhat similar to the summary / response format discussed in Chapter 7. You present your ideas and opinions about a topic in which there is disagreement or controversy, and attempt to persuade your reader that your viewpoint on the topic is correct. However, unlike in summary / response essay, you must present opposing sides of the issue and demonstrate why one side, or position, is the better one. In short, argumentation requires that you present and support your own ideas while responding to ideas that oppose them.

The viewpoint you support is called your **argument**. The opposing viewpoint is called a **counterargument**. You cannot ignore a counterargument or counterarguments. Instead, you must state and **rebut** (that is, respond to by disproving, or raising doubt about) the claims of the opposition. Acknowledging these counterarguments demonstrates to your readers your knowledge of the issue, and that you are being thoughtful, open-minded, and fair. In this way, readers are more likely to respect your point of view. However, before writing, you will need to determine who your readers are likely to be and what their stance, if any, is on the issue, which will affect how you support your position. This point will be addressed later in the chapter.

There are two common organizational patterns for argumentative essays: **block** organization and **point-by-point** organization.

BLOCK ORGANIZATION

In block organization, the counterarguments and rebuttals, and arguments and support are divided into different sections, or **blocks** of paragraphs presented separately. A diagram of block organization, with examples from Writing Model 1, looks like this:

Introductory Paragraph

The opening paragraph explains the controversy surrounding the topic, and states your position on the issue (thesis).

↓

First Group of Body Paragraphs (Block One)

In the opening paragraphs of the body (Block 1), there is a summary of the counterarguments followed by rebuttals to them. The rebuttals include explanations, evidence, and examples.

Paragraph 2: animal rights activists claim animals are tortured, research results not relevant for humans, computer simulation makes actual experiments unnecessary

Paragraph 3: rebuttal—research is important, opposing side's is emotional, and not well-reasoned

Paragraph 4: rebuttal—world is cruel to animals and humans alike; doctors trying to alleviate animal suffering

Paragraph 5: rebuttal—computer models are based on known principles; animal experiments are based on unknown principles

↓

Second Group of Body Paragraphs (Block Two)

The latter body paragraphs (Block 2) present the author's arguments and supporting evidence and examples.

Paragraph 6: lack of experimentation impacts medicine for decades

Paragraph 7: lifesaving medical procedures are created through animal research

Paragraph 8: activists have more compassion for animals than people

↓

Concluding Paragraph

The final paragraph restates your viewpoint and usually includes a summary of your argument.

POINT-BY-POINT ORGANIZATION

In an essay that is organized in a point-by-point pattern, each key idea from both sides of an issue is examined in a single paragraph. You rebut the opposing claim and provide support for your argument.

Introductory Paragraph

The first paragraph frames the issue, explains the controversy surrounding the topic, and states your position on the issue (thesis).

Body Paragraphs

In each paragraph of the body, you state a claim from the opposing side, then rebut with a claim from your argument.

Paragraph 2: statement of the other side's first counterargument and your rebuttal

Paragraph 3: statement of the other side's second counterargument and your rebuttal

Paragraph 4: statement of the other side's third counterargument and your rebuttal

---

Concluding Paragraph

The final paragraph restates your viewpoint and includes a summary of your argument. It also often includes a call to action.

Of course, these diagrams present a slightly simplified and theoretical version of argumentative essays. An essay may not follow these patterns exactly. For example, the body paragraphs may reverse the point-to-point pattern: stating the writer's argument, followed by a counterargument, and then the rebuttal.

You can use whichever organizational patterns you wish, but it may be helpful to keep these two points in mind as you decide:

- Block organization, because of its divided approach (one side, then the other), works well for short papers and issues that are not very complex.
- Point-by point organization, which allows the writer to examine issues in depth, is better suited for complex issues and longer papers.

THE INTRODUCTORY PARAGRAPH(S)

In the opening paragraph or paragraphs, it is important that you **frame the issue**, that is, introduce the arguments for and against the issue while stating your position. In short, the framing of an argument moves from "on the one hand" to "on the other hand," with the argument or counterargument occupying either position. For example, look at the opening paragraphs of Writing Model 2, which present the counterargument and the argument before moving into its thesis:

COUNTERARGUMENT The rapidly rising cost of higher education is causing many to question the value of continuing education beyond high school. . . .

INTRODUCTION TO ARGUMENT In order to determine whether higher education is worth the investment, it is useful to examine what is known about the value of higher education and the rates of return on investment to both the individual and to society.

THESIS There is considerable support for the argument that the return on investment in higher education is high enough to justify the high cost of pursuing a college degree.

Verbs for Framing an Issue

A convincing argument in part depends on a mature writing style and accurate characterization of the issues. Do not overuse the verb "says" in introducing an argument or counterargument. Aside from being repetitive, it does not indicate the attitude of the writer and the strength of his or her position. There is, for example, a great difference between "The writer insists" and "The writer suggests." The following lists of verbs will be helpful in framing an issue, introducing an argument, and responding to a counterargument.

TAKING A STRONG POSITION	TAKING A NEUTRAL OR LESS EMPHATIC POSITION
advocate	agree/disagree with
allege	favor
argue	imply
believe	indicate
claim	question
contend	recommend
deny	state
insist	suggest
maintain	support
reject	wonder

A Complete the statements with a verb from the chart.

1. I _____ that the prices we pay for fruits and vegetables are outrageous!

2. Despite all the evidence against Mr. Wilson's position, he still

   _____ that he is correct.

3. I _____ the argument of Mr. Wilson.

4. Although Mr. Wilson does not say so directly, his statement

   _____ that he has some biases against certain people.

5. I _____ that the best course of action is to stop this behavior.

6. In order to address this problem, I _____ that we take immediate action.

7. The most recent research _____ that we must change our policies.

8. No matter what Mr. Wilson _____ ,

   I _____ that his argument makes little sense.

B Work with a partner or in a small group. Compare your sentences in Part A. If you have chosen different verbs, discuss the change in meaning that results from your choice.

> *For writing guides to help you frame an argument, see Appendix A, page 193.*

BODY PARAGRAPHS

Once you have framed the issue and introduced your position on the controversy, you can follow one of two organizational patterns:

- At the beginning of each paragraph, introduce the counterargument and then state and develop your claim in response.
- At the beginning of each paragraph, state and support your claim and then present and acknowledge or respond to a counterargument.

Work with a partner or in a small group. Return to Writing Model 1 on pages 147–149 and look at paragraphs 6–8, which form Block Two of the argument. Find the arguments and counterarguments. Then summarize both.

PARAGRAPH 6

Argument: "One of the terrifying effects of the effort to restrict the use of animals in medical research is that its impact will not be felt for many years and decades...."

Counterargument: _____

_____

PARAGRAPH 7

Argument: _____

_____

Counterargument: _____

_____

PARAGRAPH 8

Argument: _____

_____

Counterargument: _____

_____

CONCLUDING PARAGRAPH

As in other types of essays, the conclusion of an argument typically returns to the thesis, summarizes the main ideas, and may make a call for action. Here are examples from the two writing models on pages 147–150.

WRITING MODEL 1

. . . But if the more radical members of this movement are successful in limiting further research, their efforts will bring about a tragedy that will cost many lives. The real question is whether an apathetic majority can be aroused to protect its future against a vocal, but misdirected, minority.

WRITING MODEL 2

. . . While it is clear that investment in a college degree, especially for those students in the lowest income brackets, is a financial burden, the long-term benefits to individuals, as well as to society at large, appear to far outweigh the costs.

Framing the argument is partly based on anticipating the responses of your audience. Some readers will easily agree with your claims. Others will demand more evidence than you have provided. Still others will disagree with your claims and offer counterarguments. Anticipating the attitude of your audience, and the arguments they might make, are essential steps in the writing process.

KNOWING YOUR AUDIENCE

Your readers can be classified into three general categories: supportive, neutral, and antagonistic.

The Supportive Audience

These readers are already familiar with the issue and tend to agree with your position. They are looking for additional reasons to support this position, especially if you can rebut the opposing arguments. Because they are receptive to what you have to say, you need not provide a great many facts, statistics, or examples—but you should provide some support for your claims.

The Neutral Audience

These readers may be interested in the issue, but have not formed strong opinions about it. They are most likely to accept your claims if you support them well and do not use overly emotional language, which would likely make them suspicious of your fairness and objectivity.

The Antagonistic Audience

These readers strongly disagree with your position. Your best approach with such readers is to strongly support your claims with facts, statistics, and examples—and avoid any emotionally charged language. Present yourself as a reasonable and logical person so they have less reason to dismiss your arguments.

Conduct a short survey about these issues. Copy and complete the form on a separate sheet of paper, and then tabulate the results. Use the results to decide whether your class is friendly, neutral, or antagonistic to each issue.

Cell phone use should be banned from public transportation.

❑ strongly agree ❑ agree ❑ neutral
❑ disagree ❑ strongly disagree

People under the age of eighteen should not be allowed to play video games.

❑ strongly agree ❑ agree ❑ neutral
❑ disagree ❑ strongly disagree

People should eat only organic food.

❑ strongly agree ❑ agree ❑ neutral
❑ disagree ❑ strongly disagree

The driving age should be raised to twenty-one.

❑ strongly agree ❑ agree ❑ neutral
❑ disagree ❑ strongly disagree

RESPONDING TO COUNTERARGUMENTS

Responding to counterarguments is essential to persuading your readers, but how, exactly, can you respond? You have several choices.

Disagree

Claim that the counterargument is wrong, because:
- it misinterprets or ignores the facts
- its claims are exaggerated
- its reasoning is not sound
- its solution to a problem will not work

In Writing Model 1, Dr. Kline maintains that the opposing argument is exaggerated and unreasonable and then responds:

> Much is made of the pain caused to these animals in the name of medical science. The animal-rights activists contend that this is evidence of our cruel and brutal nature. A more reasonable argument, however, can be advanced in our defense. Life is often cruel, both to animals and human beings.

Concede a point, but disagree nonetheless

Acknowledge that part of the counterargument is valid, but disagree with the remainder of the argument. For example, Dr. Kline concedes that the animal rights advocates have made scientists "more aware of the needs of these animals, and made us search harder for suitable alternatives." Nevertheless, he warns that limiting further research "will bring about a tragedy that will cost many lives."

Agree and disagree, but take a position

Acknowledge the validity of both sides of the issue, but then claim that one side is the better choice—or the least harmful choice. In Writing Model 2, Kathleen Porter agrees in part with the counterargument, but then expresses her disagreement:

> While it is clear that investment in a college degree, especially for those students in the lowest income brackets, is a financial burden, the long-term benefits to individuals, as well as to society at large, appear to far outweigh the costs.

For writing guides to help you respond to counterarguments, see Appendix A, page 194.

TRY IT OUT! Return to Practice 6 on page 160, in which you framed an argument. Write a full body paragraph in support of one side or the other. But also respond to the counterargument, using or adapting one or more of the guides.

PREPARATION FOR WRITING

The late United States Senator Daniel Patrick Moynihan once said, "Everyone is entitled to his own opinion, but not his own facts." So it is with writing an argument. You cannot simply state your opinion without backing it up. While some of the backing may come from your own personal experience, most will come from facts, figures, and quotations from authorities that you find through research. Likewise, since you should not—indeed cannot—ignore the counterarguments of others, you must anticipate and prepare responses to these counterarguments, which also may arise largely through research.

FINDING SUPPORT FOR YOUR ARGUMENT

Apply the research skills and methods described in Chapters 4, 5, and 6. Narrow your topic, visit the library, and search the Internet.

1. If your Internet searches produce too many irrelevant websites, experiment with different topic headings. Add the phrases "in favor of" or "supporting" (or "against" or "opposing") to the key words in your argument. For example, a Google search using the heading "against cell phones" will likely produce subcategories such as "Against cell phones in school," "Against Cell Phones While Driving," and so on.

(continued on next page)

2. Scan the articles and websites for relevant information. Download (or bookmark) the potentially most useful ones.

3. Look also for cross-references in the articles you have located. These additional sources may prove as useful as, or even more useful than, the ones you began with.

4. Then read the most relevant articles with care, looking for important data and material worth summarizing (especially if you synthesize information from more than one source). On material you download and print or photocopy, highlight or underline sections you might paraphrase or quote.

5. Keep an open mind. Quite often your research will lead you to amend your argument, especially if you discover that the issue is more complicated than you anticipated originally.

6. Use note cards to keep track of your sources and the material you have highlighted.

RESEARCH THE COUNTERARGUMENTS

Apply what you've learned about researching counterarguments.

1. Look carefully at counterarguments mentioned in the materials you have found. Note how the writer rebuts them. These rebuttals may be worth quoting.

2. Do a second Internet search for articles taking the opposing position to yours. Again, you can also add "in favor of" or "against" to the search headings.

3. Again highlight important material. Quote the passages you are going to rebut. Readers may be suspicious that short summaries or mere paraphrases have distorted the person's ideas. Keep the quotations short, however.

4. Now organize your note cards into categories such as "arguments for" and "arguments against."

These research skills apply not only to argumentative essays, but also to the writing of the term paper, which will be discussed in Chapter 9.

TRY IT OUT!   Do an Internet search on Writing Model 1. Find at least three articles in favor of and three articles against the use of animals in research. List the titles and URLs (web locations).

In Favor

1. _____

2. _____

3. _____

Against

1. _____

2. _____

3. _____

Applying Vocabulary: Using Synonyms, 2

Most words in English have more than one grammatical function: as a verb, noun, adjective, or adverb. In most cases, the word changes its form from function to function, but in some cases, it remains the same (for example, the word *love* takes the same form as both a noun and a verb). Using the forms correctly is therefore essential.

PRACTICE 7   **Using Correct Grammatical Forms**

Complete each of the following sentences with the appropriate grammatical form of the word supplied—noun, adjective, or verb. Use your dictionary if necessary.

1. *apathetic:* People are too indifferent to the suffering of the poor. We cannot allow

   such _____*apathy*_____ .

2. *therapy:* This treatment has many _____ effects.

3. *defective:* Each product must be checked carefully for _____ before it is sold to consumers.

4. *impact:* An increase in college tuition greatly _____ most students.

5. *alternative:* The main road is closed, so commuters must take an

   _____ route.

6. *initiative:* The ancient Greeks are thought to have _____ the practice of democracy.

WRITING ASSIGNMENT

Your assignment for this chapter is to write an argumentative essay on a controversial topic. Choose a topic that interests you or that you feel strongly about. Alternatively, you can use one of the topics below. Follow the steps in the writing process.

Possible Topics

- Medical research on animals should be discontinued.
- College tuition should be lowered and paid for by increases in taxes.
- There should be/there should not be quotas on the numbers and specific nationalities of people immigrating to this country.
- Computer use by children and adolescents must be carefully supervised and monitored.

Explore

STEP 1: Explore your topic, audience, and purpose.

- Write a rough draft statement of your position on the topic. You will revise it later, after investigating the issue further.
- Determine who the audience is for your argument. Are these people supportive, neutral, or antagonistic to your position?
- Decide on the goal of your argument. For example, do you want your audience merely to accept your viewpoint or to take some action regarding the issue?
- Research the issue in the library or on the Internet.

 Prewrite

STEP 2: Prewrite to get ideas.

- Brainstorm a list of the main arguments in support of your position. What evidence or examples can you provide—or do you need to find?
- Brainstorm a list of the main arguments that might oppose your position. Consider possible rebuttals to each.
- List the claims of the counterarguments, and brainstorm your responses.

Writing Tip

It may be useful to discuss the issue with another person. Hearing another viewpoint may help you understand and respond to the counterarguments.

Return to your original position statement and make any changes that are needed.

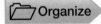 **Organize**

STEP 3: Organize your ideas.

- Use your position statement to write a preliminary thesis statement.
- Make an outline of the arguments and counterarguments based on either point-by-point or block organization.

 Write

STEP 4: Write the first draft.

- In the introductory paragraphs, frame the issue with a summary of the problem and the arguments.
- In the body, develop each claim in support of your position, using examples, facts and figures, and quotations from source material.
- Respond to the counterarguments in ways described in this chapter.
- End with a return to the summary and perhaps a call to action.

Revise

STEP 5: Revise the draft.

- Exchange papers with a partner, and give each other feedback on your papers. Use the Chapter 8 Peer Review on page 239 to guide your feedback.
- Carefully consider your partner's feedback. If you agree with it, revise your paper by marking the changes on your first draft.

 Proofread

STEP 6: Edit and proofread.

- Use the Chapter 8 Writer's Self-Check on page 240 to help you look for and correct errors in grammar, mechanics, and sentence structure.

 Write

STEP 7: Write a new draft.

- Revise the draft, incorporating all the changes you want to make.
- Make sure the draft is legible and follows the format your instructor has provided.
- Proofread the draft so that it is error free.
- Hand in the essay to your instructor.

SELF-ASSESSMENT

In this chapter, you learned to:

○ Analyze two argumentative essays

○ Examine the elements of a well-structured argument

○ Structure an argument using block and point-by-point organization

○ Use modals, phrasal modals, and the subjunctive mode

○ Rebut counterarguments effectively

○ Write, revise, and edit an essay on a controversial issue

Which ones can you do well? Mark them ✓

Which ones do you need to practice more? Mark them ⊗

TIMED WRITING

In this expansion, you will write a short argument in class. You will have 50 minutes. To complete the expansion, you will need to budget your time accordingly. Follow this procedure.

1. Carefully read the writing prompt. Make sure you understand the question or task. Then write a thesis statement reflecting your opinion on the topic. (5 minutes)

2. Brainstorm to generate ideas or make a rough outline to organize your ideas. (5 minutes)

3. Write your argument. Be sure to frame the issue in the opening paragraph, support your main arguments in the body, and respond to the counterarguments. (30 minutes)

4. Check your paper for errors. Correct any mistakes. (10 minutes)

5. Give your paper to your instructor.

Prompt: Should the current grading practices in your school be altered or remain the same? If you think they should change, how should they change, and what effects would these changes have?

> **Writing Tip**
>
> One way to save time in the early stages of writing is to omit the supporting material, inserting short notes to remind you about where to place it in the later stages of the writing process.

 TAKING THE OPPOSITE POSITION

Return to the topic of the Writing Assignment you completed earlier and advocate the opposing side to your argument. Do further research if needed. This task will require that you reverse everything you have done previously: your arguments will now become the counterarguments, and the counterarguments will become your arguments.

RESEARCH PAPERS

To write academic texts, you need to master certain skills.

In this chapter, you will learn to:

- Use point-by-point or source-by-source organization

- Find and evaluate sources

- Synthesize materials from sources

- Cite sources according to MLA and APA formats

- Use the correct sequence of tenses

- Write, edit, and revise a research paper

Mayak is a nuclear processing plant near the city of Chelyabinsk.

Many college or university courses require students to submit a **research paper** at or near the end of the term (for this reason, it is also called a *term paper*). The purpose of a research paper is to exhibit scholarship; that is, to demonstrate your ability to investigate some aspect of the course subject matter in depth. This does not mean merely gathering a collection of what others have written or said about your topic. Instead, it offers an opportunity to examine, compare, synthesize, evaluate, and even challenge these sources so you can reach an informed opinion, or thesis. The thesis you pursue in the research paper should therefore provide new, unexpected, or complex information that goes beyond the general information found in an encyclopedia.

In a sense, the research paper does not differ greatly from the kinds of essays you have done throughout the book. The main difference is in the research paper's formal treatment and acknowledgment of these sources in the body and at the end of your paper. Typically, a research paper is also longer than the essays you have written previously, ranging anywhere from five to twelve pages, or even longer. Since research writing applies to any topic, this chapter will demonstrate this diversity by examining two models about public safety.

ANALYZING THE MODEL

This model addresses an issue that was somewhat personal to the writer, as she grew up a short distance from the place where the incident she discusses occurred.

Read the model. Then answer the questions.

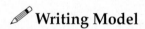 **Writing Model**

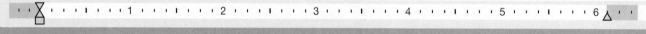

Mayak: The Unknown Disaster
Ksenia Laney[1]

1   The world knows about the Chernobyl disaster in 1986, the only nuclear event that rated the highest-level International Nuclear Event Scale. The event drew great publicity, which eventually contributed to the complete shutdown of the facility in 2000. However, many people are unaware of a comparable catastrophe at another nuclear plant on September 29, 1957, near the city of Chelyabinsk in Russia. The event has had lasting effects on both the population and the environment surrounding the facility.

2   The event is called the Kyshtym disaster, and it happened at Mayak, a nuclear fuel reprocessing plant. The plant was built hastily and secretly in 1945–1948, because its original goal was to produce plutonium for weapons. That time can be called the dawn of Russian nuclear industry because so many technologies were just being developed. However, as Alex Rodriguez states in "Cold War Secrecy's Fallout: In Russian Village, Nuclear Waste Points to Legacy of Neglect," the plant was constructed with many flaws. One such flaw required "workers to clean

---

[1] Ksenia Laney, born Senenko Ksenia Yurievna, is a former student at Truman College in Chicago. She learned of the Kyshtym disaster while she was attending high school in Chelyabinsk, Russia, just fifty-one miles from the Mayak nuclear plant.

by hand the filters that separated plutonium from other, unneeded radioactive isotopes." Other structural mistakes caused explosions of equipment and enormous consecutive spills that quickly filled the waste tanks, which eventually forced the facility officials to dump the waste in the nearby Techa River and later in Lake Karachay (Rodriguez).

3   With so many defects in its construction and maintenance, it is no surprise that in 1957 the cooling system of one of the tanks failed. The failure caused an explosion with a force of about seventy to one hundred tons of the explosive TNT and the release of seventy to eighty tons of radioactive waste. Journalist Alexander Zaitchik reports the memories of the witnesses of the disaster in his article, "Inside the Zone." Villagers heard first the loud boom away from the town and then felt shocks strong enough to rattle plates and crack the windows. As one of his interviewees, Gulchara Isnagilova, who was eleven years old at the time, remembers, "Around the smoke it was the color of sunsets."

4   The beauty of the scene masked the terrible consequences for the people in the area. Soon after the explosion, they began to fall ill, and, even after policemen arrived to "protect" them, citizens never received any explanation for their illnesses. Moreover, children and young people in the area were sent to destroy the contaminated objects: to burn crops, bury animals, and dismantle buildings. As Chelyabinsk state records show, around 1,800 adolescents worked with no protection while cleaning. In recent years after a long court process, the government was forced to compensate those people who could prove to have worked as cleaners at the time. Their compensation was 280 rubles ($11) a month (Zaitchik). Even that meager compensation was not given to people until 1990 because the Soviet government tried to conceal the event, even from the people of the region. The area was renamed the East-Ural Nature Reserve by the government and, therefore, was closed to any unauthorized access (Zaitchik).

5   Officials finally acknowledged the disaster and its effects only thirty-five years later, in 1992. It was then revealed that approximately 800 square kilometers (almost 500 square miles) of inhabited territory were contaminated long-term as a result of the explosion. Zhores A. Medvedev, an ecologist, writes that animals and vegetation suffered radiation damage from nearby stored nuclear waste released by the heat of the explosion.

6   The revelations about the previous spills and explosions eventually followed. It was admitted that a large amount of moderate to highly radioactive waste had been dumped into the Techa River from 1949 to 1956. During its entire existence, the Mayak nuclear unit released about seventy-six million cubic meters of waste into the river, which greatly affected more than 28,000 people in the area (Medvedev). Moreover, the documentary film by Slawomir Grunberg, "Chelyabinsk: The Most Contaminated Spot on the Planet," states: "Russian doctors who study radiation sickness in the area estimate that those living along the Techa River received an average of four times more radiation than the Chernobyl victims." The *BBC* (British Broadcasting Company) *News* also reported that a massive amount of waste had been "pumped from Mayak into a lake that even today is capable of delivering a fatal dose of radiation within an hour." This area is now named East-Ural Radioactive Trace, and its previously fertile soil is no longer used for agriculture (Grunberg).

7   Scientists who compare the Chernobyl and Kyshtym disasters rate Kyshtym one level lower in the International Nuclear Event Scale. However, the level of radiation emitted is less important than the government's treatment of those near the two disasters. The Chernobyl area was largely evacuated after the accident, whereas the survivors of Kyshtym and their descendants still live in the radioactive area. The consequences of this lifelong presence are terrible. "Russians in the region surrounding the plant get thyroid cancer at nearly twice the nation's average rate.

(continued on next page)

The incidence of lung cancer in the Techa region is 70 percent higher than the average for Russia; the rate of colon cancer is 44 percent higher" (Rodriguez). The worst and the saddest effect is on children. Lena Morozova, a villager in the area, comments, "We're all sick. As for the children, I don't know. It's some kind of dying generation" (Grunberg). When Grunberg was making his documentary, he met children fishing on the Techa River. His Geiger counter showed that the fish contained twenty times the normal amount of radiation. He then visited a famous osteopath whose patient told him that many, many children in the area of the Mayak complex are born without hands, legs, and feet. Physiological problems are not the only ones that occur. "At the time of Mayak's construction in the late 40s, mentally handicapped students were a rare occurrence at the school. Today, 80 out of 1,360 students are categorized as having mental handicaps" (Zaitchik).

8   Considering all the terrible consequences of the Mayak explosion, one would expect that, after the Soviet Union dissolved, the plant would be shut down completely. However, this is not the case. Mayak is still working and still dumping all the waste into the river and the lake. Moreover, the majority of the population of the area still lives there, with no meaningful support from the government, experiencing a financial ruin that is sickening and killing the population that radiation did not wipe out already.

Works Cited

"World: Analysis of Dangers of the Soviet Nuclear Legacy." *BBC News,* 23 April 1998.
    Web. 11 Feb 2011. http://news.bbc.co.uk/2/hi/world/analysis/822112.stm.

Grunberg, Slawomir, Dir. *Chelyabinsk: The Most Contaminated Spot on the Planet.*
    LogTV, LTD.: 2005, Film. <http://www.logtv.comlfilms/chelyabinsk/>.

Medvedev, A. Zhores. *Nuclear Disaster in the Urals.* New York: Norton, 1980.

Rodriguez, Alex. "Cold War Secrecy's Fallout: In Russian Village, Nuclear Waste Points
    to Legacy of Neglect." *Chicago Tribune* 20 May 2005, Chicago Final Edition: 1. Print.

Zaitchik, Alexander. "Inside the Zone." *Freezerbox Magazine.* Infocrat, LLC., 17 Oct 2007.
    Web. 28 Feb 2011. <http://www.freezerbox.com/larchive/article. php?id=523>.

Questions about the Model

1. What is the thesis statement of the paper? Circle it.

2. Find the topic sentences in each body paragraph. Which transitional phrases relate to the content of the preceding paragraph? Underline them.

3. Why does Laney make a number of comparisons in her paper?

4. What is the function of the quotations in the paper? Why are they necessary?

5. How is the paper organized—chronologically, topically, or a combination of the two?

6. How does Laney initially identify the sources in the body of the text, and how does she handle a subsequent reference to the same source?

7. Why would readers want to see a list of works cited?

Noticing Vocabulary: Antonyms

An *antonym* is a word with the opposite meaning of another word. As you saw in Chapter 1, some antonyms are formed by adding a negative prefix (*un-*, *im-*, *in-*, *il-*, *ir-*, or *dis-*) to the original word. Other antonyms, such as *slow* and *fast*, are entirely different words. You may use antonyms in writing when you contrast ideas or when you define terms—saying what something means as well as what it does not mean.

Finding Antonyms

Look at the writing model again and find each word in the writing model. Then write its antonym in the space provided. Use a dictionary as needed.

1. unaware *(paragraph 1)* _____aware_____

2. comparable *(paragraph 1)* _____

3. hastily *(paragraph 2)* _____

4. prove *(paragraph 4)* _____

5. dismantle *(paragraph 4)* _____

6. meager *(paragraph 4)* _____

7. contaminated *(paragraph 4)* _____

8. inhabited *(paragraph 5)* _____

9. capable *(paragraph 6)* _____

10. fertile *(paragraph 6)* _____

11. massive *(paragraph 6)* _____

12. descendants *(paragraph 7)* _____

ORGANIZATION

Depending on its audience, purpose, and topic, your paper will be organized in the manner of one of the genres you have studied in previous chapters: classification, process, cause / effect, argument, and definition.

For example, the writing model is a cause / effect paper that examines the multiple causes and effects of the Kyshtym disaster. The writer uses both chronological order (chain organization) and block organization in order to present the sequential events which led to the disaster, and the multiple and non-sequential effects of the disaster.

Additionally, you can organize the body paragraphs either by common key points (**point-by-point** organization) or by source (**source-by-source** organization). As always, the thesis should present the main point or claim on the topic. The body and conclusion should develop the main idea by presenting general points and synthesized information from your sources.

POINT-BY-POINT ORGANIZATION

You are already familiar with this organizational pattern from Chapter 8. As mentioned in that chapter, a point-by-point pattern is particularly well suited to complex issues and longer papers, which makes it a useful way to organize a research paper. A partial diagram of how a point-by-point organization might be used in a research paper looks like this:

Body Paragraphs

The first major point is discussed and then supported by synthesized information/views on this point taken from several sources.

The second major point is discussed in several sources, supported by synthesized information/views on this point from all of them.

The first major point is discussed and then supported by synthesized information/views on this point taken from several sources.

Further major points are developed in later paragraphs using similar support.

SOURCE-BY-SOURCE ORGANIZATION

A source-by-source organization is somewhat similar to a block organizational pattern in that it groups the information in blocks according to the source.

Body Paragraphs

The first few paragraphs contain a summary of key points covered and supported by specific information/views from one source.

The next set of paragraphs contains a summary of key points covered, supported by specific information/views from a second source.

The next set of paragraphs contains a summary of key points covered, supported by specific information/views from a second source.

Further major points are developed in later paragraphs using similar support.

Make sure to connect your sources by discussing related key points and by using transitional phrases to show similarities and differences among the sources. For an example of a source-by-source organizational style, return to the writing model from Chapter 5 on pages 87–89.

Work in pairs or small groups. Read and analyze the short research paper. Decide on its genre (process, definition, argument, and so on) and its organizational pattern.

Problems with Food Labeling
Aksana De Bretto[1]

1   When careful consumers shop for food, they inspect the packaging in order to decide which brands to buy. Each product must include a list of ingredients and a nutrition guide of vitamins and minerals. However, food companies understand that they can entice consumers with other information. Some product packaging claims that the food is "good for you" or can help reduce the risk of heart disease. Two departments of the federal government are responsible for regulating these labeling practices: 1) the United States Department of Agriculture (USDA) and 2) the Food and Drug Administration (FDA). "The USDA handles meat," writes Kent Garber, "and the FDA takes care of pretty much everything else." A growing challenge for these agencies is to ensure that the packaging is not misleading or deceptive.

2   The challenge is not simple. The companies that manufacture and sell food realize that labels are marketing tools. They use key phrases to appeal to consumers' concerns for health, nutrition, and safety. For example, Clare M. Hasler describes how companies used to claim that a certain ingredient or food promoted better heart health. Now those companies must prove that claim before receiving government approval (1217S). In addition to information approved by the USDA and FDA, however, companies may add descriptions that are true but have little value. A typical example in 2008 was the common claim that new products were "natural" (York, et al.). Other examples come from companies that have designed their own slogans or logos stressing the words "low fat" or "low cholesterol" (Hasler 1219S).

3   Such labeling can be incomplete or even misleading. Advertising foods as "natural," even if it is true, can make consumers think less about nutrition and the portion sizes of the food they eat. American Dietetic Association spokeswoman Keri Gans warns that "When someone hears, 'That's natural,' they think 'That's good for me; I can eat as much as I want'" (Eng and Deardorff). An even bigger problem arises if someone wants to know whether the food they eat contains the glutamates known as MSG. It is a food additive that flavors many processed foods, including soups and snacks like Doritos. Food labels might say "MSG Free" or "No MSG," but that only means the manufacturer did not add MSG to the final product. However, "MSG can be present and not listed because it might be part of other ingredients" (Eng and Deardorff).

4   Whether because there is too much information to digest, or because companies try to mislead consumers, the result is that consumers have difficulty understanding the information they read. Hasler examines an FDA study about labeling and concludes: "Evidence to date suggests that this mode of communication has had limited success and in fact may be misleading to consumers with regard to understanding of scientific evidence as well as overall diet choices" (1219S). Labeling is useful only if it is fully understood.

(continued on next page)

---

[1] Aksana De Bretto, whose country of birth was Belarus, is also a former student at Truman College in Chicago.

5   Consumers look to the federal government to regulate food manufacturers, but in many ways the government is not doing enough. Kent Garber reports that the FDA inspects only about one percent of the seafood and fruits imported into the United States. Moreover, one reason companies can still say that foods have no MSG, even when they really do, is that the Department of Health and Human Services has never enacted an FDA's 1996 proposed requirement in ingredient labeling (Eng and Deardorff). Privately developed slogans, like Pepsi's "Smart Spot" and Kraft's "sensible solutions" logo, were the subject of a 2007 public hearing organized by the FDA (Hasler). The USDA only recently dictated that meat raised without hormones or antibiotics, and that had never been fed animal byproducts, could be labeled "natural" (York, et al.). However, this ruling applies only to meat. Many other foods still can claim to be natural. The main agencies responsible for regulating labeling are still developing policies while the food manufacturers fight to stay a step ahead of them.

6   According to Garber, one way the government agencies try to cope with this battle is to allow third parties to do some of the work for them. "The responsibility for food safety, as it works today, lies heavily in private hands," Garber explains. Food companies hire "food safety consultants." However, the problem is that "For one thing, there's no certification system for these third-party inspectors." And the companies that use them often operate under voluntary, rather than required, guidelines for sanitation and inspection (Garber).

7   One result of this loose system is that consumers are unknowingly exposed to ingredients that are not yet clearly understood. Researchers are still not certain about the effects of MSG. They cite a 1990 FDA study that showed it could damage nerve cells in the brain and another study from 1995 that showed "though most people can eat MSG safely, 'an unknown percentage' may suffer from 'chest pain, headaches, nausea, rapid heartbeat and drowsiness'"(Eng and Deardorff).

8   In at least one way, though, private industry may be self-regulating for purely self-interested reasons. Claims that foods are "natural," for example, can be disputed to the Better Business Bureau. York, Zmuda, and Miley note that "the complaints are generally raised for competitive reasons." In other words, if a company is trying to stretch the truth in labeling a product, a competitor will likely cite the deception even if consumers do not. But the Better Business Bureau does not regulate our foods and is not accountable for our safety from hazardous or misleading products. Until the government can do a better job of ensuring that our food is safe and we are honestly told what it contains, we consumers will continue to have difficulty understanding how to make better food choices.

Works Cited

Eng, Monica and Julie Deardorff. "Navigating the MSG maze; FDA says the popular food additive is safe. But what about the chest pains, headaches and rapid heartbeat 'an unknown percentage' experiences?" *Chicago Tribune* 24 Nov 2008: 4. Print.

Garber, Kent. "Food Safety's Dirty Little Secret; Increasingly, the government is leaving the job in private hands." *U.S. News & World Report* 15 Sept 2008: 27. Print.

Hasler, Clare M. "Health Claims in the United States: An Aid to the Public or a Source of Confusion?" *The Journal of Nutrition* 138.6 (June 2008): 1216S-1220S. Print.

York, Emily Bryson, Natalie Zmuda, and Marissa Miley. "Marketers slap 'natural' label even on foods such as pizza." *Advertising Age* 19 Jan. 2009: 44. Print.

When writing a research paper, you will need to paraphrase ideas. When you paraphrase, remember to be careful with the sequence of verb tenses, especially with complex sentences that express time relationships. In complex sentences, these verb tenses fall into a sequence.

SEQUENCE OF TENSES

Use a present simple *verb*, not a future tense verb, in dependent clauses of time, usually beginning with *after*, *before*, or *once*. Use the future-tense verb in the independent clause, as in these examples:

After a nuclear plant **has** an accident, the cleanup **will be** very dangerous.

The plant **will be** carefully inspected **before** it **resumes** operation.

Once the construction **is finished**, the building **will be** ready for occupancy.

Use a present simple tense verb or a present perfect tense verb in dependent clauses establishing a future condition, usually beginning with *if* or *unless*. Again, the verb in the independent clause is in the future tense.

If the site **is** still radioactive, it **will not resume** operation.

No food **will be** safe to eat in the area **unless** the ground **is** free of radiation.

No car **will be allowed** on the road **unless** it **has passed** a thorough safety inspection.

It is also helpful to know that according to custom, specific genres of academic writing often use certain verb tenses more frequently than others:

RULES	EXAMPLES
1. The *present simple tense* (such as *show* and *shows*) is often used in abstracts, summaries, and reports on findings.	Aksana De Bretto describes the aftermath of a devastating nuclear reaction.
2. The *past simple tense* (such as *discovered* and *found*) is often used to relate details of experiments.	Scientists found the level of radiation to be extremely high.
3. The *present perfect tense* (such as *has/have done*) is used to describe ongoing processes that began in the past, to refer to completed events in the indefinite past, and to refer to sources in ongoing debates.	Researchers have reported a number of significant problems. Stephen D. Krashen (2004) has emphasized critically important practices in second language learning.
4. The *present/past progressive tense* (*is doing/was doing*) is used with adverbs such as *always*, *continually*, *sometimes*, or *often* to discuss repeated events.	Researchers are continually reviewing their findings. Marie and Pierre Curie were always underestimating the toxic effects of radiation.

Writing Verbs in the Correct Tense Sequence

Complete each sentence with the correct tense. Make sure the verb in the dependent clause is in the present tense, or the verb in the main clause is in the future.

1. Careful consumers will buy packaged food only after *they have examined the list of ingredients.*

2. Many people think that if vegetables are not labeled "organic," _____

3. The manufacturer will take a product off the shelves if consumers _____

4. A nuclear reactor will be dangerous if _____

5. After a major flood occurs, _____

6. Young people will likely get good jobs after _____

Writing Complex Sentences

Write five complex sentences using the words supplied. The independent clause in each sentence must contain the modal verb *will*.

1. If/sell _____

2. After/receive _____

3. Before/take _____

4. Unless/stop _____

5. Once/begin _____

You have already learned basic research practices in Chapter 4, page 79. Now you can build on them. Begin your research on the topic by asking yourself a question. Here are some examples.

- Have experts discovered new findings on the topic?
- Is there a debate on this topic that you should explain to readers?
- Do new studies on the topic challenge or change previously held beliefs?
- Has research revealed an important problem that is worth exploring and discussing causes or solutions that people may not have considered before?

Think about the writing model and the research questions Ksenia Laney may have asked herself when she started her research. For example, how and why did the disaster happen? What were its effects on the people, the crops, and the animals surrounding the facility?

NARROWING YOUR FOCUS

The next step is to ensure that your research question is not too broad; otherwise, you may end up writing a book instead of a five- to twelve-page paper! Note how these broad research questions have been narrowed:

TOO BROAD   What are the causes of obesity?

NARROWER   Do carbohydrates contribute more to obesity than other food groups?

TOO BROAD   What is autism?

NARROWER   Why is autism so difficult to treat?

TOO BROAD   Are artificial sweeteners dangerous?

NARROWER   What has research revealed about the long-term effects of aspartame?

PRACTICE 5   **Forming and Narrowing Research Questions**

Work in small groups. Choose a topic and generate possible research questions to pursue. Remember to ask questions that begin with *how? when? where? why? who?* and *should?* or *could?* Decide if your research question is sufficiently narrow.

TOPICS
- College admissions standards and the makeup of U.S. colleges and universities
- The wave of immigration to the United States that occurred from 1989 to the present
- Down syndrome
- Medical technology
- Music therapy for mentally or physically impaired people

Finding Information from Sources

Once you have narrowed your research question, use only sources that relate to the question, and read selectively. In books, consult the table of contents or the index to help you find the most relevant parts. Scan long articles, looking especially at the subheadings. Follow this procedure.

1. Be curious as you read, and ask yourself: Is the information important and usable in this paper? Does it raise more questions to explore? What additional research might answer these questions?

2. Annotate as you read. Underline important passages, highlight key points, and make notes in the margin about how and where the information might be used in your paper. Take notes and record your sources, along with the page numbers, on note cards. (See Chapter 6, pages 120–123.)

3. If you print out material, make notes directly on these pages. Highlight passages you may want to quote or paraphrase. Use note cards to jot down a brief summary of each important passage, abbreviate a source (using either the title or the author), and record the page numbers so you can return to them later in the original.

4. Again use note cards to write your own commentary on source material. Make sure, however, that you clearly distinguish that commentary from your source information.

5. Then organize your note cards by subtopics, especially by grouping the evidence that supports the claim of each subtopic.

Evaluating Sources

Not every source is reliable or objective. Many writers reveal a particular point of view or bias. Even the data they include or the people they quote may be influenced by their political, philosophical, or theoretical viewpoints. Moreover, with the growth of Internet use, virtually anyone can create a website, author a blog, or post an entry on a blog. Therefore, it is extremely important that you evaluate your sources for their reliability, objectivity, and stance on the issue you are researching. Keep the following guidelines in mind.

Timeliness

Your subject matter will determine whether a work is outdated. For scientific, psychological, sociological, and technical issues, the most recent publications generally provide the most useful information. However, if you are researching the life of a famous politician, author, or historical figure, older publications may be perfectly good sources of information.

Objectivity and Bias

Authors often have strong feelings about their subject matter, or even a financial or personal interest in the issue. Strongly worded opinions, though, do not necessarily mean that the author is unfair. The main test is whether the person's argument is balanced, giving equal, or nearly equal, treatment to more than one side of an issue.

Tone

When an author expresses opinions strongly, does he or she use language that is reasonable, or is it highly emotional, even angry? Does the author insult his or her opponents? These are all clues to the author's bias, degree of objectivity, and concern for balance.

The Publication

Many magazines, some newspapers, and some radio and television shows consistently exhibit a particular bias, especially in political matters. A useful practice in evaluating a source, therefore, is to examine other titles or headlines of several articles from the source. Do they reveal a consistent theme or viewpoint?

Reputation of the Author

Gather information about the author to determine his or her bias. Read the dustcover of a book or the author information in an ebook blurb to find out his or her biographical details. Is the person a recognized expert? Use a search engine to find out more information. For example, go to the author's website if he or she has one. Find out what other things the author has written.

PRACTICE 6   **Evaluating a Source**

Ⓐ Work with a partner. Return to one of these Writing Models: Chapter 2, pages 22–24; Chapter 5, pages 87–89; or Chapter 6, pages 110–112. Formulate a research question about the topic.

Ⓑ Working in pairs, find an article that relates to your question.

Ⓒ Work in small groups. Discuss how reliable your article is. Use the questions to help you evaluate it.

- What is the main point of the article?
- Who is the intended audience for this source?
- What kinds of evidence is the author using? Does the evidence seem reliable? Why or why not?
- Are there any statements you want to question? Do the author's claims and conclusions seem reliable? Why or why not?

TRY IT OUT!   For practice in identifying bias, look up "Benedict Arnold" in the *Encyclopedia Americana* or *The World Book Encyclopedia* and *Encyclopedia Britannica* and compare the entries. What is emphasized about Arnold in each? Write a one-paragraph summary of both and then explain why they differ so greatly.

DEVELOPING AN EFFECTIVE THESIS STATEMENT

After completing your research, you should formulate a thesis statement. The statement should take a debatable position; that is, it should take a side on an issue, not merely report facts or assemble quotations. You will need to:

- Build on your research question.

- Consider your intention and purpose for writing. Are you:
  - exposing a problem and offering solutions?
  - examining causes of the problem and its effects?
  - defining concepts?
  - examining arguments for and against a concept?
  - analyzing the consequences of an action?
  - weighing two sides of a debate?
  - offering a critique of an established theory or commonly held belief?

- Determine the scope of your thesis statement. Make sure it calls attention to a *specific* aspect of the topic and research; the thesis should not be too broad or too narrow in scope.

- Make sure the thesis indicates the reasoning behind your position. Why is this point worth arguing? Why is it important?

PRACTICE 7 **Evaluating Thesis Statements**

Work in small groups. Decide if each thesis statement is focused and clear. Write *G (good)* or *TB (too broad)*. Then suggest ways that the topics that are too broad could be narrowed.

_____ 1. Many sociologists, economists, journalists, and other experts have documented the positive effects that early immigrants have had on the United States. From these findings, it is clear that if recent immigrants affect the economy in ways similar to those of earlier immigrants, then they will prove to be assets rather than burdens on the country.

_____

_____

_____ 2. We should protect the health of the state's natural resources.

_____

_____

_____ 3. A university is a resource center for those who want the opportunity to develop their intellectual powers and lead more productive, useful, and fulfilling lives.

_____

_____

_____ **4.** Are U.S. policies toward Cuban immigrants fair?

_____

_____

_____ **5.** Some parents, educators, and psychologists fear that television commercials encourage children to eat bad foods, but advertisers disagree.

_____

_____

DOCUMENTING RESEARCH

As you incorporate the results of your research into your paper—whether through summary, paraphrase, or quotation—you must also document the sources. You do so for three important reasons:

- to establish that you have conducted careful research
- to allow readers to consult the original sources if they choose
- to avoid plagiarism

PRACTICE 8 **Examining a Works Cited Page**

Return to the paper on pages 175–176. Examine the Works Cited list and answer these questions.

1. In the first and fourth entries, why are the first and last names of the first author reversed but not the names of the other authors?

2. Which titles are placed in quotation marks, and which titles are in italics? Why?

3. As a general rule, where are periods placed in the entries? Where are they not?

4. Where do the page numbers appear in each entry?

5. In the third entry, why is the publication date in parentheses, but not in the other entries?

6. If the entries included the word *Web* instead of *Print*, what would that mean?

Ways of Citing Sources

The two most commonly used formats for documenting sources are those of the Modern Language Association (MLA) and the American Psychological Association (APA). Your instructor will tell you which format to use in your research paper. This chapter provides only a brief overview of both. However, you can find much more complete information on these formats in Appendix G on pages 212–220. Additionally, you might use one of the many citation machines on the Internet, which will construct source information correctly in either format. As the time of this writing, a few of the many choices include "Son of Citation Machine," "Bibme," Easybib," "Citefast," and "Citeomatic," and "Zotero."

The general principle of documentation is that whenever you quote or paraphrase source material, you must provide enough information in the text so that readers can locate the full source in the Works Cited section at the end of the paper.

The MLA Format

The MLA style is mainly used to write papers and cite sources in the liberal arts and humanities, which include subjects such as literature, philosophy, and art.

In-text citations (referring to the source in the text of your paper) of paraphrases or quotations should include the article title and the author's name in the sentence and page number, if it is relevant, in parentheses, followed by a period. Information in the humanities does not change very often. Therefore the verb introducing the material is in the present tense, implying that it still relates to the present. Here is an example from the writing model on page 170:

> However, as Alex Rodriguez states in "Cold War Secrecy's Fallout: In Russian Village, Nuclear Waste Points to Legacy of Neglect," the plant was constructed with many flaws. One such flaw required "workers to clean by hand the filters that separated plutonium from other, unneeded radioactive isotopes."

Because the source is only one page, no page number is cited.

For Works Cited citations of print materials, follow this general format:

Author's last name, first name. "Title of Article." *Title of Book* or *Source*. City of publication if available. Publisher's Name (abbreviated), Date of publication. Print.

The APA Format

The APA style is used for writing research papers in the social sciences, such as sociology, psychology, anthropology, economics, political science, and history.

For in-text citations in APA format, include the author's name and the year of publication, along with the page number if the material is quoted. Material in the sciences changes all the time. Therefore, the verb introducing the material is in the past tense or present perfect tense; this indicates that other information may be older or more recent.

BEGINNING OF SENTENCE   William Smith (2009) argued that stronger consumer protection laws are essential to prevent misleading advertising.

END OF SENTENCE   It has been argued that stronger consumer laws are essential to prevent misleading advertising (Smith, 2009).

The general format for References for print materials in APA style looks like this:

Last name of author, Initial of first name. Date of Publication. Title of Article (not quoted or italicized). *Title of Book*. Place of Publication: Abbreviated Publisher's Name.

For more information on MLA and APA format, see Appendix G on page 212.

Using the writing model on pages 170–172 to direct you, write a mini-research paper (no more than 500 words). Include a Works Cited or Reference page. This page will include only one source.

Choose one of these topics and consult an encyclopedia for information. The thesis of your paper is simply to justify why this subject deserves to be included in an encyclopedia. Summarize, paraphrase, quote, and document the source using either MLA or APA format.

TOPICS

Jane Addams	James Madison
John Wilkes Booth	NASDAQ
Indira Gandhi	Tai Chi
Stephen Hawking	Tecumseh

Applying Vocabulary: Using Antonyms

Before you begin your writing assignment, review the information you learned about antonyms earlier in the chapter. Remember that an antonym expresses the opposite meaning of another word.

PRACTICE 9 Using Antonyms

Complete each sentence with an antonym of a word in the word box. Use *in-* or *un-* to form the antonym where possible. Use your dictionary as needed.

aware	capable	fertile	inhabited	meager

1. Although many people still live in the area around Mayak, it should be

   _____ .

2. Hardly anything will grow in the area, for the radiation has made the soil

   _____ .

3. The government should have given the residents of the area

   a(n) _____ compensation.

4. The residents were _____ of the danger the radiation created for them until much later.

5. After the nuclear disaster in Japan in 2011, some people think the companies that

   construct nuclear reactors are _____ of ensuring their safety.

WRITING ASSIGNMENT

Your writing assignment for this chapter is to write a research paper of five or more pages on a topic of your choice or on one that your teacher will provide. Follow the steps in the writing process.

 Explore

STEP 1: Explore your topic, audience, and purpose.

- Do some preliminary research of the issue in the library or on the Internet.
- Select and evaluate at least five sources from books, articles, and the Internet. Is there sufficient information on the topic? Record the sources on note cards.
- Decide on the audience for your paper: Who would be most interested in the subject matter?
- Formulate an arguable thesis statement and submit it to your teacher for approval. Revise the statement if necessary.

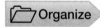 **Prewrite**

STEP 2: Prewrite to get ideas.

- Return to the sources you have located, as well as additional sources that your research leads you to.
- Take notes on your note cards, or highlight important information on photocopies and cross-reference it on note cards.

Organize

STEP 3: Organize your ideas.

- Outline your paper. Begin by returning to your initial thesis statement and revising it as necessary.
- Choose an organizational structure.
- In the body of the outline, include drafts of topic sentences, and include notes on the placement of material from sources.

 Write

STEP 4: Write the first draft.

- Frame the issue in the first paragraph and state an arguable thesis.
- Develop the claims of your body paragraphs with quotations, paraphrasing, and/or summary—or references to note cards that contain this information to include in the final draft.
- Cite sources both in the text and in a Works Cited page at the end of the paper using either the MLA or APA format.

> **Writing Tip**
>
> When writing the first draft, you need not copy all the information you wish to quote or paraphrase. Just write the number of the note card on which the information appears. You can add the quotations or paraphrases when you return to the draft in the final stages of writing. You can also use a computer's *copy* and *paste* commands to insert materials you quote directly from an Internet source.

Revise

STEP 5: Revise the draft.

- Exchange papers with a partner, and give each other feedback on your papers. Use the Chapter 9 Peer Review on page 241 to guide your feedback.
- Carefully consider your partner's feedback. If you agree with it, revise your paper by marking the changes on your first draft.
- If necessary, rewrite the first paragraph so it frames the issue clearly and establishes an arguable thesis.
- Revise body paragraphs for clarity and additional support if needed.
- Ensure that quotations and paraphrases fit smoothly and logically into your text.
- Add or revise transitions where they are needed.

 Proofread

STEP 6: Edit and proofread.

- Use the Chapter 9 Writer's Self-Check on page 242 to help you look for and correct errors in grammar, mechanics, and sentence structure.

 Write

STEP 7: Write a new draft.

- Revise the draft, incorporating all the changes you want to make.
- Make sure the draft is legible and follows the format your instructor has provided.
- Proofread the draft so that it is error free.
- Hand in the research paper to your instructor.

SELF-ASSESSMENT

In this chapter, you learned to:

○ Use point-by-point or source-by-source organization

○ Find and evaluate sources

○ Synthesize materials from sources

○ Cite sources according to MLA and APA formats

○ Use the correct sequence of tenses

○ Write, edit, and revise a research paper

Which ones can you do well? Mark them ☑

Which ones do you need to practice more? Mark them ⊘

TIMED WRITING

In this expansion, you will write a two-paragraph essay in response to a short essay or article (no more than one page). Incorporate at least one quotation and one paraphrase, and correctly cite the sources both in the text and at the end of your paper. Your instructor will choose the article. You will have 55 minutes. To complete the expansion, you will need to budget your time accordingly. Follow this procedure.

1. Read, highlight, and take notes on the article. (10 minutes)

2. Write a thesis statement indicating your opinion on the article's main point. (5 minutes)

3. Brainstorm or outline to generate and organize your ideas. (10 minutes)

4. Write your response. Summarize the article in the introductory paragraph and end the paragraph with your thesis statement. Follow with the response in a separate paragraph. Include both a quotation and paraphrase, and cite the sources both in the text and in a full citation at the end of the paper. (25 minutes)

5. Check your paragraphs for errors. Correct any mistakes. (5 minutes)

6. Give your paper to your instructor.

 EVALUATING SOURCES

Choose a social issue that is being widely discussed and debated. Find three sources on the Internet that address the issue and note the author's name (if one is given) along with the organization or sponsor of the website. Then search the Internet to find out more about the author's background and political views, and do the same for the organization or sponsor. Do they have a particular political or other kind of bias? List the sources and a short description of what you find, and discuss your results with a small group of classmates or the whole class. Give your list to your instructor.

APPENDIX A   WRITING GUIDES

The following are *writing guides*, or fill-in-the-blank sentences that can help you establish logical relationships as you write. These guides will provide you with models of wording that will make the introduction of ideas or the transition between ideas smoother. At times, you may wish to use the exact wording in the guides. At other times, you will probably need to change the language to fit your content and purpose.

Chapter 2

Guides for Reporting Statistical Results

1. Most _____ are from _____.

2. A lot of / twelve of the _____ lived _____.

3. The majority/_____ percent of the students speak _____ languages.

Guides for Thesis Statements

1. My classmates are similar in _____ ways.

2. My classmates differ in _____, _____, _____, and _____.

3. Despite many differences in their backgrounds, my classmates share _____.

Chapter 3

Guides for Describing a Process

1. The process starts when _____ .

2. Following this <u>initial / second / third</u> step, you may proceed to

   _____ .

3. Once this <u>process / operation / procedure</u> <u>is / was</u> completed, the next

   _____ <u>is / was</u> _____ .

4. The final step in the process involves _____ .

5. In summary, _____ .

Chapter 4

Guides for Introducing a Cause

1. The first cause of _____ <u>was / may have been</u> _____ .

2. One source of _____ was _____ .

3. In addition, _____ probably resulted from _____

   _____ .

4. Why did _____ happen? One possibility is that _____

   _____ .

Guides for Introducing an Effect

1. One <u>effect / result</u> of _____ was that _____ .

2. As a result, _____ probably occurred _____

   _____ .

3. These <u>causes / events</u> led to _____ .

Chapter 5

Guides for Defining by Synonym and Apposition

1. [Term being defined], or [synonym], is important because _____
   _____.

2. [Term being defined], that is, [synonym], plays a role in _____
   _____.

3. What is [term being defined]? It is / means _____
   _____.

Guides for Defining by Formal Definition

1. [Term being defined], is/ means something/someone that _____
   _____.

2. [Term being defined], can be defined as something that _____
   _____.

Guides for Defining by Negation

1. [Term being defined] is not _____; instead, it is
   _____.

Chapter 6

Guides for Introducing and Explaining a Problem

1. A (serious) problem today is _____
   _____.

2. The danger of _____ is increasing because _____
   _____.

3. One of the most important problems / obstacles / difficulties facing
   _____ today regards _____ .

Guides for Introducing and Explaining a Solution

1. The solution to _____ is / may be _____.

2. How can this problem be solved? One way / The best way is to _____

   _____.

3. Some solutions / A possible solution include(s) _____

   _____.

Guides for Introducing Agreement between Sources

1. [Author X]'s claim is supported by data / a survey from [Author Y] in [title

   of source].

2. In [title of source], [Author X] largely agrees with [Author Y].

3. In [title of source], [Author X] cites several examples that back up

   [Author Y]'s argument. For instance, _____

   _____.

Guides for Introducing Disagreement between Sources

1. Sources / Scientists / Experts disagree on the issue. For instance, [Author X]

   reports in [title of first source], that _____, while [Author Y]

   contends / asserts in [title of second source] that _____.

2. There is more than one interpretation / explanation of the issue / problem.

   In [title of first source], [Author X] states / maintains, "[quotation from

   source]." However, a study in [title of second source] by [Author Y] shows

   that _____.

Chapter 7

Guides for Introducing a Summary

1. In [title being summarized], [Author X] argues that _____
_____.

2. In his recent book, [title being summarized], [Author Y], a professor of
linguistics at _____ University, describes the results of
his research into _____.

3. [Author Z], in [title being summarized], describes her early and difficult
encounters with _____.

Guides for Introducing Responses

1. I agree with the author's viewpoint because _____.
For instance, _____.

2. I disagree / cannot agree with the thesis of this article based on my own
experience.

3. Although I accept that _____, I cannot
accept the claim that _____.

Chapter 8

Guides for Framing an Issue

1. In [title of source], [Author X] largely agrees with [Author Y].

2. The issue is whether _____. On the one
hand, [Author X] contends that _____. On the other hand,
[Author Y] argues that _____.

3. Many people believe that _____ is true / wrong /
dangerous / foolish. However, I / other people disagree.

Guides for Agreeing with a Counterargument

1. I agree with [Author X] because _____ .

2. My own experience supports this viewpoint.

Guides for Rebutting a Counterargument

1. I disagree because _____ .

2. The facts do not support this argument. For example, _____

    _____ .

3. This argument is based on the wrong assumptions, such as that _____

    _____ .

Guides for Conceding a Point to the Opposition

1. [Author X] is partially correct. However, he / she overlooks

    _____ .

2. I can see both sides of this issue. On the one hand, _____

    _____ . On the other hand, _____ .

Coordinators

Coordinating conjunctions connect grammatically equal elements. One way to remember the seven coordinating conjunctions is to use the expression "Fan Boys." Each letter of the expression represents the first letter of one of the conjunctions: *for, and, nor, but, or, yet, so.*

CONJUNCTION	FUNCTION	EXAMPLE
for	Connects a reason to a result	I am a little hungry, **for** I didn't eat breakfast this morning.
and	Connects equal similar ideas	John likes to fish **and** hunt.
nor	Connects two negative sentences	She does not eat meat, **nor** does she drink milk.
but	Connects equal different ideas	I like to eat fish **but** not to catch them.
or	Connects two equal choices	Do you prefer coffee **or** tea?
yet	Connects equal contrasting ideas	It is sunny **yet** cold.
so	Connects a result to a reason	I did not eat breakfast this morning, **so** I am a little hungry.

Correlative (Paired) Conjunctions

Correlative conjunctions are always in pairs. Like coordinating conjunctions, they connect grammatically equal elements. (Please also read the section Using Parallelism on page 77.)

CONJUNCTION PAIRS	EXAMPLE
both . . . and	**Both** San Francisco **and** Sydney have beautiful harbors.
not only . . . but also	Japanese food is **not only** delicious to eat **but also** beautiful to look at.
either . . . or	Bring **either** a raincoat **or** an umbrella when you visit Seattle.
neither . . . nor	My grandfather could **neither** read **nor** write, but he was a very wise person.
whether . . . or	The newlyweds could not decide **whether** to live with her parents **or** to rent an apartment.

Subordinators

A subordinator is the first word in a dependent clause. The following charts illustrate some common subordinators.

SUBORDINATORS FOR ADVERB CLAUSES

TIME (WHEN?)	
after	**After** we ate lunch, we decided to go shopping.
as, just as	**Just as** we left the house, it started to rain.
as long as	We waited **as long as** we could.
as soon as	**As soon as** the front door closed, I looked for my house key.
before	I thought I had put it in my coat pocket **before** we left.
since	I have not locked myself out of the house **since** I was 10 years old.
until	**Until** I was almost 12, my mother pinned the key to my coat.
when	**When** I turned 12, my mother let me keep the key in my pocket.
whenever	I usually put the key in the same place **whenever** I come home.
while	**While** I searched for the key, it rained harder and harder.

PLACE (WHERE?)	
where	I like to shop **where** prices are low.
wherever	I try to shop **wherever** there is a sale.
anywhere	You can find bargains **anywhere** you shop.
everywhere	I use my credit card **everywhere** I shop.

MANNER (HOW?)	
as, just as	I love to get flowers(,) **as** many people do.*
as if	You look **as if** you didn't sleep at all last night.
as though	She acts **as though** she doesn't know us.

DISTANCE (HOW FAR? HOW NEAR? HOW CLOSE?)	
as + (adverb) + as	We will hike **as far as** we can before it turns dark.
	The child sat **as close as** she could to her mother.
	The child sat **as close** to her mother **as** she could.

FREQUENCY (HOW OFTEN?)	
as often as	I call my parents **as often as** I can.

REASON (WHY?)	
as	I can't take evening classes(,) **as** I work at night.*
because	I can't take evening classes **because** I work at night.
since	I can't take evening classes **since** I work at night.

PURPOSE (FOR WHAT PURPOSE?)	
so that	Many people emigrate **so that** their children can have a better life.
in order that	Many people emigrate **in order that** their children can have a better life.

RESULT (WITH WHAT RESULT?)	
so + (adjective) + that	I was **so tired** last night **that** I fell asleep at dinner.
so + (adverb) + that	She talks **so softly that** the other students cannot hear her.
such a(n) + (adjective) + (noun) + that	It was **such an easy test that** most of the students got A's.
so much/many/little/few + (noun) + that	He is taking **so many classes that** he has no time to sleep.

CONDITION (UNDER WHAT CONDITION?)	
if	We will not go hiking **if** it rains.
unless	We will not go hiking **unless** the weather is perfect.

PARTIAL CONTRAST	
although	I love my brother **although** we disagree about almost everything.
even though	I love my brother **even though** we disagree about almost everything.
though	I love my brother **though** we disagree about almost everything.

CONTRAST (DIRECT OPPOSITES)	
while	My brother likes classical music, **while** I prefer hard rock.
whereas	He dresses conservatively, **whereas** I like to be a little shocking.

*This is an exception to the usual rule for commas. Many writers use a comma before *as*.

SUBORDINATORS FOR ADJECTIVE CLAUSES

The first word in an adjective clause is usually a relative pronoun or relative adverb. However, when the relative pronoun is the object of the clause, it can sometimes be omitted.

TO REFER TO PEOPLE	
who, whom	People **who** live in glass houses should not throw stones. My parents did not approve of the man (**whom**) my sister married.
whose	An orphan is a child **whose** parents are dead.
that (informal)	The man **that** is on the left in the photo is my brother.

TO REFER TO ANIMALS AND THINGS	
which	My new computer, **which** I bought yesterday, stopped working today.
that	Yesterday I received an email (**that**) I did not understand.

TO REFER TO A TIME OR A PLACE	
when	Thanksgiving is a time **when** families travel great distances to be together.
where	An orphanage is a place **where** orphans live.

Noun clauses are introduced by the words *that*, *if*, or *whether* or by a *Wh-* word.

THAT CLAUSES	
that	Do you believe **that** there is life in outer space?
IF / WHETHER CLAUSES	
whether	I can't remember **whether** I locked the door.
whether or not	I can't remember **whether or not** I locked the door.
whether . . . or not	I can't remember **whether** I locked the door **or not**.
if	I can't remember **if** I locked the door.
if . . . or not	I can't remember **if** I locked the door **or not**.
QUESTION CLAUSES	
who, whoever, whom	**Whoever** arrives at the bus station first should buy the tickets.
which, what	Do you know **which** bus we need to take?
where, when, why, how	We should ask **when** the bus arrives.
how much, how many	Do not worry about **how much** they cost.
how long, how often, etc.	He didn't care **how long** he had to wait.

Notice that some subordinators can introduce different kinds of dependent clauses. *That* can introduce either noun clauses or adjective clauses, and *where* can introduce a noun, an adjective, or an adverb clause. It normally is not important to know the kind of clause.

I can't remember **where** I put the house key.
(noun clause; direct object of *remember*)

It's not in the place **where** I usually put it.
(adjective clause; tells *which place*)

I always put it **where** I will see it when I go out the front door.
(adverb clause; tells *where I put it*)

Conjunctive Adverbs

Conjunctive adverbs can appear at the beginning, in the middle, or at the end of one independent clause, but we often use them to connect two independent clauses.

Remember to put a semicolon before and a comma after the conjunctive adverb if an independent clause follows.

CONJUNCTIVE ADVERBS	FUNCTION	EXAMPLE
also, besides, furthermore, in addition, moreover	To add a similar idea	Community colleges offer preparation for many jobs; **in addition**, they prepare students to transfer to four-year colleges.
however, nevertheless, nonetheless, still	To add an unexpected or surprising continuation	The cost of attending a community college is low; **however**, many students need financial aid.
in contrast, on the other hand	To add a complete contrast	Most community colleges do not have dormitories; **in contrast**, most four-year colleges do.
as a result, consequently, therefore, thus	To add a result	Native and nonnative English speakers have different needs; **as a result**, most schools provide separate classes for each group.
meanwhile, afterward, then, subsequently	To list ideas in chronological order	Police kept people away from the scene of the accident; **meanwhile**, ambulance workers tried to pull victims out of the wreck. The workers put five injured people into an ambulance; **afterward**, they found another victim.
for example, for instance	To give an example	Colors can have different meanings; **for example**, white is the color of weddings in some cultures and of funerals in others.
similarly, likewise	To show similarities	Hawaii has sunshine and friendly people; **similarly**, Mexico's weather is sunny and its people hospitable.
instead, on the contrary, rather	To indicate an alternative	The medicine did not make him feel better; **instead**, it made him feel worse.
instead	To indicate a substitution	They had planned to go to Hawaii on their honeymoon; **instead**, they went to Mexico. We ordered hamburgers; they brought us pizza **instead**.*
on the other hand, alternatively	To give another possibility	You can live in a dorm on campus; **on the other hand**, you can rent a room with a family off campus.
otherwise	To give a result, often bad (meaning "if not")	Students must take final exams; **otherwise**, they will receive a grade of Incomplete.
in other words, that is	To add an explanation	Some cultures are matriarchal; **in other words**, the mothers are the head of the family.
indeed, in fact	To make a statement stronger	Mangoes are a very common fruit; **indeed**, people eat more mangoes than any other fruit in the world.

* When it indicates substitution, *instead* can go at the end of the sentence.

Transition Signals

Transition Signals and Conjunctive Adverbs	Coordinators and Paired Conjunctions	Subordinators	Others: Adjectives, Prepositions, Verbs
To list ideas in order of time			
first, . . . first of all, . . . second, . . . third, . . . next, . . . then . . . after that, . . . meanwhile, . . . in the meantime, . . . finally, . . . last, . . . last of all, . . . subsequently, . . .		before after until when while as soon as since	the first (reason, cause, step, etc.) the second . . . the third . . . another . . . the last . . . the final . . .
To list ideas in order of importance			
first, . . . first of all, . . . first and foremost, . . . second, . . . more important, . . . most important, . . . more significant, . . . most significant, . . . above all, . . . most of all, . . .			the first . . . (reason, cause, step, etc.) an additional . . . the second . . . another . . . a more important (reason, cause, step, etc.) the most important . . . the most significant . . . the best/the worst . . .
To add a similar or equal idea			
also, . . . besides, . . . furthermore, . . . in addition, . . . moreover, . . . too as well	and both . . . and not only . . . but also		another . . . (reason, cause, step, etc.) a second . . . an additional . . . a final . . . as well as

Transition Signals and Conjunctive Adverbs	Coordinators and Paired Conjunctions	Subordinators	Others: Adjectives, Prepositions, Verbs
To add an opposite idea			
however, . . . on the other hand, . . . nevertheless, . . . nonetheless, . . . still, . . .	but yet	although even though though	despite in spite of
To explain or restate an idea			
in other words, . . . in particular, . . . (more) specifically, . . . that is, . . .			
To make a statement stronger			
indeed, . . . in fact, . . .			
To give another possibility			
alternatively, . . . on the other hand, . . . otherwise, . . .	or either . . . or whether . . . or		
To give an example			
for example, . . . for instance, . . .			such as an example of to exemplify
To express an opinion			
according to . . . in my opinion, . . . in my view, . . .			to believe (that) to feel (that) to think (that)
To give a reason			
for this reason, . . .	for	because	as a result of because of due to

(continued on next page)

Transition Signals and Conjunctive Adverbs	Coordinators and Paired Conjunctions	Subordinators	Others: Adjectives, Prepositions, Verbs
To give a result			
accordingly, . . . as a consequence, . . . as a result, . . . consequently, . . . for these reasons, . . . hence, . . . therefore, . . . thus, . . .	so		the cause of the reason for to cause to result (in) to have an effect on to affect
To add a conclusion			
all in all, . . . in brief, . . . in short, . . . to conclude, . . . to summarize, . . . in conclusion, . . . in summary, . . . for these reasons, . . .			
To show similarities			
likewise, . . . similarly, . . . also	and both . . . and not only . . . but also neither . . . nor		alike, like, just like as, just as as well as well as compared with or to in comparison with or to to be similar (to) too
To show differences			
however, . . . in contrast, . . . instead, . . . on the contrary, . . . on the other hand, . . . rather, . . .			instead of

As you saw in Chapter 1 (pages 10 and 11), the basic rules governing how to use articles (*a*, *an*, *the*, and no article, or Ø) are actually very simple. Unfortunately, there are exceptions to these rules, and these exceptions often make it difficult for writers to use articles correctly.

No Article (Zero Article)

The basic rule is when a noncount noun or a plural count noun is referring to something in general, then do not place an article before it.

> [Ø] Milk is good for you.

> [Ø] Dogs make excellent pets.

Exceptions

Do not use an article with these specific places: *work*, *home*, and *bed*.

> I got to [Ø] work around 8:30.

> I went [Ø] home at about 9:00 and went straight to [Ø] bed.

Use no article before the name of certain institutions, such as *church*, *college*, *court*, *jail*, *prison*, and *school*.

> She goes to [Ø] church every Sunday morning.

> After he graduated from [Ø] college, he went to work.

Use of *A* / *An*

Use the indefinite articles *a*/*an* with **singular count nouns**, such as *chair*, *car*, or *bird*. These nouns are indefinite because they do not specify a particular one. *A* precedes words that begin with a consonant sound; *an* precedes words that begin with a vowel sound.

Exception

Use *a*/*an* with time and quantity expressions to mean *each* or *every*.

> The bus runs once **an** hour.

> The grapes are on sale for only fifty cents **a** bunch.

Use of *The*

The definite article *the* is used with any specific singular or plural count noun. Use *the* to refer to specific information that you have mentioned earlier or that you expect the reader to be aware of.

> Let's ask **the** teacher.

> We bought **a** new car yesterday. **The** car gets good gas mileage.

EXCEPTIONS

The is occasionally used with generic singular nouns, especially with animal species and inventions.

The Giant Panda is an endangered species.

Les Paul invented **the** electric guitar.

The is generally not used with proper nouns. However, there are some exceptions. Here are some of them.

USE *THE* WITH PROPER NOUNS THAT . . .	EXAMPLES
1. contain an *of*-expression	The Gulf of Mexico the Republic of Korea the Statue of Liberty the Tower of London the United States of America the University of Illinois
2. are names of countries or political groups that include *kingdom*, *republic*, or *union*	the United Kingdom the Czech Republic the European Union
3. are plural names of people and places	the Alps the Philippines the Simpsons (family) the United Arab Emirates the Virgin Islands
4. are bodies of water (except a lake, waterfall, or bay)	The Amazon (River) The Caribbean The Pacific (Ocean) The Panama Canal The Persian Gulf The Straits of Hormuz
5. geographic regions or points	the Middle East the South the West coast the Gobi Desert the Equator
6. with names of buildings, bridges, highways, tunnels, towers	the Kremlin the Golden Gate Bridge the Cross County Highway/ the M16 the Chunnel the Eiffel Tower

Use *the* With Proper Nouns That . . .	Examples
7. with names of some hotels, theaters, movie theaters, libraries, museums, and banks	The Hilton The Schubert Theater The National Library The Smithsonian (Museum) The Royal Bank of Scotland
8. with names of newspapers	The New York Times The Guardian The Post
9. with names of organizations, government ministries and departments, political parties	The United Nations The Red Cross/Red Crescent The Ministry of Education The Department of State The Liberals, the Tories, the Republicans
10. with nationalities (in the sense of "the people from this country")	The British The Chinese The French The Japanese The Russians

SEPARABLE PHRASAL VERBS	INSEPARABLE PHRASAL VERBS
ask for, out	agree on
back up	allow for
blow up	amount to
break down, off, up	back out of
bring about, out	become of
build up	care about
burn up	check up on
call back	come across
call off	come along with
check out, over	come back to, out of, over to, through, with, up to
cheer up	count on
clean out, up	deal in, with
cool off, down	do without
cross off, out	drop in, on, out of
cut off, up	feel like
do over	get ahead of
drive back	get into, off, on, out of, over, through with
drop off	go into, on with
dry off, up	grow out of
dust off, up	hear about
eat up	hold on to
figure out	keep on with, up with
fill in, out, up	look at, for, out for
find out	meet with
fix up	occur to
follow up	part with
get back, down, out	plan on
give away, up	put up with
hand in, out	read about
hang up	run into, across, out of, over
have on	see about
help out	send for, away for
hold up	side with
keep on, up	speak about, for, of
leave on, out	stand by
let in, on, off, out, up	stick to
look over, up	take up with
make up	talk about, back to

SEPARABLE PHRASAL VERBS	INSEPARABLE PHRASAL VERBS
mix up	think about, back on, of
open up	try out for
pass out, up	turn into
pay off, out	wait for, on
pick out, up	watch out for
point out	work on
put aside, away, down, in, off, on, up	
set up	
shut down, off, out	
slow down, up	
speed up	
stand up	
straighten out, up	
take away, back, off, on, out, over, up	
talk over	
tear up	
tell apart	
think over	
try on, out	
turn around, down, in, into, off, on, out, over, up	
use over, up	
wear out	
work out	
write down, off	

Accept / Except

Accept is a verb. It means "to receive something offered with gladness."

He **accepted** the job.

Except is a preposition. It is used to show things or people that are not included in a statement. It means "other than."

Everybody came to the party **except** Ellen.

Advice / Advise

Advice is a noun. It means "a suggestion about what should be done about a situation."

My brother gave me good **advice**.

Advise is a verb. It means "to tell someone what you think he or she should do." When you advise you offer advice.

I'm confused. What do you **advise** me to do?

Affect / Effect

Affect is a verb. It means "to cause a change or result."

Stress **affects** people's health in negative ways.

Effect is a noun. It means "change result."

Stress has a negative **effect** on people's health.

Almost / Most of

Almost is an adverb. It means "very nearly but not completely."

The students have **almost** finished the assignment.

Most is an adjective, adverb, or quantifier. It can be followed by *of the* and a noun.

Most students finished the assignment.

Most of the students finished the assignment.

Already / Still / Yet

Already, *yet*, and *still* are adverbs. *Already* and *yet* are often used in present perfect sentences to show a completed action; *already* is generally used in positive sentences, and *yet* is used in negative sentences.

Martha has **already** had lunch.

George has**n't** has lunch **yet**.

Still is often used in positive present continuous sentences to show a continuous action.

> Leon is **still** eating lunch.

Among / Between

Among and *between* are both prepositions. *Among* is used to talk about a group of three or more people, things, or groups that are considered together.

> Mr. García's estate was divided equally **among** his four daughters.

Between is used to talk about two people, things, or groups that are considered separately.

> There needs to be better cooperation **between** the sales and customer service departments

Childish / Childlike

Childish and *childlike* are both adjectives. *Childish* is negative and means someone is immature or behaving badly.

> Politicians should stop their **childish** name calling.

Childlike is positive and means someone is innocent and trusting.

> He has a **childlike** innocence that is very charming.

Each other / One another

Each other and *one another* are both reflexive pronouns. *Each other* is used with two people or things; *one another* is used with more than two people or things.

> The two leaders shook hands with **each other**.

> All of the leaders shook hands with **one another**.

Farther / Further

Farther and *further* can be used as adjective and adverbs. *Farther* is generally used to talk about distance; *further* is used to talk about time, quantities, and amounts.

> Jupiter is **farther** than Mars from the Sun.

> This study needs **further** research.

Historic / Historical

Historic is an adjective. It describes something that will be remembered because it was very important.

> The fall of the Berlin Wall was a **historic** event.

Historical is also an adjective. It describes people or events that took place in the past.

> Gone with the Wind was a popular **historical** novel.

Lie / Lay

Lie is a verb meaning to be at rest in a horizontal position or to occupy a position. It is conjugated *lie, lay, lain*.

> The treasure **lies** between the palm trees and the river.

Lay means to put or place something or someone in a particular position. It is conjugated *lay, laid, laid*

> **Lay** the baby in the crib.

Loose / Lose

Loose is an adjective. It refers to something that is not firmly attached.

> One of my buttons is **loose**.

Lose is a verb. It means you cannot find something or you do not have it anymore.

> I **lost** my cell phone.

Lose can also mean the opposite of win.

> We *lost* a game.

Nauseated / Nauseous

Nauseated is a verb meaning to feel sick to your stomach. When something is *nauseous* it *causes* you to feel nauseated, or makes you sick to your stomach.

Suppose / Be Supposed To

Suppose is a verb that means to guess or assume.

> The committee **supposed** that she would make a good candidate.

Be Supposed to is a modal verb phrase meaning something is expected or required.

> You **are supposed to** file your taxes today.

The highlights indicate where the following words are most commonly misspelled.

absence	exaggerate	occurrence
accept	existence	opportunity
accomplish	familiar	optimist
accommodate	fascinate	parallel
acquaintance	February	particular
advertisement	foreign	Philippines
adviser	genius	possess
answer	government	prejudiced
appropriate	grammar	prescription
attendance	guarantee	privilege
beautiful	guerilla	probably
beginning	height	pronunciation
behavior	immediate	psychology
business	independence	pursue
calendar	intellectual	recommend
certainly	interest	rhythm
commercial	interrupt	scenery
committee	irrelevant	schedule
competition	judgment	secretary
conscience	jewelry	separate
conscious	knowledge	sincerely
consequently	laboratory	speech
counselor	leisure	straight
criticize	license	temperature
desperate	lightning	through
develop	maintenance	thorough
does	mathematics	tomorrow
embarrass	misspell	unnecessary
environment	niece	Wednesday
especially	occasion	weird

In academic classes, your instructors will ask you to document the sources of outside information your have used in your paper. There are two steps to this process.

1. Insert a short reference in the body of your paper. This is called an in-text citation. The purpose of an in-text citation is to refer the reader to the works-cited list at the end of your paper.

2. Prepare a complete list of your sources. This list is titled either Works Cited or References and appears as the last page of your paper.

The two most commonly used formats for documenting sources are those used by the Modern Language Association (MLA) and the American Psychological Association (APA). Each format specifies style guidelines for referring to authors with in-text citations, footnotes and endnotes, and the sources list.

The MLA (Modern Language Association) system is used primarily for documenting work within the liberal arts and humanities—literature, English, foreign languages, art, and so on. The APA (American Psychological Association) system is mainly used to document source within the social sciences—sociology, psychology, anthropology, economics, and political science, etc. The next few pages will show you only the basics of the MLA and APA styles of formal documentation. In addition, be aware that each format has differences in punctuation rules which are too numerous to be dealt with here. Consult the *MLA Handbook for Writers of Research Papers* and the *Publication Manual of the American Psychological Association* for more detailed information. You can find these books and others like them in the reference area of any library.

THE BASICS OF MLA FORMAT

In papers using the MLA system, the name of the author typically introduces a quotation, paraphrase, or summary, and the page number of the source (if there is one) follows in parentheses before the period.

In-Text Citations

In-text citations give only enough information to allow the reader to find the full reference in the list of works cited at the end of your paper. Here are some guidelines.

ONE AUTHOR

Use the last name of the author and a page number (or numbers, if the borrowed information appears on more than one page). Use no punctuation.

(Clinton 17)

TWO OR MORE AUTHORS

If there are two or three authors, give all the names. If there are four or more, use the first author's name and the Latin abbreviation *et al.* ("and others") followed by a period.

(Bamberger and Yaeger 62)

(Singleton et al. 345)

No Author

If there is no author, use a short title in quotation marks.

Encyclopedia Article with No Author

For an encyclopedia article, use the editor's name if you know it. If you don't know it, use the title of the article in quotation marks. You do not need a page number since encyclopedia articles are arranged alphabetically and a reader will be able to find the source easily.

("Climate Change")

Electronic Source

For an electronic source (online or CD-ROM), follow the same system as for print sources. If there are no page numbers, do not write a number.

(Kidder)

("2012 Olympics")

Works-Cited Lists

In the MLA format, your complete list of references is entitled *Works Cited*. To prepare a works-cited list, begin by listing all the sources you actually used in your paper. Do not include sources that you read but did not use. List them alphabetically by last name of the author or, if there is no author, by the first word of the title. Pay close attention to punctuation and capitalization, and indent the second line.

Use this format for a basic book reference. Divide the information into three parts: (1) name of the author, (2) title of the book, (3) publishing information. Put a period and one space after each part.

Author's last name, Author's first name. *Title of Book*. City of Publication: Publisher's Name*, Year of publication. Print.

Lahiri, Jhumpa. *Unaccustomed Earth*. New York: Vintage, 2008. Print.

Two or More Authors

Use reverse order for the first author's name, and then write all other authors' names in normal order. Put a comma after the last name of the first author and also between authors.

Hamilton, Tyler, and Daniel Coyle. *The Secret Race: Inside the Hidden World of the Tour de France: Doping, Cover-ups, and Winning at All Costs.* New York: Bantam, 2012. Print.

---

*The Publisher's name can be abbreviated. For example, Oxford University Press, William Morrow, and Bantam Books can be abbreviated to Oxford, Morrow, and Bantam.

More Than One Edition

Put the number and the abbreviation "ed." (2nd ed., 3rd ed., 4th ed., and so on) after the title, followed by a period.

Slavin, Robert. *Educational Psychology: Theory and Practice*. 10th ed. Boston: Pearson, 2012. Print.

Encyclopedia Article

Use the author's name if it is given. If there is no author, put the title of the article first. Enclose the title in quotation marks. Underline or italicize the title of the encyclopedia. Put the edition number if there is one; if there is none, use the year.

"Intelligence Test." *New Encyclopedia Britannica: Micropedia.* 15th ed. Print.

Magazine Article

Put the title of the article inside quotation marks. Underline or italicize the name of the magazine. Include the day, month, and year for weekly magazines followed by a colon and the page number or numbers on which the article appears. Abbreviate the names of months except May, June, and July.

Rapoport, Abby. "School for Success." *Mother Jones. July/Aug. 2012*: 44–49. Print.

Newspaper Article

This article appeared on page A–22 of the newspaper.

"An Unfinished Campaign Against Polio." Editorial. *New York Times*. 29 Sep. 2012: A–22. Print.

Personal Interview

Give the person's name, last name first, and the date of the interview.

Jones, John. Personal interview. 31 Oct. 2003.

Online Source

Citations for online sources need the same basic information as print sources: author, title, and date of publication. The date of publication for an online source is the date it was put online or the date it was last revised.

In addition, you need to write the word *Web* followed by your date of access. Because online sources are often revised, you need to show exactly which version you used. Put the date you accessed (visited) the site at the end of your entry.

If you include the exact electronic address, copy the address from the top of your computer screen and enclose it in angle brackets (< >). Copy the exact address of the webpage you used, not just the home page address. If you must divide an address because it is too long to fit on a line, divide it only at a slash mark (/).

Kispert, Robert J. "Universal Language." *World Book Online Reference Center*. 2004. World Book, Inc. Web. 25 Mar. 2004 <http://www.aolsvc.worldbook.aol.com/wb/Article?id=ar576960>.

The Works-Cited Page

The works-cited list appears on a separate page as the last page of a paper. Use the following format.

- Capitalize the title of the works-cited list and center it on the page.
- Put the list in alphabetical order by author's last name (or title of the work, if there is no author).
- Double-space everything.
- Indent the second line of each citation 5 spaces or 1/2 inch.

Works Cited

Baugh, Albert C., and Thomas Cable. *A History of the English Language.* 5th ed. Upper Saddle River, NJ: Prentice Hall, 2002. Print.

Bonner, Jessie and Heather Hollingsworth. "Single-Sex Classes Popular As More Public Schools Split Up Boys and Girls." *Huffington Post.* 8 July 2012. Web. 1 Oct. 2012. <http://www.huffingtonpost.com/2012/07/08/more-public-schools-split_0_n_1657505.html>.

Downie, Andrew. "Brazil Considers Linguistic Barricade." *Christian Science Monitor* 6 Sep. 2000. Web. 13 Sep. 2004. <http://csmonitor.com/cgi-bin/durableRedirect.pl?/durable/2000/09/06/fp7s2-csm.shtml>.

Hamilton, Tyler, and Daniel Coyle. *The Secret Race: Inside the Hidden World of the Tour de France: Doping, Cover-ups, and Winning at All Costs.* New York: Bantam Books, 2012. Print.

Henderson, Lynne, and Philip Zimbardo. "Shyness." *Encyclopedia of Mental Health*. San Diego: Academic Press, 19 pp. 4 May 2004. <http://www.shyness.com/encyclopedia.html>.

Kispert, Robert J. "Universal language." *World Book Online Reference Center.* 2004. World Book, Inc. 12 Sep. 2004. Web. 1 Oct. 2012. <http://www.aolsvc.worldbook.aol.com/wb/Article?id=ar576960>.

Slavin, Robert. *Educational Psychology: Theory and Practice.* 10th ed. Boston: Pearson, 2012. Print.

"The 2000 Olympics: Games of the Drugs?" *CBSNEWS.com* 9 Sep. 2000. Web. 30 Mar. 2004. <http://www.cbsnews.com/stories/2002/01/31/health/main326667.shtml?CMP=ILC-SearchStories>.

PRACTICE 1   **Preparing a Works-Cited List**

On a separate sheet of paper, write the heading "Works Cited." Then list each of the following sources in MLA style and in alphabetical order.

1. A book entitled *Learning Disorders* by Robert W. Henderson published by Morris & Burns in Chicago in 2005.

2. A magazine article entitled "How to Live to Be 100" by Richard Corliss and Michael D. Lemonick on pages 40–48 of the August 30, 2004, issue of *Time* magazine.

(continued on next page)

3. A newspaper article entitled "Biology of Dyslexia Varies with Culture, Study Finds" on page D7 of the September 7, 2004, issue of the *New York Times* newspaper. The author's name is Anahad O'Connor.

4. An article in an online encyclopedia. The title of the article is "Dyslexia." The site's address is http://www.aolsvc.worldbook.aol.com/wb/Article? id=ar171010. The author's name is Michel W. Kibby. The website is *World Book Online Reference Center*. The publisher is World Book, Inc., and the copyright date is 2004. Use today's date as your date of access.

5. A website published by the U.S. Food and Drug Administration's Center for Food Safety and Applied Nutrition. The website contains an article titled "Tattoos and Permanent Makeup." The website's address is http://www.cfsan.fda.gov/~dms/cos-204.html. The article was updated on July 1, 2004. Use today's date as your date of access.

THE BASICS OF APA Format

In-Text Citations

The main difference between the MLA and the APA citation system is the identification of the author, the use of the publication date, and the tense of the verb introducing the reference. Unlike the MLA system, the APA system typically does not emphasize the author, but instead includes only his or her last name, along with the year of publication.

ONE AUTHOR

Use the last name of the author and the year of publication, separated by a comma. Include page references when citing an exact quotation.

(White-Hooel, 2006) [For a paraphrase]

(White-Hooel, 2006, p.152) [For a quotation]

TWO OR MORE AUTHORS

When a work has two authors, always use the last names of both authors. Do not spell out the word *and*. Instead, use an ampersand (&).

(Oshima & Hogue, 2013)

When a work has three, four, or five authors, always cite all of the authors, the first time they are referenced. The next time, use the first author's name and the Latin abbreviation *et al.* ("and others") followed by the year.

(Biber, Johansson, Leech, Conrad, & Finegan, 1999) [Use as a first citation]

(Biber et al., 1999) [Use for subsequent citations]

When a work has six or more authors, only use the last name of the first author, followed by *et al.*, followed by a comma and the publication year.

(Barnes et al., 2013)

No Author

If there is no author, use a short title in quotation marks, followed by the year of publication.

> ("Study Finds," 2010)

If the author is listed as "Anonymous," use the word *Anonymous*, followed by a comma and the year of publication.

> (Anonymous, 2011).

Encyclopedia Article with No Author

For an encyclopedia article, use the editor's name if you know it. If you don't know it, use the title of the article in quotation marks, and the year of publication. You do not need a page number since encyclopedia articles are arranged alphabetically and a reader will be able to find the source easily.

> ("Climate Change," 2012)

Electronic Source

For an electronic source (online or CD-ROM), follow the same system as for print sources. If there are no page numbers, use the paragraph symbol "¶" and the paragraph number.

Lists of References

In APA format, your list of sources is titled *References*. Like a works-cited list, your references list appears on a separate page as the last page of your paper. The title of the References list should be capitalized and placed flush left on the page. Your references should be alphabetized by the last names of the first author of each source. All references should be double-spaced. They should use a hanging indentation: the first line of each reference should be flush left, but each additional line of the reference needs to be indented by about five spaces. In article titles, only the first letter should be capitalized. If a colon appears in the title, the first letter after the colon should also be capitalized. The title should not be placed in quotations, underlined or italicized. All major words in the title of a journal should be capitalized; for example, *The Journal of Personality and Social Psychology*. Longer works such as books and journals should appear in italics.

Use this form for a basic book reference. Pay close attention to punctuation and capitalization:

Author's last name, Initials of Author's name. (Year). *Title of Book*. City of Publication: *Publisher's Name.

> Pinker, S. (1994). *The Language Instinct*. New York: Morrow.

---

*See note on the bottom of page 213.

Two or More Authors

Oshima, A. & Hogue, A. (2014). *Longman Academic Writing Series 2: Paragraphs.* (pp. 10–11). White Plains: Pearson.

Churchill, R., Ferguson, P., Godinho, S., Johnson, N. F., Keddie, A., Lets, W., & Mackay, J. (2013). *Teaching: Making a difference.* Sydney: John Wiley & Sons.

No Author

If the author is an organization or government agency, cite the title first, then the year of publication, followed by the full name of the organization.

Cancer facts and statistics. (2012). American Cancer Society.

More Than One Edition

Put the number and the abbreviation "ed." (2nd ed., 3rd ed., 4th ed., and so on) after the title, followed by a period.

Wade, C. & Tavris, C. (2011). *Psychology.* 10th ed. Boston: Pearson.

Encyclopedia Article

Use the author's name if it is given. If there is no author, put the title of the article first. Only capitalize the first letter of the article title. Italicize the title of the encyclopedia. Put the edition number if there is one; if there is none, use the year. Add the volume number and the page numbers of the article.

Bergman, P.G. (1993). Relativity. In *The new encyclopedia britannica:* (vol. 26, pp. 501-508). Chicago: Encyclopedia Britannica.

Magazine Article

Only capitalize the first word of the title. Include the year and month and the page number or numbers on which the article appears. Abbreviate the names of months except May, June, and July.

Rapoport, A. (2012, *July/Aug*). School for success. *Mother Jones*, 44–49.

Newspaper Article

Hutcheon, S. (2011, March 25). iPad 2 leading the charge. *The Brisbane Times.*

Online Source

A reference to an electronic source is very similar to that of any other reference; however, you need to also include the URL of the document.

Kazilek, C.J. (2012). A matter of scale. *Ask a Biologist.* Retrieved from http://askabiologist.asu.edu./explore/matter-scale

Bernstein, M. (2002). 10 tips on writing the living Web. *A List Apart: For People Who Make Websites, 149.* Retrieved from http://www.alistapart.com/articles/writeliving

Greenhouse, S. (2013, May 13). Major retailers join Bangladesh safety plan. *New York Times.* Retrieved from: http://www.nytimes/2013/05/13/world/asiapacific/retailers-agree-to-safety-plan

References Page

Remember to use the following format:

- Capitalize the title of the References list and place it flush left on the page.
- Put the list in alphabetical order by author's last name (or the title of the work if there is no author).
- Double-space everything.
- Indent the second line of each citation 5 spaces or 1/2 inch.

References

Bergman, P.G. (1993). Relativity. In *The new encyclopedia britannica:* (vol. 26, pp. 501–508). Chicago: Encyclopedia Britannica.

Biber, D., Johansson, S., Leech, G., Conrad, S., & Finegan, E. (1999). *Longman Grammar of Spoken and Written English.* Harlow: Pearson

Churchill, R., Ferguson, P., Godinho, S., Johnson, N. F., Keddie, A., Lets, W., & Mackay, J. (2013). *Teaching: Making a difference.* Sydney: John Wiley & Sons.

Greenhouse, S. (2013, May 13). Major retailers join Bangladesh safety plan. *New York Times.* Retrieved from: http://www.nytimes/2013/05/13/world/asiapacific/retailers-agree-to-safety-plan

Hutcheon, S. (2011, March 25). iPad 2 leading the charge. *The Brisbane Times.*

Kazilek, C.J. (2012). A matter of scale. *Ask a Biologist.* Retrieved from http://askabiologist.asu.edu/explore/matter-scale

Oshima, A. & Hogue, A. (2014). *Longman Academic Writing 2: Paragraphs.* (pp. 10–11). White Plains: Pearson.

Pinker, S. (1994). *The Language Instinct.* New York: Morrow.

Rapoport, A. (2012, July/Aug). School for success. *Mother Jones*, 44–49.

Rick, T. C., & Erlandson, J. M. (2009, August 21). Coastal exploitation. *Science*, 325, 952–953.

Wade, C. & Tavris, C. *Psychology.* (2011). 10th ed. Boston: Pearson.

PRACTICE 2 **Using APA Format**

Using the information above to help you, change each MLA format Works Cited entry into an APA format Reference.

1. Bennett, Jeffrey and Seth Shostak. *Life in the Universe.* 3rd ed. San Francisco: Addison-Wesley, 2012. Print.

   APA format: _____

   _____

2. Fallows, James. "Mr. China Comes to America." *Atlantic.* 2012: 54–66. Print.

   APA format: _____

   _____

(continued on next page)

3. Horner, Bruce, et al. "Toward a Multilingual Composition Scholarship: From English Only to a Translingual Form." *College Composition and Communication.* 63.2 (2011): 269–300. Print. [The other authors are Samantha NeCamp and Christianne Donahue.]

APA format: _____

_____

4. Rich, Motoko. "For Young Latino Readers, an Image Is Missing." *New York Times* 5 Dec. 2012, National Edition Sec.A:10,16. Print.

APA format: _____

_____

5. Leonard, Andrew. "How Consumer Brainwashed Are You?" *Salon.com.* Salon Media Group, 4 Dec. 2012. Web. 5 Dec. 2012.

APA format: _____

_____

6. "Demographic Profiles of the Island Areas: 2010 Census." *Census Bureau Homepage.* United States Census Bureau, 29 Nov. 2012. Web. 5 Dec. 2012.

APA format: _____

_____

| PRACTICE 3 | **Creating an APA References Page** |

On a separate sheet of paper, write the heading "References." Then list each of the following sources in APA style and in alphabetical order.

1. A book entitled *Sociology: A Down-to-Earth Approach* written by James M. Henslin published by Allyn & Bacon in Boston in 2010. This is its 10th edition.

2. A magazine article entitled "Utopia for Beginners" written by Joshua Foer which appeared on pages 86–97 of the December 24, 2012 issue of *The New Yorker* magazine.

3. A newspaper article entitled "World's tallest dam approved by Chinese officials" on page A1 of the May 17, 2013, issue of the *Guardian* newspaper. The author's name is Jonathan Kaiman.

4. An article in an online encyclopedia. The title of the article is "What is Biodiversity?" The author's name is Alexandra Mushegian. The website is *Encyclopedia of life*. The copyright date is 2011 and the site's address is http://eol.org/info/about_biodiversity

5. A website published by the U.S. State Department. The website contains an article titled "Tips for Travel Abroad." The website's address is http://travel.state.gov/travel/tips/tips_1232.html. The article was updated on February 28, 2013.

6. A website published by the U.S. Food and Drug Administration. The website contains an article titled "How to Report a Pet Food Complaint." The website's address is http://www.fda.gov/AnimalVeterinary/SafetyHealth/ReportaProblem/ucm182403.htm. The article was updated on February 24, 2012.

SYMBOL	MEANING	EXAMPLE OF ERROR	CORRECTED SENTENCE
P	punctuation	*P* *P* I live, and go to school here	I live and go to school here.
^	missing word	*am* I working in a restaurant. *^*	I am working in a restaurant.
——	rewrite as shown	*some of my* I go with ~~my some~~ friends.	I go with some of my friends.
cap	capitalization	*cap* It is located at main and *cap* *cap* *cap* baker streets in the City.	It is located at Main and Baker Streets in the city.
vt	wrong verb tense	*vt* I never work as a cashier *vt* until I get a job there.	I never worked as a cashier until I got a job there.
s/v agr	subject-verb agreement	*s/v agr* The manager work hard. *s/v agr* He have five employees.	The manager works hard. He has five employees.
pron agr	pronoun agreement	Everyone works hard *pron agr* at their jobs.	All the employees work hard at their jobs.
⌣	connect to make one sentence	We work together. So we have become friends.	We work together, so we have become friends.
sp	spelling	*sp* The maneger is a woman.	The manager is a woman.
sing/pl	singular or plural	She treats her employees *sing/pl* like slave.	She treats her employees like slaves.
✕	unnecessary word	My boss ~~she~~ watches everyone all the time.	My boss watches everyone all the time.
wf	wrong word form	*wf* Her voice is irritated.	Her voice is irritating.
ww	wrong word	The restaurant has great *ww* food. Besides, it is always crowded.	The restaurant has great food. Therefore, it is always crowded.

(continued on next page)

Symbol	Meaning	Example of Error	Corrected Sentence
ref	pronoun reference error	The restaurant's specialty is *ref* fish. They are always fresh. The food is delicious. *ref* Therefore, it is always crowded.	The restaurant's specialty is fish. It is always fresh. The food is delicious. Therefore, the restaurant is always crowded.
wo OR ~	wrong word order	*Friday always is our busiest night.*	Friday is always our busiest night.
ro	run-on sentence	*ro* [Lily was fired she is upset.]	Lily was fired, so she is upset.
cs	comma splice	*cs* [Lily was fired, she is upset.]	
frag	fragment	*frag* She was fired. [Because she was always late.] *frag* [Is open from 6:00 P.M. until the last customer leaves.] *frag* [The employees on time and work hard.]	She was fired because she was always late. The restaurant is open from 6:00 P.M. until the last customer leaves. The employees are on time and work hard.
prep	preposition	We start serving *prep* dinner 6:00 P.M.	We start serving dinner at 6:00 P.M.
conj	conjunction	Garlic shrimp, fried *conj* clams, broiled lobster are the most popular dishes.	Garlic shrimp, fried clams, and broiled lobster are the most popular dishes.
choppy	choppy writing	*choppy* I like the work. I do not like my boss. I want to quit.	Even though I like the work, I do not like my boss, so I want to quit.
not //	not parallel	Most of our regular customers are *not //* friendly and generous tippers.	Most of our regular customers are friendly and tip generously.

Symbol	Meaning	Example of Error	Corrected Sentence
sub	subordinate	sub The tips are good, and all the employees share them.	The tips, which all of the employees share, are good.
art	article	Diners in the United States art expect glass of water when ^ they first sit down.	Diners in the United States expect a glass of water when they first sit down.
Ⓣ	add a transition	The new employee was Ⓣ careless. She frequently spilled coffee on the table.	The new employee was careless. For example, she frequently spilled coffee on the table.
¶	start a new paragraph		
nfs/nmp	needs further support/needs more proof; you need to add some specific details (examples, facts, quotations) to support your points		

Peer Review and Writer's Self-Check worksheets are designed to help you become a better writer.

Peer Review

Peer review is an interactive process of reading and commenting on a classmate's writing. You will exchange rough drafts with a classmate, read each other's work, and make suggestions for improvement. Use the worksheet for each assignment and answer each question. Write your comments on the worksheet or on your classmate's paper as your instructor directs. If you exchange rough drafts via email instead of hard copy, it may be easier to make comments in the document. Check with your instructor to find out how you should exchange and comment on drafts.

Advice for Peer Reviewers

- Your job is to help your classmate write clearly. Focus only on content and organization.
- If you notice grammar or spelling errors, ignore them. It is not your job to correct your classmate's English.
- Don't cross out any writing. Underline, draw arrows, circle things, but do not cross out anything.
- Make your first comment a positive one. Find something good to say.
- If possible, use a colored ink or pencil if you are working in hard copy.
- The writer may not always agree with you. Discuss your different opinions, but don't argue, and don't cause hurt feelings.

Here are some polite ways to suggest changes:

Do you think it is important/necessary/relevant?

I don't quite understand your meaning here.

Could you please explain this point a little more?

I think an example would help here.

This part seems confusing.

I think this part should go at the end/at the beginning/after XYZ.

Maybe you don't need this word/sentence/part.

Writer's Self-Check

Becoming a better writer requires that you learn to edit your own work. *Self-editing* means to look at your writing as a writing instructor would. The Writer's Self-Check worksheets contain questions about specific elements that your instructor hopes to find in your paragraph or essay—a strong thesis statement, clear topic sentences, specific supporting details, coherence, an effective conclusion, and so on. Self-editing also requires attention to every aspect of your writing. It involves proofreading to check for and correct errors in format, mechanics, grammar, and sentence structure. By answering the worksheet questions thoughtfully, you can learn to recognize the strengths (and weaknesses) in your rhetorical skills as well as to spot and correct errors.

Reader: _____   **Date:** _____

1. Is the essay interesting?   ☐ yes   ☐ no
   If you answered *yes*, write a comment about a part that was especially interesting to you.

   _____

   If you answered *no* and you have some ideas to make it more interesting, write them below.

   _____

2. Do you understand everything?   ☐ yes   ☐ no
   Circle or underline any part that you do not understand and write a comment about it.

   _____

3. How many claims does the writer make? Number: _____

4. Does the writer introduce each claim in the body of the essay with a clear topic sentence?
   If not, which paragraph(s) are missing topic sentences? _____

5. Does each claim have supporting details?   ☐ yes   ☐ no
   Write one detail that you especially like:

   _____

6. What kind of supporting details does the writer use (facts, examples, quotations, statistics, etc.)? _____
   If you would like more information about anything, indicate that below.

   _____

7. Do you understand everything?   ☐ yes   ☐ no
   If your answer is *no*, what part(s) or sentence(s) don't you understand?

   _____

   _____

8. Is there anything unnecessary or that seems "off topic"?   ☐ yes   ☐ no
   If your answer is *yes*, write a comment about it (them).

   _____

9. Is there a strong conclusion?   ☐ yes   ☐ no
   If your answer is *no*, suggest another way to conclude the essay.

   _____

10. What do you like the best about this essay? Write one positive comment here:

    _____

    _____

    _____

CHAPTER 1 WRITER'S SELF-CHECK

Writer: _____   Date: _____

Format

My essay has a title.	☐ yes	☐ no
The title is centered.	☐ yes	☐ no
The first line of every paragraph is indented.	☐ yes	☐ no
There are margins on both sides of the page.	☐ yes	☐ no
The essay is double-spaced.	☐ yes	☐ no

Mechanics

I put a period, a question mark, or an exclamation mark after every sentence.	☐ yes	☐ no
I used capital letters correctly.	☐ yes	☐ no
I checked my spelling.	☐ yes	☐ no

Content and Organization

The first paragraph has a clear thesis statement.	☐ yes	☐ no
Each body paragraph has a topic sentence that makes a claim.	☐ yes	☐ no
Each body paragraph contains several specific and factual supporting sentences for its claim.	☐ yes	☐ no

Grammar and Sentence Structure

Every sentence has at least one subject-verb pair and expresses a complete thought.	☐ yes	☐ no
I have used articles correctly.	☐ yes	☐ no
I have used negative prefixes with adjectives correctly.	☐ yes	☐ no

Every student has his or her own personal grammar trouble spots. Some students have trouble with verb tenses. For others, articles are the main problem. Some find it hard to know when to use commas. In the next section, write down items that you know are problems for you. Then work on them throughout the course. As time passes, delete items that you have mastered and add new ones that you become aware of.

Personal Grammar Trouble Spots   **Number found and corrected**
(verb tense, articles, word order, etc.)

I checked my essay for:

- _____   _____

- _____   _____

- _____   _____

Reader: _____   **Date:** _____

1. Is there a thesis statement?   ☐ yes   ☐ no
   If you answered *yes*, copy it here.

   _____

2. Does the opening paragraph contain a specific criterion?   ☐ yes   ☐ no
   Copy the topic sentence here.

   _____

   _____

3. Do you understand everything?   ☐ yes   ☐ no
   If your answer is *no*, what part(s) or sentence(s) don't you understand?

   _____

   _____

   _____

4. Would you like more information about anything?   ☐ yes   ☐ no
   If you answered *yes*, what information would you like to see?

   _____

5. **Unity:** Do all the sentences develop the claim in each paragraph?   ☐ yes   ☐ no
   If you answered *no*, circle the sentences that seem to be "off topic."

6. **Coherence:** Does the paragraph flow smoothly from beginning to end?   ☐ yes   ☐ no
   If you answered *no*, underline the places where the flow between ideas needs improvement.

7. In your opinion, what are the best features of the essay? In other words, what is this writer's best writing skill?

   _____

   _____

   _____

CHAPTER 2 WRITER'S SELF-CHECK

Writer: _____   Date: _____

Format

My essay is correctly formatted (title centered, first line indented, margins on both sides, double-spaced).   ☐ yes ☐ no

Mechanics

I checked punctuation, capitalization, and spelling.   ☐ yes ☐ no

Content and Organization

My first paragraph includes a thesis statement and each body paragraph includes a topic sentence that makes a claim.   ☐ yes ☐ no

Each body paragraph includes support (observations, data, and explanations) for its claim.   ☐ yes ☐ no

Unity: All sentences develop the topic.   ☐ yes ☐ no

Coherence: Each paragraph flows smoothly from beginning to end.   ☐ yes ☐ no

I repeat words where necessary.   ☐ yes ☐ no

I use pronouns consistently.   ☐ yes ☐ no

I use some transition signals.   ☐ yes ☐ no

How many? _____

Grammar and Sentence Structure

I checked my paper for correct use of quantifiers.   ☐ yes ☐ no

Personal Grammar Trouble Spots   **Number found and corrected**
(verb tense, articles, word order, etc.)

I checked my paragraph for:

- _____   _____

- _____   _____

- _____   _____

Reader: _____   **Date:** _____

1. What is the thesis of this essay? Copy it here.

   _____

   _____

2. Does the essay establish its purpose?   ☐ yes   ☐ no

3. Does the essay define key terms and indicate the materials or parts needed?   ☐ yes   ☐ no

4. Do you understand everything?   ☐ yes   ☐ no

   If your answer is *no*, what part(s) or sentence(s) don't you understand?

   _____

   _____

   _____

5. Does the writer present the steps in a clear sequence?   ☐ yes   ☐ no

6. Does the writer correct any run-on or comma-spliced sentences?   ☐ yes   ☐ no

   If your answer is *no*, write the beginning of the sentence(s) with errors.

   _____

   _____

7. What do you like the best about this essay? Write one positive comment here.

   _____

   _____

   _____

CHAPTER 3 WRITER'S SELF-CHECK

Writer: _____   Date: _____

Format

My essay is correctly formatted (title centered, first line indented, margins on both sides, double-spaced). ☐ yes ☐ no

I wrote a clear summary or abstract. ☐ yes ☐ no

Organization

My introduction names the process, states its thesis, and establishes the goal of the process essay. ☐ yes ☐ no

I define all key terms and indicate the parts or materials needed. ☐ yes ☐ no

The steps in the process are presented in sequential order. ☐ yes ☐ no

The conclusion restates the goal of the process or summary of the process. ☐ yes ☐ no

Vocabulary

I use the correct forms of irregular nouns from Latin and Greek. ☐ yes ☐ no

I have checked my spelling. ☐ yes ☐ no

Sentence Structure

I have checked for run-ons, comma splices, and fragments. ☐ yes ☐ no

Personal Grammar Trouble Spots
(verb tense, articles, word order, etc.)

Number found and corrected

I checked my paragraph for:

- _____   _____

- _____   _____

- _____   _____

© 2014 Pearson Education, Inc. Duplication for classroom use is permitted.

Reader: _____   **Date:** _____

1. Does the opening paragraph contain a clear thesis statement?   ☐ yes   ☐ no
   If you answered *yes*, copy it here.

   _____

   _____

2. Does the essay establish a clear pattern of chain reaction or
   block organization?   ☐ yes   ☐ no

3. Are the writer's claims backed up and illustrated well?   ☐ yes   ☐ no
   Write one example of backing you especially like.

   _____

   _____

4. Do you understand everything?   ☐ yes   ☐ no
   If your answer is *no*, what part(s) or sentence(s) don't you understand?

   _____

   _____

   _____

5. What do you like the best about this essay? Write one positive comment here.

   _____

   _____

   _____

CHAPTER 4 WRITER'S SELF-CHECK

Writer: _____ **Date:** _____

Format

My essay is correctly formatted (title centered, first line indented, margins on both sides, double-spaced). ☐ yes ☐ no

I establish a clear relationship between causes of an effect or of effects of a cause or causes. ☐ yes ☐ no

Organization

My opening paragraph includes a clear thesis statement. ☐ yes ☐ no

I established a clearly organized chain or block organization. ☐ yes ☐ no

I have researched my subject matter in print sources and/or on the Internet. ☐ yes ☐ no

I support my claims appropriately with surveys, statistics, examples, specific descriptions, explanations, and/or quotations. ☐ yes ☐ no

I establish logical relationships between ideas with transitional signals. ☐ yes ☐ no

Grammar and Sentence Structure

I use separable and inseparable phrasal verbs correctly. ☐ yes ☐ no

I use parallelism correctly in and between sentences where appropriate. ☐ yes ☐ no

I use correct punctuation and capitalization of quotations. ☐ yes ☐ no

I checked my spelling. ☐ yes ☐ no

Personal Grammar Trouble Spots
(verb tense, articles, word order, etc.)

Number found and corrected

I checked my paragraph for:

- _____ _____

- _____ _____

- _____ _____

© 2014 Pearson Education, Inc. Duplication for classroom use is permitted.

Reader: _____   **Date:** _____

1. Is the writer's definition of the term clear?   ☐ yes   ☐ no

2. How does the writer define the term: by synonym, apposition, negation, or formal definition?

   _____

3. Does each claim have adequate support?   ☐ yes   ☐ no

4. Does the writer use at least one paraphrase?   ☐ yes   ☐ no

5. Do you understand everything?   ☐ yes   ☐ no

   If your answer is *no*, what part(s) or sentence(s) don't you understand?

   _____

   _____

   _____

6. What do you like the best about this essay? Write one positive comment here.

   _____

   _____

Writer: _____   Date: _____

Format

My essay is correctly formatted (title centered, first line indented, margins on both sides, double-spaced).   ☐ yes ☐ no

Organization

My opening paragraph contains a clear thesis statement and establishes a reason to define a term.   ☐ yes ☐ no

My essay includes a clear definition of the term by synonym, apposition, a formal statement of definition, and/or definition by negation.   ☐ yes ☐ no

I support my claims with reasons, examples.   ☐ yes ☐ no

I establish logical relationships between ideas through clear transitions.   ☐ yes ☐ no

Grammar and Vocabulary

I paraphrase source material correctly, and blend quotations with paraphrase when appropriate.   ☐ yes ☐ no

I match synonyms with the same parts of speech.   ☐ yes ☐ no

Personal Grammar Trouble Spots   **Number found and corrected**
(verb tense, articles, word order, etc.)

I checked my paragraph for:

- _____   _____

- _____   _____

- _____   _____

Reader: _____   **Date:** _____

1. Is the problem clearly introduced and explained?   ☐ yes   ☐ no

2. Does a transition clearly introduce the solution?   ☐ yes   ☐ no
   If you answered *yes*, copy the transition below.

   _____

3. Is the solution clearly explained?   ☐ yes   ☐ no

4. Does each claim have adequate support?   ☐ yes   ☐ no

5. Do you understand everything?   ☐ yes   ☐ no
   If your answer is *no*, what part(s) or sentence(s) don't you understand?

   _____

   _____

   _____

6. What do you like the best about this essay? Write one positive comment here.

   _____

   _____

   _____

CHAPTER 6 WRITER'S SELF-CHECK

Writer: _____   Date: _____

Format

My essay is correctly formatted (title centered, first line indented,
margins on both sides, double-spaced).   ☐ yes   ☐ no

Organization

My opening paragraph includes a clear thesis statement that introduces a
problem and states or suggests a solution.   ☐ yes   ☐ no

I researched and synthesized multiple sources.   ☐ yes   ☐ no

My beginning of the body of the essay explains the nature of the problem. ☐ yes   ☐ no

I use a clear transition to introduce a solution.   ☐ yes   ☐ no

I back up my claims with data, examples, and/or quotations.   ☐ yes   ☐ no

I establish clear relationships between ideas with transitions. ☐ yes   ☐ no

Grammar and Sentence Structure

I vary my sentence structure by shortening some adverbial clauses to phrases. ☐ yes   ☐ no

I correctly use a variety of intensifiers.   ☐ yes   ☐ no

Personal Grammar Trouble Spots   **Number found and corrected**
(verb tense, articles, word order, etc.)

I checked my paragraph for:

- _____   _____

- _____   _____

- _____   _____

Reader: _____   **Date:** _____

1. Is the summary clear and objective?   ☐ yes   ☐ no

2. Is the transition to the response clear?   ☐ yes   ☐ no

3. Does the response contain a thesis statement?   ☐ yes   ☐ no
   If you answered *yes*, copy the thesis statement below.

   _____

4. Is the response clearly explained?   ☐ yes   ☐ no

5. Does each paragraph develop a single claim?   ☐ yes   ☐ no

6. Does each claim have adequate support?   ☐ yes   ☐ no

7. Do you understand everything?   ☐ yes   ☐ no
   If your answer is *no*, what part(s) or sentence(s) don't you understand?

   _____

   _____

   _____

8. What do you like the best about this essay? Write one positive comment here.

   _____

   _____

   _____

CHAPTER 7 WRITER'S SELF-CHECK

Writer: _____   Date: _____

Format

My essay is correctly formatted (title centered, first line indented,
margins on both sides, double-spaced).   ☐ yes   ☐ no

Organization

My opening paragraph summarizes the material and includes the author's
name (if one is mentioned) and the title.   ☐ yes   ☐ no

My summary is objective; it does not contain any of my opinions.   ☐ yes   ☐ no

I introduce my response through a thesis statement.   ☐ yes   ☐ no

My response continually addresses the summary.   ☐ yes   ☐ no

I back up my claims with quotations, paraphrases, and examples from
the source.   ☐ yes   ☐ no

I establish clear relationships between ideas through transitions.   ☐ yes   ☐ no

Grammar and Sentence Structure

I checked my paper for awkward use of passive voice.   ☐ yes   ☐ no

I used the correct forms of nouns, verbs, and adjectives. ☐ yes   ☐ no

Personal Grammar Trouble Spots   **Number found and corrected**
(verb tense, articles, word order, etc.)

I checked my paragraph for:

• _____   _____

• _____   _____

• _____   _____

Reader: _____   Date: _____

1. Is the argument clearly framed?   ☐ yes   ☐ no

2. Is the thesis clearly stated?   ☐ yes   ☐ no
    If you answered *yes*, copy the thesis below.

    _____

3. Does the body of the paper follow a clear structure of argument to counterargument or argument to response to a counterargument?   ☐ yes   ☐ no

4. Does each claim have adequate support?   ☐ yes   ☐ no

5. Do you understand everything?   ☐ yes   ☐ no
    If your answer is *no*, what part(s) or sentence(s) don't you understand?

    _____

    _____

    _____

    _____

    _____

6. What do you like the best about this essay? Write one positive comment here.

    _____

    _____

    _____

    _____

Writer: _____   Date: _____

Format

My essay is correctly formatted (title centered, first line indented, margins on both sides, double-spaced) ☐ yes ☐ no

Organization

My opening paragraph frames the issue, introducing the argument and counterargument. ☐ yes ☐ no

My thesis is clearly stated. ☐ yes ☐ no

The body of my paper follows a clear pattern of counterargument to response or argument to response to a counterargument. ☐ yes ☐ no

My response continually addresses the summary. ☐ yes ☐ no

I back up my claims with quotations, paraphrases, and examples from the source. ☐ yes ☐ no

I establish clear relationships between ideas through transitions. ☐ yes ☐ no

Grammar and Sentence Structure

I have checked my paper for the correct use of modals, semi-modals, and the subjunctive. ☐ yes ☐ no

I checked my paper for the correct forms of nouns, verbs, and adjectives. ☐ yes ☐ no

Personal Grammar Trouble Spots   **Number found and corrected**
(verb tense, articles, word order, etc.)

I checked my paragraph for:

- _____   _____

- _____   _____

- _____   _____

Reader: _____   Date: _____

1. Is the thesis of the research paper clearly stated? ☐ yes ☐ no

   If the answer is *yes*, copy the thesis statement below.

   _____

2. Does each body paragraph develop a central claim stated in a topic sentence? ☐ yes ☐ no

3. Is each claim adequately supported with material quoted, paraphrased, or summarized from sources? ☐ yes ☐ no

4. Are multiple sources synthesized clearly, showing similarities or differences between or among them? ☐ yes ☐ no

5. Is the documentation of the sources correct? ☐ yes ☐ no

6. Do you understand everything? ☐ yes ☐ no

   If your answer is *no*, what part(s) or sentence(s) don't you understand?

   _____

   _____

   _____

   _____

7. What do you like the best about this essay? Write one positive comment here.

   _____

   _____

   _____

   _____

Writer: _____   Date: _____

Format

My research paper is correctly formatted (title centered, first line indented, margins on both sides, double-spaced).   ☐ yes   ☐ no

Organization

My opening paragraph includes a clear thesis statement.   ☐ yes   ☐ no

Each paragraph in the body of my paper includes a clear topic sentence that the paragraph develops.   ☐ yes   ☐ no

I back up my claims with quotations, paraphrases, and examples from multiple sources.   ☐ yes   ☐ no

I have correctly documented the sources in the body of the paper.   ☐ yes   ☐ no

I establish clear relationships between ideas through transitions.   ☐ yes   ☐ no

I have correctly documented sources on the Works-Cited page.   ☐ yes   ☐ no

Grammar and Sentence Structure

I have checked my paper for the correct use of quotations and paraphrases of the source material.   ☐ yes   ☐ no

I have synthesized sources, showing similarities or differences between or among them.   ☐ yes   ☐ no

Personal Grammar Trouble Spots   **Number found and corrected**
(verb tense, articles, word order, etc.)

I checked my paragraph for:

- _____   _____

- _____   _____

- _____   _____

INDEX

CREDITS

Photo Credits:

Cover: BrAt82/Shutterstock (quill pen), Evgeny Karandaev/Shutterstock (laptop).

Page xiii: UnoL/Shutterstock; **1:** Wavebreakmedia/Shutterstock; **2:** Auremar/Shutterstock; **5:** Raisman/Shutterstock; **17:** Pressmaster/Shutterstock; **21 (top):** Delmas Lehman/Shutterstock; **21 (bottom):** Rokfeather/Shutterstock; **23:** Patricia Hofmeester/Shutterstock; **41:** Directphoto Collection/Alamy Stock Photo; **43:** UnoL/Shutterstock; **44:** Wunschmedien.de/Shutterstock; **64:** Chrisdorney/Shutterstock; **69:** Everett Historical/Shutterstock; **86:** Voinakh/Shutterstock; **88:** Prostock-studio/Shutterstock; **109 (top):** Shutterstock; **109 (bottom):** Mandy Godbehear/Shutterstock; **110:** Sweet Memento Photography/Shutterstock; **111:** Sylvie Bouchard/Shutterstock; **122:** George Dolgikh/Shutterstock; **124:** Cherezoff/Shutterstock; **128:** Sirtravelalot/Shutterstock; **133:** PlusONE/Shutterstock; **134:** Ashwin/Shutterstock; **146:** Bespaliy/Shutterstock; **150:** Yuttana Jaowattana/Shutterestock; **155:** Alexwhite/Shutterstock; **176:** Shutterstock.

Text Credits

Pages 22–24, 29, 30: "The Amish: An Intimate Society" Henslin, James M., *Sociology: A Down-to-Earth Approach*. 10th Ed., © 2010. Reprinted and Electronically reproduced by permission of Pearson Education, Inc., Upper Saddle River, New Jersey.

Pages 42–44: "What Scientists Do" CJ Kalizek and David Pearson, "Using the Scientific Method to Solve Mysteries." ASU Ask A Biologist. http://askabiologist.asu.edu. Reproduced under a Creative Commons Attribution-ShareAlike 3.0 Unported License.

Pages 68–69: "The Explosive Growth of The Cities" Carnes, Mark C.; Garraty, John A., *American Nation, A History of the United States*, Combined Volume, 14th Ed., © 2012. Reprinted and Electronically reproduced by permission of Pearson Education, Inc.

Pages 88, 104: "What is Language" Wade, Carole; Tavris, Carol, *Psychology*, 10th Ed., © 2011, pp. 75–80. Reprinted and Electronically reproduced by permission of Pearson Education, Inc., Upper Saddle River, New Jersey.

Page 88: "Things No Amount of Learning Can Teach," Noam Chomksy, Interviewed by John Gliedman. *Omni*, 6:11, November 1983.

Pages 110–112: "Bullying in Schools in The United States" Powell, Sara Davis, *Your Introduction to Education: Explorations in Teaching*, 2nd Ed., © 2012, pp. 254–256. Reprinted and Electronically reproduced by permission of Pearson Education, Inc., Upper Saddle River, New Jersey.

Page 112: Olweus, D., Limber, S., & Mihalic, S. (1999). *The Bullying Prevention Program. Blueprints for Violence Prevention. Boulder*, Colo.: Center for the Study and Prevention of Violence.

Page 134: "Arranging a Marriage in India," Author: Serena Nanda. Reprinted by permission of Waveland Press, Inc. from DeVita, *Stumbling Toward Truth: Anthropologists at Work*. Long Grove, IL: Waveland Press, Inc., © 2000 all rights reserved.

Page 140: "Material and Nonmaterial Culture" Henslin, James M., *Sociology: A Down-to-Earth Approach*, 10th Ed., © 2010, p. 37. Reprinted and Electronically reproduced by permission of Pearson Education, Inc., Upper Saddle River, New Jersey.

Page 141: "A Cultural Mosaic" Popple, Philip R.; Leighninger, Leslie, Social Work, *Social Welfare and American Society*, 8th Ed., © 2011, p. 144. Reprinted and Electronically reproduced by permission of Pearson Education, Inc., Upper Saddle River, New Jersey.

Page 147–149: "A Scientist: I Am the Enemy,"Ronald M. Kline, MD, Medical Director, Pediatric Division, Comprehensive Cancer Center of Nevada. Reprinted with permission.

Pages 170–172: "Mayak: The Unknown Disaster" Mayak: The Unknown Disaster by Ksenia S. Laney.

Pages 175, 176: "Problems with Food Labeling" Problems with Food Labeling by Aksana DeBretto.

Illustration Credits:

TSI Graphics: pgs: 95, 169